# TEXAS SCHLOCK

Bret McCormick

**LECR Press**

Bedford, Texas

*Texas Schlock* copyright ©2018 by Bret McCormick

All applicable copyrights and other rights reserved worldwide.
No part of this publication may be be reproduced, in any form
or by any means, for any purpose, without the express,
written permission of the author, except by a reviewer, who
may quote brief passages in a review, as provided by
the U.S. Copyright Law.

Under section 107 of the Copyright Act of 1976, allowance is made
for "fair use" for purposes such as criticism, comment, news reporting,
teaching, scholarship, education and research. The illustrations accompanying
this text are utilized in accordance with the "fair use" provision provided by law.
The purpose of this publication is to present historical information and promote
interest in the works described herein.

Contact the author at
Texaswriterman2014@gmail.com

Interior Design and Cover Art by Russell C. Connor

ISBN:
978-0692069950

First Edition: 2018

# Thanks to

Patrice Kleypas for her loving support,

E.R. Bills for suggesting this book into reality,

Glen Coburn for his kind assistance and contributions to this and other projects and his lovely wife, Kay Bay, for putting up with these shenanigans,

Joe Bob Briggs for being the first real movie critic ever to give my films some positive ink,

Larry Buchanan, S.F. Brownrigg, Russ Marker, Edgar G. Ulmer, Pat Boyette, Hal P. Warren, Jim Sullivan, Robert Burns, Terry Lofton, Jesse Sherman, Mike Minton, Justin Powers, Sal Hernandez, Jacob Grim and anyone else who ever took up a camera with Schlockish intent in the Great State of Texas,

Michael H. Price for guidance,

Russell Connor for a fine book design,

Jeff Buchanan, C. Ross Burns, Art Ettinger, Libby Brownrigg, Gary Kennamer, Benton Jennings and Daniel Redd for adding their thoughts and memories to the mix,

Greg Goodsell for letting me use his excellent interview with Jackie Neyman Jones,

Jackie Neyman Jones for allowing use of her artwork,

David Szulkin for sharing his discoveries and encouraging me,

Adrian J Smith of horrorpedia.com for his editorial contribution and friendly cooperation in bringing this book to the attention of readers,

Tim Harden for providing some excellent photos,

Chris Cerreta for loaning me a copy of Hugh Gallagher's magazine *Draculina*, so I could rediscover the Brownrigg interview I did in a lost time,

All the enthusiastic mutants who enjoy these flicks as much as I do.

I'm pretty sure I've overlooked someone who deserves to be on this page. If you are that person, please accept my sincere apology.

# CONTENTS

| | |
|---|---|
| INTRODUCTION | 4 |
| RATIONALE | 9 |
| LARRY BUCHANAN | 11 |
| EDGAR G. ULMER | 40 |
| PAT BOYETTE | 53 |
| RUSS MARKER | 61 |
| HAL P. WARREN | 72 |
| JIM SULLIVAN | 88 |
| TOM MOORE | 95 |
| S.F. BROWNRIGG | 108 |

| | |
|---|---|
| ROBERT A. BURNS | 144 |
| GLEN COBURN | 162 |
| TERRY LOFTON | 183 |
| BRET MCCORMICK | 196 |
| SHERMAN AND MINTON | 218 |
| JUSTIN POWERS | 233 |
| GRIM AND HERNANDEZ | 245 |
| AFTERWORD | 251 |
| INDEX | 253 |

# INTRODUCTION

Though my mother would probably be mortified if she heard me make this claim, I was a TV baby. My folks were teenage parents and there was a good deal of struggle built into their pursuit of the American Dream. Money was short, but we had a little black and white Montgomery Ward brand television set. This was the babysitter my parents could afford. Some of my earliest memories include *Tarzan*, *Flash Gordon*, Steve Reeves as *Hercules* (I could not understand how they got their mouths to move out of sync with their words,) *Godzilla* (ditto on the mouth movement thing), *Three Stooges*, *Bowery Boys*, *Perry Mason*, *Twilight Zone* and *Outer Limits*. Most of the time I was content to passively absorb this action-packed, imaginative fare. When I wasn't watching it, I was acting it out with my friends, improvising props and costumes from whatever I could find around the house. Later, Mom would be screaming for her spatula and scolding (too mild a word) me for using all of her clean towels and safety pins to array myself and my companions as the *Sons of Hercules*.

By the time I was in third grade, I was spending virtually every Saturday afternoon in either the Poly or the Gateway, the two neighborhood theaters on the Eastside of Fort Worth. I'd watch a double feature while my mother got the laundry and grocery shopping done. Spending all those hours in the dark, engaged in fantasies the good folks in Hollywood (and elsewhere as it turned out) had created, no doubt took a toll on my social and physical skills. Who had time for sports, when *The Green Slime* (1968) was playing at the Poly? Who wanted to attend a church or school function when *Dracula Has Risen from the Grave* (1968)? Often, when I exited the theater to go home, I would suffer a sort of post-cinematic depression on realizing I was back in the 'real world.' This was the place where adults didn't like being pestered by kids, where people had to change tires and mow lawns. I longed for a pirate, astronaut or cowboy lifestyle, full of adventure.

When I became old enough to work, I was unfit for employment anywhere but a movie theater. In 1975, I landed my second job as an usher at Cineworld, Fort Worth's first multiplex movie house. One day a guy named Randy walked into the lobby. I recognized him immediately, though I had not seen him since I was seven years old. In the mid-1960s he was my next-door neighbor, but his family had moved away. Randy was there to see *Jaws* (1975) with a couple of his buddies. He said, "I remember you. You're that weird kid!" He launched into a detailed account of how he'd come over to my house to play. My mom had sequestered us in my bedroom, where I forced him to act out "space stories." We had approximated Flash Gordon-style costumes by pinning towels to our shoulders for capes and pulling Fruit of the Loom briefs over our blue jeans. I had placed the tornado illustration from my storybook of the *Wizard of Oz* under an opaque projector and we threw ourselves around the room, pretending we were on a planet with severe atmospheric disturbances.

Did I remember doing this? No, not specifically. Still, I'm certain his story was true because that's the sort of thing I did every day as a kid. He remembered it because, to him, it was insanely different. I did not remember it because it was just another day in the world I was constructing despite the steady opposition from reality.

My parents, God bless them, did everything within their power to encourage my creativity. When my twelfth birthday rolled around, my father who was in Vietnam sent me a great Canon Super 8 movie camera he purchased from the PX. He also encouraged me to enter the *Stars and Stripes* Short Story contest, which I did, receiving an Honorable Mention (maybe everybody got one of those, I don't know.) Mom bought me a projector and I was in business. My friends and I began making monster and superhero movies in the backyard.

At Eastern Hills High School, I met a kid with incredible artistic talent. His name was Bob Camp and we became really good friends. We shared a love of movies, animation, underground comics and extreme vulgarity. Bob and I, and our close circle of cohorts, made a series of Super 8 films involving psychedelic hallucinations, skateboarding werewolves, vampires who dug themselves out of the grave on Halloween and a Blob-like stop-motion creature known as Splot! (Our answer to the animated Christian propagandist *Jot*.) We were nothing, if not irreverent, in every aspect of our lives. Little wonder that Bob went on to become the Creative Director of a groundbreaking animated program on the Nickelodeon Network known as *Ren and Stimpy* (TV series 1991-1996).

After High School, Bob and I enrolled in filmmaking classes at UT Arlington, under Andy Anderson. Andy, no slouch as a filmmaker himself, told us he admired our enthusiasm, but felt he just didn't have the energy to tackle a feature length film.

I was really pissed a few years later when I learned he'd done exactly what Bob and I had suggested – assembled the students into a rag-tag crew and shot a sort of sci-fi thriller called *Interface* (1985). The film which cost around thirty thousand to produce, using slave (read that 'student') labor, was licensed to Vestron for 90K. That was the sort of deal I wanted to be a part of!

The summer following our first year at UTA, I went to visit my father in Isfahan, Iran. Bell Helicopter was footing the bill, since I was still a dependent. I was there about six months. I returned with a young woman from Hawaii whom I intended to make my wife. Her name was Carolyn Thompson and in addition to giving birth to my three sons, she starred in three of the ultra-cheapie-direct-to-video films I produced, *Highway to Hell* (1990), *The Abomination* (1986), and *Ozone: Attack of the Redneck Mutants* (1986) performing under the screen name Blue Thompson.

My father had agreed to pay for my college education and now that I was seemingly starting a family, he wanted me to get that over with pronto. And as cheaply as possible. At his suggestion, I enrolled in Brooks Institute in Santa Barbara, California and completed their course in Motion Picture Production. The first time I ever heard the word "schlock" occurred one idle afternoon in the library at Brooks. By chance I picked up a book called *Kings of the Bs* (Dutton 1975). My life would never be the same.

Sure, I'd heard of Roger Corman. He was the token B-Movie guy who got all the press attention, while his partners in crime remained well under the radar. In *Kings of the Bs* I found a whole book dedicated to the unsung directors of such cinematic enigmas as *Blood Feast* (1963) and *Mudhoney* (1965). In the chapter on Sam Katzman, a Poverty Row producer known for his extensive use of stock shots, I became acquainted with the word "schlock." Allegedly this word referred to shoddy goods. And, by some peoples' standards, that was an accurate assessment of Katzman's output. But, I'd seen a lot of Katzman's movies on television when I was a kid. I had a fondness for the stuff and I wasn't so certain that joining the ranks of the Schlockmeisters was a bad thing. My fellow film students thought I was nuts, high or both. Katzman had left his mark on cinematic history, something many respected directors had failed to do. He was also credited, according to the book, with coining the term "beatnik." I really dug him for that!

I knew I wanted kids, but I didn't want to raise them in Los Angeles. My Bible-Belt upbringing still had a fence around my mind, so after Brooks, Carolyn and I moved back to Texas and shortly thereafter, had our first son, Joshua. I was trying to make a living *and* put together some sort of production deal for a low budget movie. For three years I just drifted, working as a printer, a cab driver (for about two days) and as a film inspector at the glamorous Allied/WBS facility in the Las Colinas Communications Complex.

During this slump, I never lost my taste for cheesy cinema nor abandoned my aspirations to schlockdom. I hooked up for a short time with a group of five guys who were eking out meager livings on the fringes of the entertainment industry. Like me, they wanted to make movies. One was a magician, one a juggler; two were Blues Brothers impersonators and the last videotaped Little League Baseball games. We rented a warehouse in Deep Ellum and printed some business cards with the name Productions West Communications. It was a wild time of flailing about and grasping at straws. We established a school for Santa Clauses and placed them in paying venues around the Dallas / Fort Worth Metroplex. We produced a gameshow for local cable access. Most importantly to me, I began writing a book on B Movie directors. I started interviewing people like Larry Buchanan (*Mars Needs Women* (1967), *Zontar: Thing from Venus* (1966), *It's Alive!* (1969)), S. F. "Brownie" Brownrigg (*Don't Look in the Basement* (1973), *Keep My Grave Open* (1977), *Poor White Trash Part 2* (1975)) and Larry Stouffer (*Horror High* (1973)). I happened upon a young fellow named Glen Coburn who had just directed a movie he called *Bloodsuckers from Outer Space* (1984). Productions West never even came close to getting a movie done. The fellows just couldn't quit fighting among themselves long enough to make something productive happen. So, I left the PWC warehouse/studio one day in 1984 and never went back.

A friend helped me land a gig through a local ad agency for the Marriott Corporation. They'd just purchased the very retro hamburger diner franchise known by different names in various regions of the country. In my hometown we called it Kip's Big Boy. The mascot was a beefy cartoon guy in red checkered overalls holding an enormous burger on a platter. There was a fiber glass statue of the Big Boy in front of each of the restaurants. Marriott decided to run a campaign in which people would vote on whether the Big Boy should stay or go. Our leader organized a band of pro-Big Boy picketers who would demonstrate in public, holding signs and shouting phrases like, "No, No, the Boy can't go!" or my favorite, "He's stupendous, he's colossal, if not for us he'd be a fossil!" We got a (pardon the Texanism) shitload of free press. We held demonstrations in Fort Worth, Dallas, Tulsa, Oklahoma City, Wichita, and Houston. By day, I was a Big Boy supporter. But, by night I was part of a sinister plot to do away with the big guy. Two other accomplices and I rented a U-Haul truck and in the wee hours, we kidnapped four of the Big Boy statues and incarcerated them in a friend's garage. We took Polaroid photos of ourselves, wearing terrorist garb and wielding chainsaws, threatening to dismember the pudgy mascots if our demands were not met. The name of our covert organization was Federation Against Ridiculous Trademarks (F.A.R.T. for short). It was fun and lucrative. I got paid $200 a day to do the sort of stuff I'd pretty much always done for free.

On the cusp of my exciting Big Boy adventure, one day my step father, a successful commercial real estate broker, out of the blue, offered to finance a movie concept I'd come up with called *Tabloid!* I was off to the races. I graduated from the ranks of mundane humanity into the privileged status of schlockmeister. With confidence, I moved forward and never looked back.

# RATIONALE

Why do good people like bad movies? Good question. I'm glad you asked.

Pauline Kael once wrote "movies are so rarely great art, that if we can't appreciate great trash, there is little reason for us to go." She admitted to the guilty pleasure of enjoying those hideous biker movies Hollywood cranked out, in lieu of cheesy westerns, during the 1960s. Kael is a respected name in the field of film criticism. If we accept her assessment as valid, the question is not, "Why do some people like bad movies?" Maybe the question is, "Why do we disagree on what constitutes a bad movie?" Or, "Why do some of us think we only watch good movies?" Or as Bill Murray (as Dr. Peter Venkman) said in *Ghostbusters* (1984), "I'm a little unclear on this whole good/bad thing."

Marshall McLuhan said, "Good taste is the first refuge of the non-creative. It is the last-ditch stand of the artist."

All of us possessing a passing familiarity with the history of the twentieth century know that Hitler and his Nazis attacked what they called "degenerate art" with a vengeance.

Admittedly, bad films are an acquired taste, much like cigarettes, liquor and the stinkiest of cheeses. No one starts out liking bad movies. But those who admire abysmal films, like smokers, drunks and people with cheese breath, are sending a signal loud and clear: *I don't give a damn!*

Generally, film viewers start out enjoying only good films, the ones they deem worthy of praise. The appetite for truly good films, music, literature or even food, far outstrips the supply. There are always mercenary characters willing to fill that gap. This is what we're taught, but I think there's more to it than that.

I think many bad movies arise from the same swamp that birthed punk rock, rap, tattoos, piercings and graffiti. I think the music of Roky Erickson and Lou Reed have much in common with the films of Ed Wood and Ray Dennis Steckler. Like the underground comix of R. Crumb, bad movies are a way of rubbing noses in the bogus standards society claims to promote. They scratch at the veneer of civilization to expose the rotten structure beneath. These are the rag-tag hooligans raiding the house, uncovering the hidden perversions in June Cleaver's panty drawer. These are the people your parents warned you about, the ones your father couldn't stand or understand. These are the explorers who pointed the way out of the Norman Rockwell painting.

Andy Warhol knew the game was rigged, so he created his own world in which to operate. Does anyone really think his soup cans and silk screens of Monroe are great art? If not, why are they so incredibly expensive? The game is rigged. His paintings are worth that kind of bread because an illusion has been carefully constructed around them by the "in crowd."

Jack Kerouac stared at the nauseating object on the end of his fork and proclaimed it the "naked lunch." In doing so, he gave William S. Burroughs the title of his most famous novel. Did Jack Kerouac eat that tidbit? Refusing to play the game, refusing to eat the scuz is what the "bad" musicians, artists, writers and filmmakers do. We've been encouraged to seek a seat at the table where there aren't enough chairs to go around. More and more bright young people are too smart to chase the soiled carrot.

Bad movies are a way of telling the establishment to take a long walk on a short pier. People with a rigid idea of what makes "good" art, literature or films, often operate under the mistaken assumption that purveyors of the "bad stuff" are unsophisticated, undiscerning. My own experience, indicates they are more likely to be operating outside the soul-stunting box set up by the guardians of good taste.

Bad art is an act of rebellion. In truth, it's a healthier path than the ones chosen by "normal" folks; cigarettes, liquor, drugs or Limburger. It's a way of saying, "You're not fooling anyone with that over-the-rainbow stuff."

Guys like Larry Buchanan and David Friedman got a kick out of creating the illusion, the lure that pulled people into the theater. Roger Corman made a fortune doing exactly the same thing. The difference between Corman and the others is that he was savvy enough to create his own distribution network. In the early days of his film career, Larry Buchanan was told by Claude Alexander, "They pay on the way in." *Who cares if the movie's bad? Make them pay on the way in and see where it gets you.*

Of course, some bad movies are accidental constructions created by incompetence. Even these may be subconscious acts. The human ego is an enigmatic beast. Certainly not every film discussed in this book represents a conscious act of intellectual rebellion ... or does it?

Do I still appreciate finely crafted movies? Sure, I do! But, I have to say, finding a great novel to read seems easier than finding a great American film. Hollywood is mostly a brainless carnival of expensively produced gimmicks. Those are fine, too, but don't try to convince me that the latest multi-million-dollar-graphic-novel-based-extravaganza has any more long-term legitimacy than *Bloodsuckers from Outer Space*.

# LARRY BUCHANAN

He was born Marcus Larry Seale, Jr. in the poetically named little town of Lost Prairie, Texas, to farmer and part-time peace officer, Marcus Larry Seale and Maude Dove Seale. Head of casting for 20th Century Fox, William Mayberry, said "Sounds like a circus act!" Axing the Seale, Mayberry chose instead the surname of one of Larry's grandmothers; Buchanan. "We'll start a whisper campaign that you're the bastard son of Jack Buchanan!" Jack Buchanan was a major entertainer in the United Kingdom. So, for all practical purposes, Larry Buchanan was "born" January 31, 1943 when the struggling actor from Texas signed on with 20th Century Fox.[i]

My earliest exposure to a Buchanan movie was *It's Alive* (1969) a truly bizarre slice of weirdness featuring a couple of stalwart Texas talents; Annabelle Weenick and Bill Thurman. I was spending the night at the home of best friend, Herb Hays. We stayed up very late to catch it on KXAS Channel 5's *All Night Movies*.

**Author's Note:**
Larry Buchanan is unquestionably in a category of his own. His eccentric approach to cinema and his prodigious output are legendary. For this chapter dealing with Buchanan's films, I have deviated from the format used in the other chapters. I could not see giving a detailed description of each of Larry Buchanan's science fiction and horror productions, along with three examples of criticism for each. Had I done so, this chapter would have mushroomed into a virtual book of its own. Instead, I've hit the high notes and provided any unique observations I had to offer. Much has been written about his oeuvre. Those who want critiques of his titles will find the internet teeming with clever and sometimes insightful examples.

The thing didn't even kick off until about 2 am, which was way past the usual bedtime for a twelve-year-old. As I recall it, the experience had a surreal impact on my young mind. Really loud commercials for Smith Brothers' Carpets and Sigel's

[i] *It Came from Hunger!* by Larry Buchanan, McFarland & Company, Inc, 1996; pg. 7

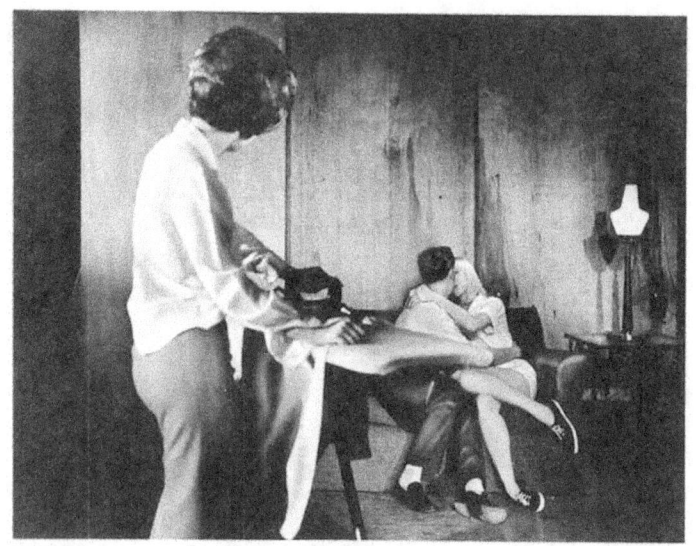

*Under Age*, an early Buchanan exploitation title.

wine of the week hammered us relentlessly every ten minutes. It was tougher than shucking oysters, but we were determined to stick it out. Our sleep-deprived, pre-pubescent minds were strangely impacted by Buchanan's opus. I remember feeling as if I'd been bludgeoned.

The next morning, Herb's folks took us to a local pancake restaurant. Over breakfast we joked about *It's Alive*. I'd say we were struggling for a context into which we could place the film. That's when Herb's dad told us the thing had been made by a man from Dallas. News flash! That simple fact made a huge difference in our assessment of it. It wasn't just a weird piece of crap anymore. It was *our* weird piece of crap! Sure, we told ourselves, if we ever got our hands on a 16mm camera and enough film to shoot a feature, we'd certainly do a better job than this Buchanan dude. Still, we admired him enormously for being a local son who'd managed to do what we so desperately wished to do. He'd shot a monster movie in Dallas, Texas! Armed with this knowledge, we continued to shoot our own Super 8mm epics in the environs of east Fort Worth.

In 1982 someone from the Dallas film community gave me Larry Buchanan's phone number. With a bit of youthful trepidation, I telephoned and was pleasantly surprised to find him, charming, witty, encouraging and cooperative. Talking with the man was a pleasure. The enthusiasm in his repertoire of tales was contagious. He may have travelled through the sleazy back alleys of the film industry, but somehow, he had remained unsullied by the experience.

That first interview I did with Larry was highly informative, entertaining even, especially to a recent film school grad who wanted to follow in his footsteps. We spoke long enough to fill a 60-minute cassette tape on both sides and a few minutes on a second tape. (My wife would surely raise her eyebrows at the long-distance charges on the next phone bill!) I wish I still had those tapes or even a transcription, but they were lost somewhere along the twisting path I call my life. To this day, my memories of in-person and phone conversations with the man remain cherished memories.

Buchanan certainly was educated in the school of hard-knocks. His mother died while he was a child and his father placed Larry and siblings in the Buckner Children's' Home in Dallas. Ever the storyteller, Larry made sure I understood his father was a lawman and present at the ambush which claimed the lives of famed outlaws, Bonnie and Clyde.

At the orphanage, the young Buchanan developed a love of motion pictures. He spoke with obvious passion of learning to thread and operate the old 35mm projector that was used to screen movies at the Buckner home. The film prints were often loaned by local exhibitors. Skinny little Larry willingly shuttled the metal cases containing the movies on buses between the theaters and the orphanage. Recalling this time, he referred to himself as the "fanatic of film row."

On more than one occasion, Larry admitted his overwhelming and even irrational attraction to motion picture production. "Filmmaking's a disease, an obsession, and there's no cure for it."

As my own endeavors in cinematic schlock progressed, I found Larry was always curious and genuinely supportive. We met in person a couple of times and spoke via phone a handful of times between 1982 and 1996. In reality I guess you could say I barely knew the guy, but I considered him a friend nonetheless. Over the years, Larry told me many amusing tales from his life experience. All the stories he told me (and many more) can be found in his auto-biographical memoir, *It Came from Hunger!* (McFarland 1996). Larry Buchanan was, without a doubt, a kindred spirit.

I think it was in 1984 that a friend and I arranged a public screening of Christian Blackwood's documentary film, *Roger Corman: Hollywood's Wild Angel* (1978). We showed the film in a nightclub called *Tahiti's* on Dallas's Lower Greenville Avenue. The establishment was owned by the entertainment attorney we were working with as we put together our first feature film. We printed up some garish flyers and invited Roger Corman, Larry Buchanan and local film distributor, Tom T. Moore, to attend. Moore, and possibly Buchanan, were interested in attending in order to share the company of Corman as featured guests. At the last minute Corman's people notified us that Roger appreciated the invitation, but he would be in South America overseeing the fringes of his cinematic empire on the date in question. Moore and Buchanan seemed happy to attend. This was the first time I met Larry face to face. He and his wife Jane were charming people, well-spoken and entertaining. I considered the event a success.[ii]

After completing my first feature film *Tabloid!* (1985), I contacted Larry for input on avenues of distribution. He was as helpful as he could be given his own situation at the time. "Was it shot on 35mm?" No. "Can you get a blow-up?" Not unless the distributor pays for it. "I'll check around and let you know if I come up with any promising leads." I ended the conversation with a sense that Larry and I were basically in the same boat. Hollywood was changing rapidly as a result of new technologies. Home video had taken the place of the drive-ins. We were in uncharted waters in the indie film world and, as always, there were plenty of sharks ready to devour naïve filmmakers.

One of the things that stands out in my memory of the first phone interview I did with Larry was his use of the word "matriculated" in reference to his attendance at Baylor University in Waco, Texas. I had never heard the word before. I chuckled to myself many years later when I finally got to read Larry's autobiography, *It Came from Hunger!* for there in a chapter about his schooling was that word. I don't believe I had heard or even read that word in the thirty-plus years between the conversation and reading the book. Larry was a class-act with a slick vocabulary. He had been groomed by Buckner Children's Home for the ministry, after all.

Things in Los Angeles in the mid-1940s were not to Larry's liking, so he packed his bags and caught a train to New York. He lucked into a connection with the prestigious Thornton Model Agency and things began looking up.[iii]

---

[ii] I didn't realize it at the time, but in the audience that night, was a very talented young musician and filmmaker who would go on to score my film *Highway to Hell* and to direct the Vanilla Ice video for *Ice, Ice, Baby*, none other than Greg Synodis.

[iii] *It Came from Hunger!* by Larry Buchanan, McFarland & Company, Inc, 1996; pp. 23-24

Soon he was appearing in Broadway and off-Broadway productions and forming friendships with other talented up-and-comers. He scraped together enough money to produce and direct his first film, a short subject called *The Cowboy* (1949), which at least broke even thanks to some friendly assistance from Max Youngstein at United Artists.[iv] Serving as an assistant director to George Cukor on the Judy Holiday vehicle *The Marrying Kind* (1952) he met and fell for a lovely young actress who was an extra in the film, Jane McVayne. He was so smitten with her that he engaged in some creative shenanigans throughout the course of the production to get the young lady multiple days of work, despite director Cukor's explicit instructions to the contrary. On the final day of the shoot, thinking he had pulled the wool over the eyes of the veteran director, he was astonished when Cukor commented sardonically, "Lawrence, dear boy, why don't you marry the girl?"

He did.[v]

When Jane informed him that they were having a child, Larry decided to relocate to warmer (and more affordable) climes. He accepted a job as producer of commercials, training and instructional films for the renowned Jamieson Film Company of Dallas. Back in his hometown, life became increasingly more com-

[iv]Ibid, p. 32
[v]Ibid, p. 34

**The Eye Creatures** and **Zontar** double video

fortable and predictable for the Buchanan family.

The motion picture business is rife with tales of disappointment. For the fledgling director, there are ample opportunities to be exploited, cheated or hoodwinked. One of the most memorable stories in Buchanan's canon was about the production of a softcore porn film he titled *Venus in Furs*. The only print of this lost erotic flick now rests at the bottom of Lake Dallas.

While employed at Jamieson, Larry

was approached by a wealthy oil man who wanted to produce a cheapie/nudie flick, the sort of thing that Harry Novak's Boxoffice International was releasing to art houses like the Lido in Dallas and the Capri in Fort Worth. The man was in the throes of a passionate extra-marital affair with a lovely vixen who had set her sights on a career in the movies. To prove his love, she demanded he finance a vehicle to display her ample talents.

The financing was all cash under the table. Buchanan wrote, produced and directed on a whirlwind schedule, "winging it" with a "script" that was little more than one extremely long paragraph detailing the sordid antics to be captured on film. He borrowed the premise from one of the writings of the Marquis de Sade and called the movie, *Venus in Furs*.[vi]

Things went rather well on the shoot and Larry managed to carry the project through to an answer print, cutting and scoring the epic himself in a week's time. The budget may have been miniscule, but savvy Larry was hanging onto as much of that cash as possible for himself and his family. When the film was screened for the man who'd financed it, he was most complimentary. He asked if everyone had been paid; were there any outstanding debts on the project? The books were clear, Larry assured the man. They loaded the film into the trunk of the man's car and drove to his weekend place on Lake Dallas. The astounded Buchanan watched as the wealthy oil man threw the only copy of his underground epic into the deep, dark waters of the lake. He'd paid for it and was entitled to do with it as he pleased. After the ritual disposal, he explained his paramour had skipped town the night before with a prominent disc jockey.[vii]

The late 1950s and early 1960s were a time of transition for movies in America. TV was stealing more of the audience the major Hollywood Studios had come to rely on. Pornography had been around since the earliest days of silent cinema, but nudity was excised from all general release films thanks to the influence of the Catholic Church and what was sometimes called "the Hays Code." The gradual introduction of foreign films into American "art house" cinemas, proved there was big box office in skin flicks! Our man in Dallas, Larry Buchanan, hitched his wagon to the art house star and compiled a number of cheapie flicks out of documentary footage from all over the world. He said he never took credit on these projects because, "a credit would cost the producer more money and anyway, credits only bored the audiences who were waiting for the skin."[viii]

---

[vi] Not to be confused with films of the same title by Jesus Franco and Roman Polanski. Works by the Marquis de Sade provided the basis for many ultra-low-budget efforts over the years, partly because they were known works with exploitation potential, but also because they were in the public domain.

[vii] Ibid, pp. 46-47

[viii] Ibid, pp. 49

In 1957, Larry received a call from bottom-of-the-barrel indie road-show distributor, Claude Alexander. Alexander was the last of a dying breed of entrepreneurs who would hit town in a Cadillac, trunk full of lurid promo materials and as few prints of the movie as the release could get away with. Local media would then be saturated with enticing claims of hitherto unseen forbidden delights. It didn't matter if the films were stinkers (*They paid on the way in!*) as long as they contained a scene or two of naked women. The films often were just the bait to get people into the drive-in. The real profits would be made from the sale of condoms and other "adult novelties."

This guy Alexander, wanted to do a "real movie." No more scrap footage hack jobs. He wanted a real movie shot in color, with a story, plenty of nudity, a lurid title and most importantly, a price tag of no more than $8,000.[ix] Larry was reticent, but intrigued. Sure, it was slim pickings, but he'd always enjoyed a challenge and he'd rarely walked away from a long-shot. After an in-person meeting, over a bowl of chili, Buchanan was taken with the man's suave demeanor. He wasn't the usual poorly educated grindhouse hack. He regaled Larry with tales of his exploits in years as a bare-bones indie distributor.

Buchanan dragged out an old script that had been inspired by the picturesque little Texas hill country town of Luckenbach. (Yes, the same place Waylon Jennings sang about in 1977). It was based on a German folktale of a witch who returns from the grave for vengeance. The working title for the project was *The Luckenbach Witch*, but of course, that was entirely too tame for Claude Alexander. When the 59-minute epic made a splash in America's drive-in theaters, it was known as *The Naked Witch!* The modest project racked up $80,000 in domestic box office receipts. This was the gig that put Buchanan on the map as "that guy in Texas, who gets 'em done cheap!"

Following the indie success of *The Naked Witch*, Buchanan focused on lurid titles that would draw the rubes into the art houses and drive-ins. *A Stripper is Born* (aka *Naughty Dallas*, 1958), *Common Law Wife* (aka *Swamp Rose*, 1960), *Free, White and 21* (1963), *Under Age* (1964) and *The Trial of Lee Harvey Oswald* (1964) kept him busy for seven years and away from the horror and science fiction genres. As the titles indicate, Buchanan was not above pandering to the morbid curiosity of the masses in matters of sex, racial inequality and even the assassination of a president.

The life of an indie film producer is a roller-coaster at best. One year, you're in the chips, the next you're struggling to get

---

[ix] Ibid, pp. 48-49 Though Buchanan claims Alexander insisted on an eighty-minute running time for the film, all known versions of **The Naked Witch** weigh in at a scant 59 minutes.

Promo art from Buchanan's **The Naked Witch**.

another project rolling. After he was leveraged into an alliance with Sam Arkoff at American International Pictures for the distribution of *Free, White and 21*,[x] Buchanan saw AIP as an answer to the question of continuity of work. In the interest of moving up the ladder and providing a steadier stream of reliable income for his family, Larry accepted an offer from Arkoff to produce a series of 16mm color remakes of AIP flicks from the previous decade for exclusive distribution on television. It was steady work, but the budgets were set at a mandatory $35,000 per picture. There was no wiggle room, no hope of gradually increasing the budgets. "Sam knew what they could expect to make off the TV syndication deal, so he wasn't willing to spend a penny more per picture," Buchanan told me, "I wasn't making movies, I was grinding out sausages!"

*Invasion of the Saucermen* (1957), directed by Ed Cahn, had been a reasonably successful sci-fi comedy in its original release, though no one could've imagined at the time it would ever be considered worthy of a remake or that a remake could take it so far down the scale of cinematic respectability. Arkoff sent Buchanan a copy of the old screenplay and told him to recreate the movie Dallas-style. Teenagers were still interested in parking on Lover's Lane in 1965 and UFOs were still a mysterious topic of interest if not the furor they had been in the 1950s. In all fairness, the film that came to be called *The Eye Creatures* (1965) was a worthy effort considering the budgetary constraints. Buchanan and his Texas film crew gave it their all. Though, certainly not the most well-known of the AIP remakes, *The Eye Creatures* may have the highest production value of the series; but even this

[x]Ibid, pp. 65-66

distinction can seem like splitting hairs. These cinematic upstarts in Dallas were determined to put their city on the film production map. Arkoff was delighted to have a feature-length movie, in color no less, delivered into his hands for a paltry 35 grand. He sent Larry and the Dallas troupe more Hollywood tripe to transform into tasty late-night TV sausages.

Arkoff reached a bit further back into the American International archives and fished out Roger Corman's *It Conquered the World* (1956). This was perhaps even less remake-worthy than the Saucermen. At least that film had never pretended to be anything other than a sci-fi spoof. Corman had created a space alien from a world with a much greater gravitational pull. He reasoned the thing would be short and squat. Logical? Perhaps. Scare-inspiring? Hardly. The monster from *It Conquered the World* had a comical underbite and resembled nothing more than a huge, mutant dim sum from another planet. *It* was transformed into the legendary *Zontar, the Thing from Venus* (1966), Buchanan's best-known picture and the source of on-going derision, confusion and awe. Many thousands of words have been written about *Zontar*, often from a highly academic perspective.

The thrill of having an on-going production contract was rapidly fading. Buchanan insisted on selecting his own talent and made major revisions to the script to make it more "doable." In the 1980s, while I was working at Allied + WBS in Las Colinas, I met Jack Kelly. Jack was a salesman for Allied, but had been a crew member on *Zontar*. He entertained me with recollections of himself and Brownie Brownrigg cobbling together the alien creature out of found objects, including an old umbrella. "I thought you guys were in the sound department," I said, "were you also part of the special effects team under Jack Bennett?"

"I don't know where Jack Bennett was that day. All I remember is me and Brownie frantically scrambling to come up with something that could pass for a monster from outer space. That's just the way it was, working for Larry. There were no strict job descriptions, that's for sure. It wasn't like a union picture."

The appearance of John Agar in *Zontar*, allowed the film a modicum of respectability it otherwise would never have had. Agar had appeared in many of the best-known sci-fi flicks of the 50's, Universal Studios' classics like *Tarantula* (1955) and *Creature from the Black Lagoon* (1954). I can imagine many fans tuned into *Zontar* thinking they were in for an obscure treat, only to be caught up in the enigma. Here are a few of the questions and comments I heard from my own friends and family who had seen the movie; *Why would Agar do that? He used to be a pretty good actor! Did you* know he was married to Shirley Temple? He was great in those westerns with the Duke. How far the mighty have fallen! I've heard he has a drinking problem.

*Mars Needs Women* (1966) is the second best-known title in the Buchanan oeuvre, though accorded much less attention than *Zontar*. This was the third in the series of made-for-TV AIP flicks and Larry reasoned he could have more control over the budget and instill a greater sense of production value if he wrote his own screenplay. He was tired of being limited to properties that had been produced a decade earlier in black and white for much larger budgets. Arkoff signed off on *Mars Needs Women* and arranged for Tommy Kirk to play the lead.

The same Jack Kelly who'd told me about fashioning an umbrella into a space alien, commented, "Working with Tommy Kirk was a trip!" How so, I wondered. "He was just totally off-the-wall." I asked if Jack meant he was flamboyant. This was conservative Dallas of the 1960s and it was common knowledge that Disney had dropped Kirk's contract because he was a well-known homosexual. "No, I don't mean that at all. I mean he was absurdly childlike. We'd be in the middle of production and he'd want to play patty-cake. If you said no, he would absolutely insist. I'm trying to run sound and here's this grown man forcing me to play patty cake on the set." I asked how he handled the situation. "I tried to keep him happy and do my own job at the same time. It was always something like that, working for Larry."

One of the women Mars needed was the lovely, Yvonne Craig, who played Batgirl on later episodes of TVs *Batman* (1966-1968) starring Adam West and Burt Ward. Craig was under contract to AIP where she'd played in a few of the zany beach comedies with the likes of Frankie Avalon and Annette Funicello.

If the effects in this sci-fi oddity seem sparse or even nonexistent, it's for good reason. Buchanan had this to say: "Our effects budget for *Mars* was zero, zip, nada. But, with characteristic enthusiasm, we plodded on. In one scene, we actually used a Frisbee as a spaceship. It was thrown up into the fog and the camera was over-cranked[xi] to give the movement a threatening reality. It worked."[xii]

While the production of made-for-TV features continued, Buchanan found time for other indie films like a western called simply, *Sam* (1966). The demands placed on Buchanan's time and talent may be why he reverted back to using old AIP properties for his next micro-budget sci-fi epic. *In the Year 2889* (1967) was based on *The Day the World Ended* (1956) which trailers had proclaimed "the Screens New High

[xi]To over-crank the camera was to speed up the rate at which it exposed frames of film. This resulted in a slow-motion rendition of the action.
[xii]Ibid, pg. 101

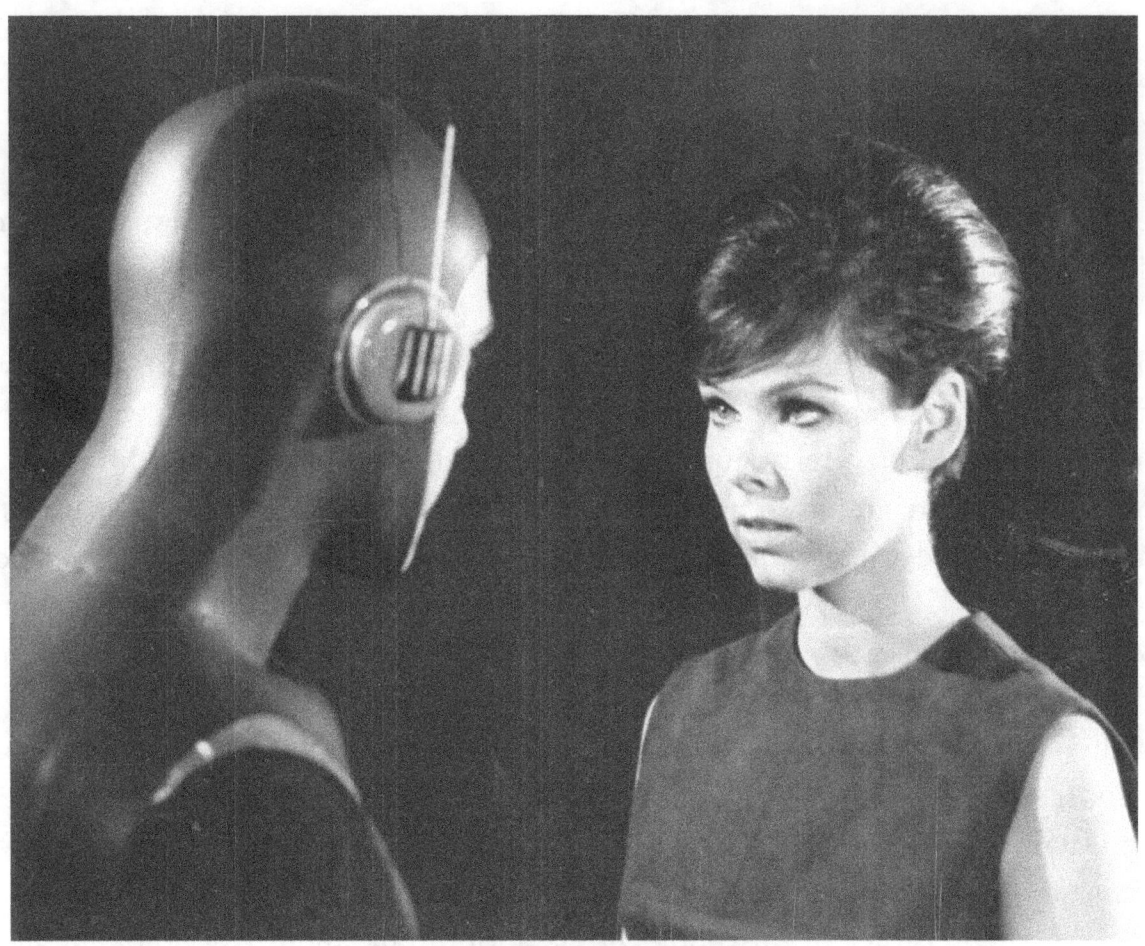
Yvonne Craig in **Mars Needs Women**.

in Naked Screaming Terror!" Neither original nor remake offered even a hint of terror, but the plot centering on isolated scientists battling a single radiation mutant, was ideal for a limited budget. AIP had always been about making silk purses from sows' ears, but with Buchanan on board they were pushing their own envelope. Another beach party girl, Quinn O'Hara, and Paul Petersen who had attained fame portraying the son of television's Donna Reed, starred in the film.

Next up in the Buchanan parade of remakes was *Creature of Destruction* (1967), based on one of my childhood favorites *The She Creature* (1956). The original film had featured decent performances from Marla English, Chester Morris and Tom Conway in a story of hypnotism, reincarnation and the unknown origins of humanity. A dose of common mayhem was thrown in to spice things up. It was the perfect recipe to captivate my six-year-old mind the first time I watched it on television. The Paul Blaisdell monster design was imaginative if not highly plausible.

Les Tremayne puts in his trademark competent performance as the hypnotist and Pat Delany, of *Zontar*, was brought back to play the hypnotist's subject who reverts into the prehistoric *Creature of Destruction!* The creature costume seems to be a wetsuit embellished with neat scissor-cut scales attached to it. If the costume had been a kid's stab at replicating the *Creature of the Black Lagoon*, it would have garnered applause and been given an 'A' for effort. Television audiences, however, were not much impressed with the beast and its unblinking ping-pong ball eyes.

Buchanan was clearly tiring of Arkoff's treadmill. *It's Alive!*[xiii] (1969) was allegedly written by Buchanan and based on a short story from Richard Matheson, *Being* (1954), though neither of them receive on-screen credit as writers. I've spoken of the movie earlier in this book. It is surreal. As inept as it appeared at first glance, I was unable to stop watching. Greg Goodsell, writing in *Zontar, the Magazine from Venus*, said, "*It's Alive! Is* the most enigmatic of Buchanan's sci-fi canon. For once, the technical shortcomings in the series produce unintentional results that strike ominous chords in the viewer."[xiv] When I read Goodsell's words, I felt strangely vindicated for my own enigmatic response to the film. Goodsell says the results were "unintentional," but who can say for certain? Was Buchanan conjuring from a playbook known only to sorcerers who dared manufacture realities from hunger?

It's clear that Larry was loyal to his troupe of actors and technicians in Dallas. He was a dedicated family man, determined to provide both materially and emotionally in ways his own father never had. He was a man of his word who fulfilled his contractual obligations. *It's Alive!* was to be the last of the made-for-TV cheapies he would create for Arkoff. Costs of production had continued to rise during the 60s. Inflation meant everything was going up. The only thing not rising was the amount of money AIP was willing to fork out for these flicks. When Larry began making them there had been a lot of talk about AIP becoming increasingly active in television production. By 1969 Larry's string of cheapies were the only films Arkoff's company had produced specifically for television.

Buchanan delivered what he promised; a full-length movie, in color with a monster. Most of it was easily staged "non-action" in a car or a cramped bedroom, with relentless dialog laid over the silent footage. The monster was supposed to be a dinosaur in a cave. Buchanan's answer to this special effect dilemma was to shoot close-ups of the ping-pong-eyed beast from *Creature of Destruction* in such a way as to make the beast seem huge in compari-

---

[xiii]Not to be confused with schlockmeister Larry Cohen's film of the same name.

[xiv]*It Came from Hunger!* by Larry Buchanan, McFarland & Company, Inc, 1996; pg. 117

son to the actors. In terms of actual effectiveness, he might better have used a dinosaur toy from the five and dime.

Larry Buchanan and his tribe were restless. They'd had enough and they weren't going to take it anymore. For several years, they had all paid dues in hope that doors would open. Those doors were still locked and many of them felt they were being taken advantage of; not by Buchanan, but by the system. They simply couldn't afford to keep making these terrible little films for Larry. There was neither money nor prestige in the venture, so folks were ready to move on.

Buchanan told Sam Arkoff he was done making pictures for $35,000. He was more than a little surprised when his Executive Producer allowed him to choose his next film and name his own budget. He was given $300,000 to produce *A Bullet for Pretty Boy* (1969) starring rock and roll heartthrob Fabian Forte. The success of Warner Brothers' *Bonnie and Clyde* (1967) had spawned a trend of depression-era gangster films. That cycle was still going strong in 1969. Buchanan's movie, loosely based on the real-life exploits of Charles Arthur "Pretty Boy" Floyd, was a hit. The success of that film gave Buchanan a little breathing room. It was no longer a mad rush to be making that next movie.

In the decade following *A Bullet for Pretty Boy*, Larry made five pictures; a *Bergmanesque* indie intended to please the arthouse crowd, a movie about Jesus Christ from a controversial perspective, films about Marilyn Monroe, Howard Hughes, Jean Harlow and even a quirky sexploitation piece about a good-hearted female anthropologist who shares her body with a tribe of missing links. It was not until 1982 that Larry would return to the horror/sci-fi genre with a movie called *The Loch Ness Horror*, shot at Lake Tahoe which straddles the California/Nevada border.

**The Loch Ness Horror.**

I'm truly pleased to have known Larry Buchanan. He was something of a trailblazer, no matter what you think of his movies. This orphan set his sights on a career in the movies and, by god, he pulled it off. Though I had a limited number of conversations with the man, I certainly felt his influence on the path I took. And, I believe I had a bit of an impact on him in some small measure.

In 1991, I produced a three-part series for Irving Community Television called *Guerilla Cinema*. One of the episodes dealt with Larry's work. I interviewed him for the project and when it was finished, sent him a VHS copy. When I first asked him to be a part of the program, he asked, "Why are you calling it Gorilla Cinema?" I explained it was a different sort of guerilla. We both had a laugh. Sometime later when he was teaching seminars for aspiring young filmmakers, he told me he'd borrowed my title for his workshops. He asked if I minded and of course I didn't care one bit.

Larry found out I'd been the subject of a chapter in John McCarty's book, *The Sleaze Merchants*. He winced at the word "sleaze." I understood. I'd grown up in the Bible Belt, too. I told him Ted V. Mikels had refused to be a part of the book because he would not have his work referred to as sleaze. In the same conversation, I mentioned that there was a growing appreciation for "bad cinema," that I'd always felt I was following in the footsteps of the Poverty Row producers like Sam Katzman. I made him understand that I took pride in my chosen path as a schlockmeister. In fact, I said, "If I ever write a memoir, I'm calling it *Confessions of a Schlockmeister*." When Larry wrote his own memoir, he let me know he was borrowing that word "schlockmeister."

When I began work on this book I was reminded of the *Guerilla Cinema* program I'd done for ICTN in 1991. I contacted their office in Irving and asked if the programs still existed. After an exchange of emails, I learned that the ¾" masters did still exist, but were unplayable.

In 1991, I had a sense that these interviews had some sort of historical significance, but no one else seemed to think so. It was a little disheartening twenty-plus years later to think that the interviews were lost. The ICTN engineer informed me that we could send the faulty masters away to be "baked." My involvement with media has been extremely limited for about twenty years, so I had no idea what this baked thing was. Still, I agreed to pay for it and asked them to go ahead with it.

On January 11, 2017, I received word that the tapes had been baked and DVDs were ready for me to pick up. I've just spent the afternoon listening to Larry Buchanan and Tom Moore talk about their love for cinema. It was a heart-warming experience. I'd almost forgotten how much I adored these two guys and what an influence they were on me.

Here is a transcript of everything Larry Buchanan told us in episode one of Guerilla Cinema.

*LB*: Film is a kind of infection. I think it's a real infection … and there's no cure for it.

I was an orphan. My dad was a famous Peace Officer. As a matter of fact, he was after Bonnie and Clyde, like a lot of others. He was at the site in Gibsland, Louisiana when they were shot. I lost both my mother and father early. We were put into an orphanage in Dallas called Buckner Orphan's Home. You may have heard of it.

I was unofficially adopted by the Variety Club of the US. The Variety Club is made up of show business members, owners of theaters, producers and directors. I was unofficially adopted, so any time I went into Dallas, I had a free pass to any movie house in the city.

I was able to pick up clips from the junk behind the theaters. Have you seen a picture called *Cinema Paradiso*? Be sure to see it. It's my life story, although it's set in Italy. I would piece them together, all sorts of montages and show them at the orphanage on Saturday night. I'd be in the projection booth. We had a little theater. I was eleven, making these strange montages.

When it came time to graduate I had a choice. I had a scholarship to Baylor in Waco, provided I studied for the ministry and I had an introductory letter to Darryl Zanuck who was then head of Fox Studios. The Fox lot on Pico. I matriculated to Waco, Baylor. Bored with it in three days, I hitch-hiked to California.

I got a job at Fox. I was trying to get into acting. I was in the prop department. I wanted to be an actor too, because they were all making the money. In those days it was very hard to break in as an actor, so I went to New York.

I started doing theater and making Army Training films at the Army Signal Corps, Astoria. There it was wide open. A person as young as I was could write, he could direct and edit. They had a tremendous facility there. And I was also doing plays in the evening.

I did a film called *The Cowboy*. A one-reel short subject that won a Peabody Award. I also did a thing called *The Wetback* for CBS. Ed Murrow narrated, Fred Friendly produced it. My work was heard about by the Jamieson Film Company of Dallas. They called me in New York and said, "We understand you're a Texan." I said, "Yes." "Do you ever intend to come back home?" "Yes."

The reason I was saying, "It comes from hunger" was we'd just had our first son. I didn't want to bring him up in the mean streets of New York. We didn't even talk money. It was Bruce Jamieson calling. Jamieson was very good for me. It was hard work. Not a lot of money, but we made a lot of commercials, a lot of industrial films. The one condition was that I could continue to work toward the independents. I knew I wanted to make independent films. I'm happiest when I'm doing that, even if it's something that costs fourteen dollars and sixty-seven cents. I'm happier doing that than anything.

I did a thing called *The Naked Witch*, a feature film, in color for $8,000! That's my classic! That one was incredible!

The thing that got me international… I mean real international notoriety was a film called *Free, White and 21*. It was the story of a famous rape case in Dallas. A real story. We worked from the transcripts of the trial. It became a very big hit for AIP (American International Pictures.) Sam (Arkoff) saw it and said, "We want the picture." Sam Arkoff and Jim Nicholson, who was his partner, the *late* Jim Nicholson.

They did so well with that, they said, "We'd like to talk about some other pictures." So, we made one, we made two, we went on to three. I got back to this idea of continuity. I said, "This can't go on."[xv] I told them, "Okay, I'll do these little pictures." They were all shot locally on color film, for virtually no budget, using talent that had, for the most part, done their best work. I'm not saying they were bad. I'm just saying they were cheap. We got some good people from Hollywood who'd come down to play the two principle roles.

John Agar did three for me. Tommy Kirk did two. Suddenly they began to get a sort of "culty" color to them. There was an ambience about the films. The urgency and the difficulty of making them somehow bled into what they looked like. Suddenly they had a different look. The people looked at them and said, "Well, can they be that bad?" Because they always found a certain strain of intelligence running through them.

I do like to throw people off a little bit. Once in a while, someone will say something with a certain amount of intelligence. They weren't used to that in this genre. In this genre, the girls are usually bad actors. The guys are bad actors. The camera work looks like it's a blow up from 8mm. It looks rotten.

But, they got better and better. You know the story; if you play softball only one day a week, on Saturday afternoon, you're not very good. If you play softball every day, you get to be pretty good. So, we were playing a lot of softball. We were working every day on films. And weekends. We didn't recognize weekends.

People do not believe these stories, but they're true. Just check with the crews. We did not have the time to plan weeks for a picture, the way it's done now. Even on

[xv]Buchanan felt like AIP was stringing him along. They knew how desperately he wanted to make movies, so they'd only call on him at their convenience. He wanted a regular gig making films for them.

the cheapest picture, you'll have three or four weeks of pre-production. We didn't have that time. We didn't have that kind of money.

I'll give you one example. It's true, in *Mars Needs Women*, we actually went out on the first shot ... I did, I threw a Frisbee in the air and we shot it and over-cranked it. Later, I did get a model and used that and showed the people coming out of this little hulk when we did inserts. But the actual space ship was a Frisbee.

When we would come across a special effect, we'd talk about it. I'd say, "Jack, do you have any powder?" He'd say, "Yeah, I got some powder." It was so erratic. When I look back now at the dangers that we did working with this stuff. Jack got where he knew enough about it to be safe. I look back and think, "My god!" today we'd have a special effects man with a permit and all this business. Of course, he (Jack Bennett) has one now.

In *Eye Creatures*, there was a case in which we had lightning coming in on John Ashley in an old house. We did not have enough of an exposure between the lightning flashes. So, we under-cranked our camera. Our 16mm. We went to a wild motor and under-cranked and made him walk slower to get the exposure. Now, no one's ever heard of that. But, that's the only way we could get it.

We wanted it to have that eerie look. And we'd done many things like that, just on short notice. Really it was seat-of-the-pants stuff. Like I mentioned earlier about the explosion at the ice house at White Rock Lake. We didn't know how much powder to use. I mean, we just guessed at it and of course, it was much too much.

But, by the time we got to *Pretty Boy Floyd* (*A Bullet for Pretty Boy*, 1969) Jack had it licked. It had great effects, that were very well done. The picture, if it were done in LA today, it would be a very expensive film. Everybody threw in and worked so hard. Because we were fresh and new and because we were beginning something really in Texas. Remember, there was only Jamieson when I started. Now, you have twenty, thirty different companies.

We would go to the fire department, for example and they would, just to get their name on the screen, they'd have a fire engine standing by if we were going to blow up a filling station or a farmer's cabin. They'd say, "Well, gee, you'll put us on the map. We'll be glad to be there." You just can't be that informal anymore. Insurance? Well, we kind of looked the other way.

Horror films! That genre is primary for a beginner's film. Whether you're talking about me or anyone else. The reasons are very simple. It is a film that, if it is well made at all, cannot help but be released. That's number one: Be Released. Number two: if it has something unique about it, it's not only going to be released, it's go-

Early VHS sleeve for *Zontar, the Thing From Venus*. Photo courtesy of vhscollector.com

ing to make some money. And that brings you to a second film, which is very good. They do not have to have stars.

Let me tell you about horror films; they're very forgiving. Very forgiving. Because if you are under terrible constraints, with money and time, terrible constraints – it comes out with a certain kind of unvarnished, untutored originality. Like the guy that did *The Legend of Boggy Creek* ... Charles B. Pierce. I like Charles. He's cut of the same cloth I think I am, in that, if we can't work over here for some reason, we go over there and work. Nothing's going to stop us. But, *Legend of Boggy Creek* is a very crude picture. Very crude. It shows its origins. It didn't have stars, but it had a scary quaintness about it. The same with *Chain Saw*, although he got a lot of nice action elements in there, Tobe Hooper did.

These elements…there is such a fantastic audience for violence. From Schwarzenegger's *Total Recall* (1999) to all the way back to the first films in France with (Georges) Méliès. Even then they'd put some kind of horror in them, as much as they'd allow back then. They didn't have blood-letting because it was not allowed. Had it been allowed, it certainly would've been there, because it would've guaranteed release of their pictures.

So, you take something like *The Curse of the Swamp Creature* … we shot that on Caddo Lake on the Louisiana border. That was one of my favorite places to shoot. I shot three pictures there in those swamps. I like swamps. It's a southern thing. Billy Thurman was the monster and he used the same ping-pong ball eyes that I'd used on three other monster suits! Now, here's the problem with low-budget monsters. You're going to make an 8-reel picture. You only get to about reel five with these suits and they're torn up. Every night you spend more time patching this suit with gaff tape or whatever than you do rehearsing the actors. They were made so cheaply and we didn't have the materials then. The monster has to come first.

There's a remarkable thing about audiences ... it's kind of a cheat on them, but you can have a monster walking for twenty minutes as long as there's a pay-off somewhere. So, you get your screen time. If you're delivering a picture as I was, I was delivering sausages and the sausage had to be 80 minutes long. I ran out of story at 60 minutes many times. Because I'd try to get some pace into a scene and find out, geez I shouldn't have done that. All of a sudden, I've got a 60-minute picture. What am I going to do? So, we'd go back and shoot some more monster.

*Creature of Destruction* was kind of an intellectual thing using, I think, the same monster. One of the monster suits we used three times. My green, gilled monster.

The monster that has generated the loftiest comments from the critics ... (chuckles) ... I was interviewed at Cannes by an Israeli crew who had seen *Zontar, the Thing from Venus*. And they came up to the hotel room, doing just what we're doing now, but they were talking intellectually about *Zontar, the Thing from Venus*! They read into it all kinds of things, which of course I didn't have in there, at least not consciously. We had a lot of people compare it to Satan with the wings coming up.

All we had done, was Sam Arkoff wanted one real fast. I said, "I don't have a script right now." He said, "Well, we've got a lot of scripts here that Roger (Corman) did. Can you rewrite one?" I said, "Well, yeah, can you get it down here?" He Express-Mailed it to me. *Zontar* was based on another movie where the pod things attacked people from behind. It's a classic black and white film that Roger made. (*It Conquered the World!*) We just remade that. I asked how much I could change and he said, "Change whatever you want."

I made the thing called *The Naked Witch*, I mentioned. Years later I'm being interviewed about these little pictures and a guy came up to me and said, "Did you know there was a film called *Die Nakte Zauberin*? German, in 1915 or something, a silent film. Same idea. A witch returns after 100 years to wreak vengeance on the people who put the stake in her. I'd never seen the picture.

No matter how bad you make the film, and I've done this, I set a rule that no matter how poor the budget or how bad the actors or how little time we had, there was *a day that was Buchanan's day*. I don't care if the schedule's 15 days. One of those days is mine. Jessup wonders, "You're not rushing me." No, this is my day. We're going to do this as if we are really doing it right. If the sound's not right, I'd listen to it, "All right, let's do it over." If the actor's not right I might even pay them off and bring in another actor on short notice. Call somebody to come on over. I've done it. Because, this day, there's going to be a scene that no one's going to find fault with. And that has been very rewarding to me.

If you were to see *Hughes and Harlow*, we shot a 1920s picture, with aircraft! Dogfights in the air and everything. It's an expensive-looking picture. It looks like 3 to 5 million dollars. We shot it for $240,000. There was one day. A scene in a Mexican shack, supposedly in Ensenada, where he has trouble with his plane and they go in to an old friend. I said, "This is Buchanan's day!" And everybody wondered, "Well, Jesus, this is a piece of cake! Here it is lunch and we've only done two or three set-ups." That was my day. That scene looks fantastic. I'm very proud of those scenes. In every one of them, there's been a scene that I felt was flawless, technically and histrionically. That's been very rewarding over the years, to have one of those scenes pop up. I'd say, "Let's just watch this scene, then we can go back to having our peanuts or something. We don't have to watch the rest of the picture."

TS: Have you ever regretted not having an entire feature film like that?

LB: I have. I came closest on *Hughes and Harlow*, because I thought it was to be a feature film, but came to find out it was a tax shelter. It's good as my pictures go, but that one day was mine!

I say this, for the record, I don't want to start another picture unless it's like that. A lot of film makers boast, like Sam (Arkoff), saying "The bottom-line is making money." And yet they always say that so wistfully. I sometimes feel that if you could talk to them a few minutes, you would find out, yes, they'd like to make a good one. There's something more than just the praise of your peers. I think that in your own private and loneliest moment, when you're not even trying to impress your peers, you can sit there and smile and say, "I did it. I made a good film." It's a great feeling. The danger, I think is to wait too long to do it. I know people older than I am – if you talk to them any length of time – they've done some marvelous commercial films. But, if you talk to them a few minutes, you find that their whole life was directed toward doing this one film and for some reason they never did it. Then, with an edge of bitterness, he says, "Well, I don't want to do that anymore." But, really, I think it's still there.

In 1995 I attended my last American Film Market[xvi] in Santa Monica. I was killing time in the bar and noticed a man about my age standing nearby. We exchanged greetings and glancing at his

---

[xvi] The American Film Market (AFM) is an industry sponsored event held, in Santa Monica, California, during which motion picture distributors license rights to foreign territories.

badge, I noticed his name was Jeff Buchanan. I asked if he was related to Larry Buchanan. "Yeah, he's my dad." Jeff was a bit surprised that I even knew who Larry Buchanan was. I explained that I was from the Dallas/Fort Worth area and that I had often been compared to his father. We had a nice visit and I didn't run into him again for over twenty years.

As this book was going through the editing process, I noticed one of my youtube videos, an interview with Larry Buchanan, had received a comment. It was Jeff Buchanan! I had tried to contact him when I began writing the book, but all my leads had been dead-ends. Serendipitously, he showed up in time to contribute to the chapter on his father.

In mid-September of 2017 I had a wonderful two and a half-hour conversation with Jeff Buchanan. Like his father, I found him to be genuine, knowledgeable and both interesting and interested. Our phone conversation has been heavily edited for the purposes of this book.

*JB*: I was always amazed at how much my father knew about the process of filmmaking. For instance, Dad was good about going to sets in advance of the time he'd actually be shooting on them. As the art department people were putting something together, he'd come in and say, "I'll be shooting this area and this area. Don't worry about finishing out that part over there, because we'll never even see it." That was considerate! I had art department people tell me, "Your dad just saved us so much work!"

He always did all of his sound work at Cinesound, this no-frills place that had great engineers. The whole place including the cigarette machine was like from the 1940s. They did great work. Occasionally there would be a problem and we'd have to go do sound work at a different facility. The sexy secretary in a short skirt would be offering you cappuccinos. Dad was not impressed with that. He'd say, "Remember son, we're paying for all this." I really learned from him to find the people who can do the work. Disregard the flash and bling.

A lot of people don't realize how fragmented the film industry is. They just think, "I want to get into film" without realizing the many areas of specialization. People outside looking in think it's this one big monolithic industry. It's radically diverse, as I'm sure you discovered.

Regarding those Dallas made-for-TV movies Dad did for AIP; he always thought, "Oh, I'll just do this crap to stay busy and pay the rent. Eventually, I'll get to do my *Bridge Over the River Kwai* sort of thing." He didn't realize he had pigeon-holed himself. Although he had a lot of fun doing those films, he really did want to be a serious filmmaker. He had some scripts and several books optioned that he wanted to do and unfortunately, he never got the chance.

Often, when he was interviewing cast and crew, he was so eager to get going that the first person who walked through the door, he'd say, "Yeah, they'll be wonderful." It was frustrating to me. I was always trying to get him to slow down, take a little time.

TS: In the beginning, the opposite was required of him. Doing things fast and cheap, ensured his success in ventures like *The Naked Witch* and other titles destined for drive-in theaters.

JB: You know Dad felt like the drive-in was a truly American phenomenon and that its decline represented the end of an era. We were fascinated by them. On road trips, whenever we saw one in disrepair, we'd stop and look at the weeds growing up through the asphalt. He'd say, "There's nothing sadder than a closed down drive-in theater." And it's kind of true in a way.

The last ten or twelve years of his life I was really trying to help him craft something. A good film. I suggested the idea *Hurry Sundown*. It's the story of the last night of this Texas drive-in theater before it falls prey to the wrecking ball and the plans of real-estate developers. They decide to have an all-night marathon of films. There was some debate over whether we should have it be a Larry Buchanan marathon at the theater. Then we talked about it being a really major film from

When John Agar made this film for Universal, he never dreamed he'd be in Buchanan's **Curse of the Swamp Creature**.

each decade, like *Jaws* and other blockbusters, the thinking being it might have a broader appeal than just Buchanan films.

The projectionist is dreading the return of all these people who have gone on to Hollywood and Milan and made it big. During the course of the evening they all come to see him in the projection booth. The old girlfriend who became a successful model ends up to have a drug problem. The guy who made a fortune on Wall Street is now so broke he actually asks to borrow money. By the end of the marathon this projectionist realizes, "Hey, my life's actually been pretty good!"

The final scene was designed as a cameo for my father. The projectionist goes out to the one remaining car after the sun comes up and it turns out to be Larry Buchanan. They discuss their mutual love of film and he ends up encouraging the projectionist to make a film. Now that Dad's gone, I'd be hard-pressed to find someone to play that role.

*TS*: What was it like growing up the son of Larry Buchanan?

*JB*: My dad enjoyed doing even those super low-budget films. I'll tell you though, I was always personally a little ashamed of them. When I was eighteen or nineteen, I had a life-changing experience. I was visiting my parents and an aunt showed up. One of my dad's sisters whom I'd never met.

During the course of a conversation with this aunt, she said to me, "I gather you don't really respect what your dad does."

I said, "Well, no. It's a little embarrassing."

She set me straight very quickly. She told me about growing up in the orphanage. All the children had to pick cotton out in the Texas sun. These kids are dragging around these canvas bags that are eight feet long. They had to fill those up. It took a long time to fill up one of those bags. They may have gotten fifty cents for it.

My aunt said, "At lunch we would sit under the tree to eat. Your dad, who was a little kid, would entertain us with stories about how he was going to go to Hollywood and make movies. Imagine that. We're sitting in the shade just trying to cool off and your dad is telling us these stories and as far as you can see behind Larry, all the way to the horizon, all you can see is cotton fields." She thought to herself, it's wonderful that our little brother has such wild dreams, even if they'll never be realized. "So, think about that," she said, "He left that orphanage, hitch-hiked to Hollywood and ended up doing what he did. The fact that your dad has ever been a welcome visitor on a soundstage, let alone a director, is absolutely amazing."

Have you ever had one of those moments? One of those cathartic moments in life when you just completely shift your thinking? When I thought about that little kid in Texas, it was just amazing. I suddenly had this completely new respect for him. I've thought about that many times.

My dad would project movies for the others at the orphanage. He noticed that watching a movie on Saturday night people could completely forget about their situations in life. He thought, okay, this is what I want to do. I want to help people escape. There's a place called Hollywood where they make these things and I'm going to go there.

That's pretty bold if you think about it. He came out of that Texas orphanage with a new suit and a ten-dollar bill. He walked down that gravel road and hitched to Hollywood.

He was such a refined gentleman and yet he had no education. He loved books. If you ever went to the library with him, that was it. You'd be there for hours. He was well-read, self-taught. He grew up in a pretty rough orphanage. With all the time I spent with my dad, I still find myself asking, where did he get that education? How did he become that cultured, refined gentleman?

**TS**: Why don't you fill us in a bit more on your experience as a filmmaker?

**JB**: I wanted very much to be an editor for a time. Dad kept saying, "No son, you don't want to be an editor." Years later when I was directing, he said, "See, you're not the sort of guy who's going to be happy sitting in a dark editing room on a beautiful summer day."

I was never into the horror films or those slasher flicks. When I was in fourth grade, around 1967, I watched *Bridge Over the River Kwai* with my family on its television premiere. I remember asking my dad if there was more than one director on that film. I'd been around those schlocky little Dallas productions and I couldn't imagine something as immense as *Bridge Over the River Kwai* could be done by a single director. It seemed to me you'd need a fleet of directors. It was so absolutely amazing.

I always loved the process of filmmaking. I loved the actors and the crews. I hated the business end, the distributors, the financing. My dad was always encouraging about my aspirations.

I was actually offered a slasher film one year at Cannes. A friend of my father pulled me aside and said, "We need a director." I turned him down. Later, my girlfriend asked me why. I told her, "Anything that guy touches will be a career killer."

When I decided to get serious about film, originally, I wanted to be a cinematographer. I started at the bottom, became an electrician, moved up to second unit gaffer. I quickly came to see that as a Director of Photography you are hard-pressed to ever find a director who will hire you. The majority of my cinematographer friends end up shooting industrial productions.

Working in various positions, I came to admire my father even more for the fact that he'd worked pretty much every position on the crew. He gained a lot of respect from crews over the years because of his ability to quickly trouble-shoot problems and provide solutions. Many of the directors I worked with had never done anything. They did not understand what any of the crew positions entailed. I wanted to be one of those guys who knew what each position required.

I realized the only way I'd have any control would be to create my own projects. When I was about twenty-eight I told my dad I thought I wanted to direct. He got very serious and said, "Son, you'd better be very sure that's what you want. Even if it's the only thing in the world you want to do, you're going to find its very difficult to get there."

My dad gave me my first chance to produce. I produced *Good Night, Sweet*

*Marilyn* for him. It was only two weeks of shooting. He took all the outtakes from *Goodbye, Norma Jean* and just wrapped a film around it. Technically, it gave me a credit as a producer. That led to me producing a few projects.

Soon, I was complaining that I wanted to work on something with a real budget. I was hired as Unit Production Manager on a Japanese film shooting in Monterrey. It was like a nine-million-dollar film. I learned there was no difference! Wow! As far as the chaos and the problems; you imagine a bigger budget's going to help. It didn't.

My dad always said, "Work expands to fill the time allotted for its completion." We had nine million to spend, so we spent every bit of it.

In 1992 I was hired as Line Producer on a film for American Playhouse. We did *Shimmer* (1993) up in Iowa. I had always considered American Playhouse to be the zenith of mini-arthouse-type studios. I came away from that experience just so bewildered. I found myself asking if there was a safe-haven anywhere out there where people were sane and gracious about making movies.

I was an Assistant Director for many years. I worked for 3DO the game company for a good long while. We racked up a series of hits for them. I won two Telly Awards for work I did there. An associate and I started our own advertising agency and immediately after that 9/11 happened. Everyone was so uncertain after that and all of our clients put everything on indefinite hold. Our phone stopped ringing for close to a year.

*TS*: Any current projects in the works?

*JB*: The project I'm developing now arises from something I've noticed on every big-budget film I've ever worked on. I can't tell you how many times this has happened. Inevitably, there would come a day during shooting when you had to quickly move up on the side of a hill somewhere to catch the last light of the day and shoot a scene to stay on schedule. One particular situation, we grabbed the leading man and lady, ran up the hill, sat them in the grass. We had one reflector, camera with sticks and the sound guy. We got the scene.

The whole time we were shooting, I'm looking down the hill at this vast community of people, all earning good wages. And we didn't even need them. I remember thinking. You could bring everything we're using right now in the back of a station wagon. Why not just write scripts that play into this reality? So, you only have five or six or eight people working on a film.

Invariably, when you were watching the dailies, the scene we shot on the fly in the last moments of sunlight would be the best-looking stuff in the film! That really made an impression on me. Why not just build a film from the ground up to do it that way? I had a sort of conceptual rebirth.

I have always wanted to work with someone like a David Lean or a Stanley Kubrick; people who pay attention to every detail. I've found very few filmmakers in my time who are willing to do that. I've met a lot of very loud people who are really good at selling themselves, but not the sort of talent I've imagined working with.

*TS*: What are your thoughts on film versus digital?

*JB*: Oddly enough, my dad was very pro-new technology. He'd say, "You watch, cameras will become so good, you won't even need to rent a lighting package. You'll be able to carry your entire production around in your car. Some unknown guy in Mississippi will make a brilliant masterpiece of a film." This was twenty-five years ago that Dad was predicting this.

As you know, this came true. It's very liberating, but it's also produced a glut of films. A lot of them are not very good. The problem is the public has to sift through them to find out what's good and what's not.

I remember the first time I attended the American Film Market, back when they had it at the Beverly Hilton, before it got moved to Santa Monica. I was blown away by the number of movies there were being offered up. Admittedly, many weren't very good, but I saw some stellar films that could not get any traction. It was an important wake-up call.

*TS*: Did you ever network with any of the distributors your father had worked with? AIP for instance?

*JB*: At that same market Sam Arkoff was holding court, cigar in hand as always. He said, "Your dad tells me you want to make a film." I told him about a pet project concerning the time that Frederic Chopin spent on the island of Majorca. "My god!" he exclaimed, "How did the son of Larry Buchanan manage to hang onto his idealism?"

Sam said, "Back when your dad was making films with me, the market was so dry and needed product so badly. Imagine that; a time when the networks are calling saying, 'Do you have anything?' If you walked through my door with the dream of directing and an idea for a film, you got a job."

That's really what got that whole thing started with Roger Corman and the rest of the AIP troupe. They were just trying to fill up those available slots on TV and at the drive-ins. Speaking of Roger Corman, he gave me some excellent advice. He told me to pick a company name and stick with it until it gains some recognition. He said it's a mistake when people feel the urge to reinvent themselves every so often. And another thing he told me was no matter how long the term of a contract, whether it's four years or fourteen years, make sure the rights revert back to you in the end.

*TS: Is there anything you'd like to say about your father – maybe something that hasn't already been said before on the many internet sites that have written about him?*

*JB:* Dad had this little office at 9255 Sunset. He was finishing up a film. I was twelve years old and wanting to learn. He'd keep me busy by giving me outtakes and having me assemble them together so I could practice my splices. I'll never forget one day he was leaning over the viewer, he had his sleeves rolled up and his tie was hanging down. He turned to me with a big grin and said, "Just think, there are people going to jobs that they don't want to be at." He was excited like a little kid and I thought, that's what I want to be.

He was the most compassionate and gracious man I've ever met. You probably know this, because you said he would call you once in a while. You know firsthand, when he said 'How are you doing?' It wasn't just an intro. He really wanted to know how you were doing. He would *really listen*.

I wish he had really had the proper opportunity to make one of the period films he wanted to make.

I remember my dad directing a couple of girls one day on the film *Down on Us*. At the end of the scene they were wrapped and he said, "All right, you've done a great reading and I'm happy. In a few minutes we're going to release you. You'll

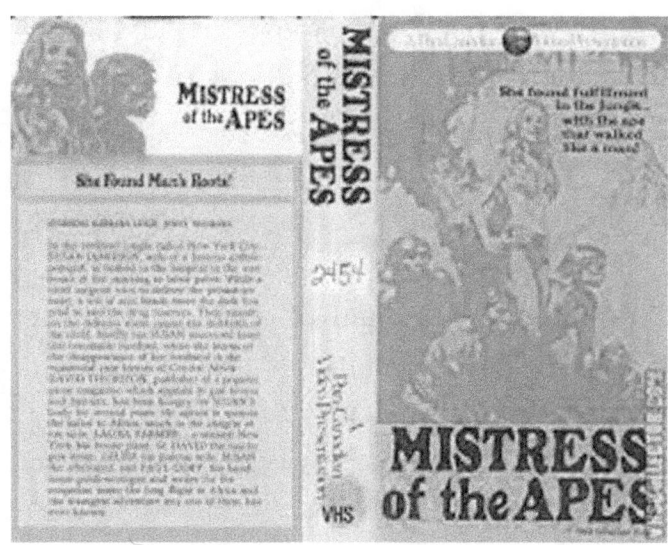

Buchanan's sexploitation classic ***Mistress of the Apes***. Photo courtesy of vhscollector.com

sign out, you'll walk down that hall and get out of your make-up and wardrobe. In a few minutes, when you're getting in your car, you're going to say to yourself, 'Shoot! If I could do that scene again I'd hit it out of the park.' So, why don't we do just one more and give you that chance to hit it out of the park right now?" They did it again and improved it. I thought to myself, 'Damn! I've got to remember that!'

David Lean had a version of that. He'd say to actors, "Give me the performance you gave to the bathroom mirror this morning."

Over the years I've met a lot of filmmakers who are familiar with my dad's work. Once they find out I'm related to Larry Buchanan, it's not like they're thinking what a bunch of crap my father made. It's more like they want to know how on earth he exposed enough film to tell a story on those kinds of budgets! They have respect for him.

You hear stories about other low-budget filmmakers of the era, people like Russ Meyer for instance. And this may be horribly judgmental of me, I never met the guy, but you hear stories that their films were a reflection of who they were as people. My father was nothing like the films he made. He was a caring and often inspirational man.

Cheese becomes riper with time. *It* became *Zontar*.

My dad had a very cathartic experience writing his memoir. He had always resented his father for putting them in the orphanage. When he wrote about that he finally came to the realization that his father was just doing what he honestly thought was best for his kids. It wasn't that he just didn't want to deal with them. His wife had died and he honestly thought this was the best thing to do.

I don't know if you've heard this, but there were six kids. And there was a stipulation; you couldn't adopt just one. You had to take the whole family. There was no way anybody was going to adopt that many kids.

People don't realize what a great writer my dad was. That's why I was after him the last twelve years or so of his life to write a really great script. He'd say, "Oh, I can write a script in a weekend."

I'd say, "No, you can write a *poor* script in a weekend. Take your time, make it perfect."

But he was really a master of storytelling. Some of the descriptions in his screenplays were beautiful and some of the suggestions he made for changes in my own work showed me what a great writer he was.

Gunning and running all the time can sort of do a number on your head after a while. It's like can you actually relax and take your time? Even if you have the money?

My brothers and I were with him at the end. Even after he was in hospice he'd look out the window and talk about the westerns he was going to make someday. He'd be talking about doing this and how he was going to do that. I was like wow! I mean I was glad he was still dreaming, but at one point I said, "Dad, I need you to be serious with me for a moment." He agreed and I asked, "Have you had a good life?"

He said, "Oh, my god, I've had a glorious life!" He went on and on about meeting my mom, about making movies. He said, "I wish I could've done a few things differently," and I'll never forget this, he said, "I'm ready for whatever's next. Whether it's the classic heaven we all prepare for or if it's pitch black or if it's the Elysian Fields, I'm ready for it."

It was the most remarkable closure for a father/son relationship I could imagine. It was sad when he passed away. It's good talking to you about this. I miss him. When he was in Tucson and I was in Malibu, he was always my Sunday phone call. For months after he died, I'd reach for the phone on a Sunday afternoon thinking 'I need to call Dad' and then catch myself. I'm sure it comes through that I loved the man; as a father, as a friend and as a mentor.

# EDGAR G. ULMER

## BEYOND THE TIME BARRIER (1960)

The opening credits for *Beyond the Time Barrier* could easily have been the inspiration for George Lucas' disappearing-into-the-distance screen crawl in the opening of *Star Wars*, but the X-80 aircraft in outer space sequences are cartoonish and unconvincing, even by 1960 standards. Still it is interesting to note that when the craft "breaks the time barrier" it splits into two separate images, anticipating a future quantum physics model of time travel, where things can simultaneously exist in parallel universes.

An abandoned Marine Corps Air Station at Eagle Mountain Lake (north of Fort Worth) is used effectively as a stand-in for the air base U.S. Air Force test pilot Major Bill Allison (Robert Clarke) took off from some sixty years before. The lonely scenes of Allison exploring the ghost base, trying to understand, evokes comparisons with no small number of *Twilight Zone* (TV series 1959-1964) episodes. The haunting musical score is competent and meets the standards of the

"Today's atomic tests and research may spell the doom of the human race 65 years from now as forecast in American International's *Beyond the Time Barrier*—which provides a grim look into the future; a future without children, with horrible half-people, without hope—an entirely possible world of tomorrow."
  -- *The Pocono Record*, September 17, 1960

"A prime example of low-budget mid-century cheese, more valuable now as an artifact of that era than for any supposed entertainment value it might have possessed in 1960. It can only be enjoyed ironically."
  -- *Sarasota Herald-Tribune*, Christopher Lloyd, May 2, 2013

"Every so often one finds a film that is so perfectly trite, poorly acted, and predictable, in every imaginable way, that its very boldness into badness is forgivable. Such was my thought whilst recently watching Edgar G. Ulmer's 1960 schlocksterpiece film *Beyond the Time Barrier*."
  -- *thespinningimage.co.uk*, Dan Schneider

Edgar G. Ulmer

day. Unfortunately, the films rendering of the futuristic "Citadel," where the inhabitants of Ulmer's apocalyptic vison dwell, falls short.

By the time *Beyond the Time Barrier* was filmed, Americans had been exposed to decades of science fiction art on book and magazine covers at the local drugstore. The project's low budget may have forced director Edgar G. Ulmer to decide that if he couldn't beat them, he'd join them. But the unconvincing matte painting of the futuristic city on the horizon undermines the verisimilitude Ulmer established by utilizing the abandoned base. The Citadel matte painting is as good as many of the aforementioned sci-fi magazine illustrations; it just doesn't fit with the rest of the film. And then there's the fact that it's just entirely too futuristic for only sixty years in the future. Black and white stock footage from bombed European cities after World War II probably would have worked better.

The inhabitants of this futurescape observe the bewildered Major Allison closely, and then fell him with an invisible ray. When he regains consciousness, he's inside a large glass tube. He asks questions, but his captors don't seem to understand. He gets into a scuffle with a couple of guards, but when a beautiful young woman (Princess Trirene played by Darlene Tompkins) touches his shoulder, he stops fighting and says, "Sorry, I didn't mean to do that."

As with many low-budget filmic efforts striving to attain a respectable running time, there's a lot of walking around, ostensibly to show off the high-tech set dressing.

Vladimir Sokolov, a character actor with a recognizable face (he portrayed the extremely likable old man in the Mexican village in the original *Magnificent Seven* (1960)), plays "The Supreme." *No, he's not a pizza.* But he is the head honcho of the Citadel. Radiation exposure has reduced the surviving human population to deaf-mutes—which naturally helped the film's production budget, by limiting the number of speaking roles. Though Allison has returned to Earth only 60 years

Promo art for **Beyond the Time Barrier**.

into the future, everyone at the Citadel has forgotten about the United States and everything that came before, so his queries and proclamations seem like nonsense. It's at this point that astute sci-fi fans begin to wonder if plot lines in the *Planet of the Apes* (1968) and *Beyond the Planet of the Apes* (1970) were cribbed from *Beyond the Time Barrier*.

During a brief incarceration in the Citadel's hoosegow with a number of hairless mutants, Major Allison is attacked, but prevails and extracts some much-needed background intel from his angry, fellow prison-mates. They claim they are victims of a "cosmic plague" and blame their condition on the citizens of the Citadel. Meanwhile, The Supreme's granddaughter, Trirene, has developed something of a crush on Allison and convinces The Supreme that the apple of her eye is no real threat. Trirene is a deaf-mute, but telepathic and likes what she sees in Allison's head. The Supreme acquiesces to his grand-daughter's wishes and Allison is given run of the Citadel.

Ulmer clearly tapped his old contacts from his days with Universal for this picture, because Jack Pierce—the man who transformed Karloff into the *Frankenstein* monster, is credited for make-up. Unfortunately, the mutants of *Beyond the Time Barrier* offer little in the way of visual shock. They're basically bald, shirtless guys, held captive behind bars, not much different from the gaggles of white supremacists you might find in your nearest state prison. Excepting the evocative wide shots establishing the dungeon-like prison, wherein the mutants look more like hairy denizens of a lunatic asylum. These clips appear to be stock footage borrowed from some older film.

Allison encounters three time travelers from other timelines: a Russian, female cosmonaut, Captain Markova (played by Ulmer's daughter, Arianne) who hails from 1973; General Kruse and Professor Bourman who arrived from colonies on other planets in 1994. After pleasantries, Cap-

The lovely Trirene from **Beyond the Time Barrier**.

tain Markova informs Major Allison that he has landed back on Earth in the year 2024 and The Supreme needs him to serve as the prime fecundator in the repopulation of the human race. It's tough job, but mostly great work if you can get it. Unless they intend to extract semen mechanically as happened with Don Johnson in *A Boy and His Dog* (1975), which also coincidentally features a healthy American stud roaming a post-apocalyptic, wasteland in 2024 and was financed by money from Texas investors.

Allison's breeding partner will be Trirene (naturally).

Everyone else living in the Citadel is sick with radiation poisoning and subject to mutation. But even a 21st century telepath wants to be romanced. Trirene is so embarrassed by the matter-of-fact discussion of the Citadel-saving coital romp-to-be that she blushes and runs away.

Since the primary set pieces in the futuristic city are pyramid-shaped, Ulmer makes use of a triangular wipe as a transition device between scenes. This gives the film a definite campy feel as it evokes memories of sci-fi serials from the 1930s like *Buck Rogers* and *Flash Gordon*.

Crosses and double crosses ensue as each of the three captive scientists make their case for being the one who goes back with Major Allison to a time before the worldwide radiation plague. In a last-minute struggle, a stray bullet kills Trirene, the Citadel's only hope of human survival. Allison delivers her body to The Supreme who helps him get back to his aircraft, giving him Trirene's ring as a sign of good faith. The reverse time-barrier breakage goes as planned and Allison lands on Earth in the year 1960.

Problem is, now he's an old man. He rants about the irradiated future society and offers Trirene's ring as proof that his story is true. The military officials present are unconvinced by his account, but express their intent to think it over. So, our time travel saga comes to a close.

## THE AMAZING TRANSPARENT MAN (1960)

In *The Amazing Transparent Man*, Douglas Kennedy as safecracker Joey Faust, escapes from a penitentiary with the help of Laura Matson (played by the tough and lovely Marguerite Chapman.). A disenchanted, former military man, Major Paul Krenner (James Griffith) is behind the jailbreak. Krenner has an axe to grind. His career ended when he was injured by the blast from a grenade. Now, he's fond of tossing a bit of shrapnel that was removed from his body not unlike the way Jimmy Cagney would toss a coin relentlessly when playing a gangster.

On a remote ranch, Major Krenner is experimenting with radioactive isotopes.

"The director Edgar G. Ulmer's science-fiction B-movie, *The Amazing Transparent Man*, from 1960, is a bare-bones riot of visual invention. Ulmer's camera eerily conjures the invisible Faust's presence by taking his point of view. The simple yet striking optical effects contrast wildly with the story's apocalyptic implications."
   -- *The New Yorker*, Richard Brody, "Anthology Film Archives," August 1 2017

"This little film is a product of famed science fiction director Edgar Ulmer, though an unfortunate example of his work later in life. By 1960, Ulmer was outside the mainstream Hollywood gravy train, reduced to directing low-budget (or no-budget) films starring C-list stars and often shot in just days out the back of a truck."
   -- *millionmonkeytheater.com,* Nathan Decker, April 2005

"Of the Ulmer-directed movies I've seen thus far, *The Amazing Transparent Man* is easily the best. Jack Lewis's rather top-heavy screenplay is never allowed to seem as ridiculous as it probably should, what with its combination of mad science, crime, and insane world-domination conspiracies. Ulmer's long-evident flair for visual composition is also in full effect, even in spite of the poverty-row budget."
   -- *1000misspenthours.com,* Scott Ashlin

The scientist he's holding captive in his secret lab, Dr. Peter Ulof (Ivan Triesault) is made up in old-guy style and calls to mind a perennial supporting player in *Three Stooges* shorts, Emil Sitka (*"Hold hands, you love-birds."*).

When Faust insists on being "clued-in" about the operation, Professor Ulof straps an anxious guinea pig into a cute little harness beneath a contraption designed to focus the strange rays he's discovered. He turns knobs and adjusts instruments to the accompaniment of some well-known sci-fi sound effects and the guinea pig disappears. When Faust suspiciously asks what becomes of the animal, Major Krenner tells him the process has been perfected to the point that no ill effects befall the subject. On the way out of the lab, Faust asks what lies behind a closed door. "No concern of yours," Krenner replies, but the sinister background music tells us it's something creepy.

Faust, a consummate tough-guy, stages a ruse to lure an armed guard into his bedroom. He knocks the guy unconscious, ties him up with strips torn from a bedsheet and goes back to the lab to get a look at whatever is behind the door. His skills as a master safecracker guarantee he'll have no trouble getting in.

He's confronted by Professor Ulof, who sleeps on a small bed in the lab. Faust understands that Ulof is being held against his will and drops the tough-guy routine.

Ulof explains that his own daughter is being held captive behind the locked door to ensure his cooperation. Faust wants the full story, so the professor relates his tragic tale of being forced by the Nazis to perform experiments on hooded human subjects in a prison camp. One of the hooded test subjects was his own wife. Ulof cannot bear the thought of losing his daughter, too.

Before Faust can release the girl, Laura Matson shows up with a gun.

Back downstairs, Faust tries to convince Laura that they could make a fortune robbing banks with the professor's invisibility gizmo. The armed guard, Julian, wakes up and overhears their conversation. Soon Major Krenner, Julian and Laura are all suspicious of one another. Which of the potential double-crosses will achieve fruition?

Now, it's Faust's turn to go under the invisibility ray. Though he's been told the ray has no harmful effects, Ulof, Matson and Major Krenner watch from a shielded observation room with foot-thick lead walls (remind you of those X-rays you get at the dentist?).

Faust's transformation into invisibility is fairly interesting for such a low-budget film. Many a poverty row producer would've accomplished this with a simple dissolve. Ulmer opts for a multi-stage effect in which, first, Faust's face appears as a negative image, then his extremities vanish, with his torso being the last part of his body to become invisible. I imagine this effect in the movie trailer was responsible for luring legions of teens into the theater to see *The Amazing Transparent Man*.

With all his scheming and secret technology, Major Krenner hasn't spent enough time considering how he's going to control the criminal Faust once he's invisible. Faust takes advantage of this lapse and slaps Krenner around, just to show he's not going to be a mindless slave. He steals a kiss from Laura while he's at it. Finally, he makes sure Krenner realizes he's not so much as lifting a finger for chump change.

That night, at a government installation, Faust breaks into a vault where radioactive isotopes are kept. He outwits a couple of security officers, knocking one unconscious. The senior officer is played by familiar Texas character actor, Pat Cranshaw. They've got the radioactive material they need, but the plot thickens as Professor Ulof reveals to Major Krenner that the guinea pig has died. It's only a matter of time before Faust meets the same fate.

Krenner sends Laura and Faust on a daytime mission to get more isotopes. The two are getting real cozy and Laura suggests they discontinue their association with Krenner and run. They'll need getaway cash, so Faust insists on rob-

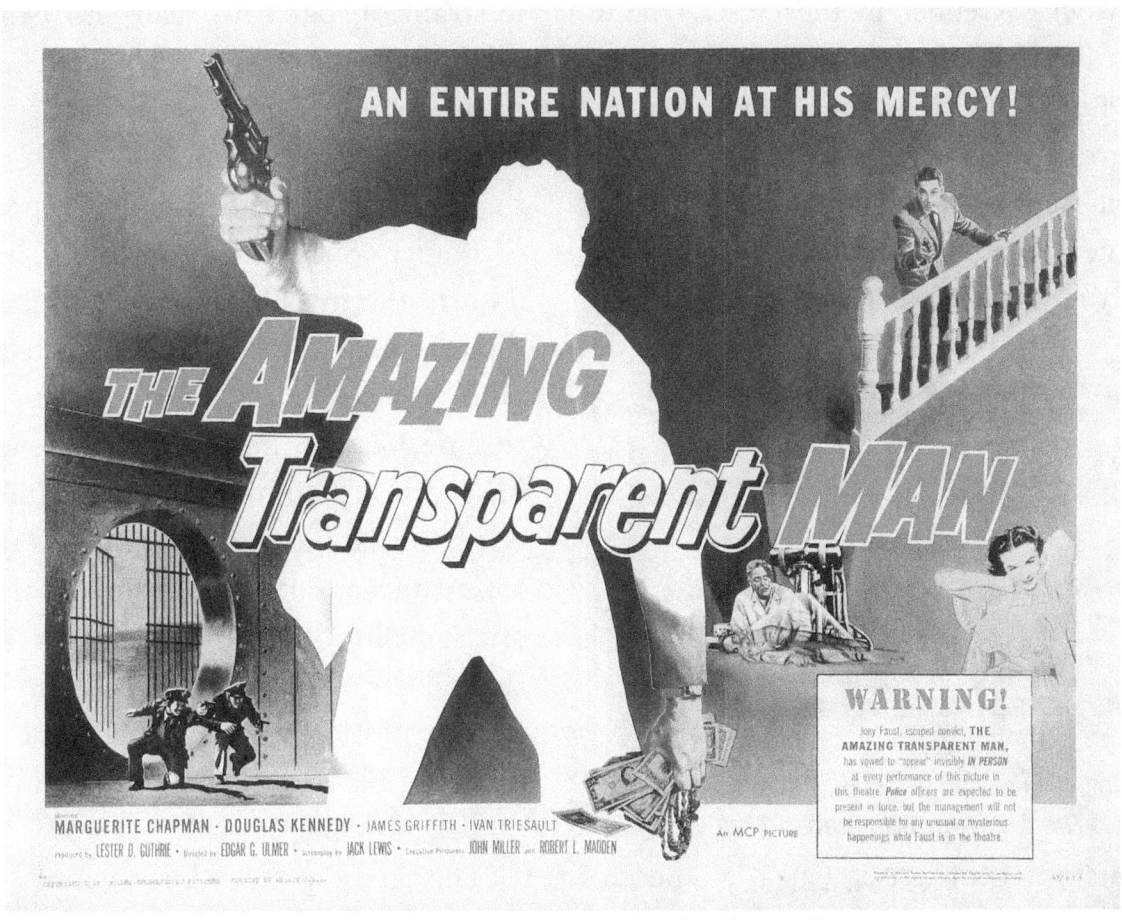

Promo art for **The Amazing Transparent Man**.

bing a bank. The heist begins well and it looks like they'll get away with it, but in the bank lobby, Faust's invisibility begins to wear off. Tellers and customers are astounded to see his various appendages and body parts eerily reappear and disappear. A young woman exclaims "Oh, my lord!" The now fully visible Faust barks at the bank customers and runs to a waiting convertible.

Faust is quickly identified as the thief. Investigators realize he is the one behind the theft of the military's X-13 radioactive isotope and that he's figured out a way to make himself invisible. But, what can they do?

Back at Major Krenner's place, he and Julian, listen to a ridiculously detailed radio report that tells everything that happened at the bank.

Laura and Faust want to return to invisibility ray HQ, but cannot do so while Faust is a visible quantity. Faust divides the money and starts to run out on Laura but, just as he's about to hop in the convertible and ditch her, his invisibility returns. Laura is angry, but she and Faust visit Major Krenner's lab and the still transparent

Faust locks Krenner in the closet where Ulof's daughter had been held captive. Faust becomes visible again which annoys him greatly. Julian gets the drop on the gang as they're trying to escape, but lets them go when he learns that Krenner had been lying to him, using him all along.

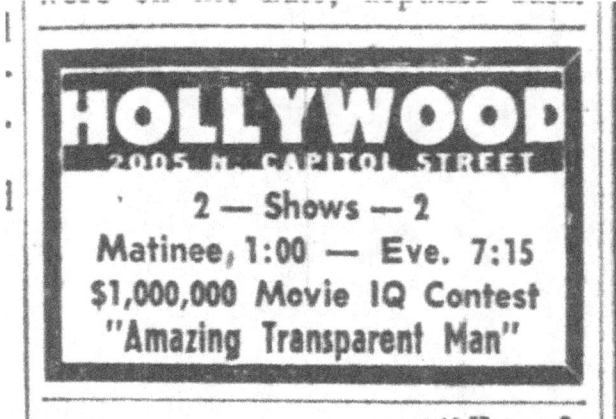

A contest was used to increase attendance for **The Amazing Transparent Man**.

Outside, Ulof gives Faust a speech about justice and the sort of world we should all be building for our children. Faust drives away but, inspired by Ulof's speech, heads back. He tells Julian, Ulof and the professor's daughter to go on without him. Inside the house, Krenner shoots the lock off the door of his temporary prison and escapes, just as Faust and Laura are settling their differences. Krenner shoots Laura and Faust pursues him to the lab. The Major breaks a bottle of acid on Faust's arms, incapacitating him long enough for Krenner to knock him semi-conscious.

Up until now, the film has been cheesy, but pretty much sensible, with a B-movie strain of logic. It's really no better or worse than an episode of the television show *Topper* (TV series 1953-1955). But now, Major Krenner (and presumably the screenwriter) abandon any pretense of sanity. Suddenly unhinged, Krenner adjusts the invisibility ray equipment to direct a lethal dose of radiation to Faust who is writhing on the floor. Activating the mechanism, he hides in the shielded observation room, but then returns to open the safe and remove the X-13 isotope canister. But Krenner's plans are shot and it's all too much. He screams maniacally and strangles the prone Faust. There is an explosion which destroys the farmhouse and leaves a huge mushroom cloud on the horizon. *Whew!*

The two police investigators who threw up their hands helplessly after Faust robbed the bank, show up on the road leading to Major Krenner's vaporized former abode. They show their IDs to officers at a road block, but are told they cannot proceed because of the radioactive fallout from the explosion.

Looking through binoculars they see what appears to be stock footage from an actual nuclear test site where technicians take radiation readings. Dr. Ulof apologizes to one of the investigators for "blowing up half the county." Then, Ulof delivers a monologue about weighing the potential dangers against the possible benefits of technology. He closes by staring directly into the camera and asking, "What would you do?"

Larry Buchanan wasn't the only proficient schlockmeister prowling the streets of Dallas, Texas in 1960. In only two weeks' time, veteran B-movie auteur, Edgar G. Ulmer gave birth to not one but two ultra-low-budget sci-fi flicks; *Beyond the Time Barrier* and *The Amazing Transparent Man*. Great titles and trailers reminiscent of films from an earlier decade, promised much more than the duo delivered, but you still had to admire a man who could put together two feature films in an equal number of weeks.

I knew Ulmer's work from his association with the filmic masterpiece *Metropolis* in 1927. Like Texas' own Robert A. Burns, Ulmer had started out in the art department, creating fantastically original sets for Fritz Lang's stylized silent German expressionist film. And Ulmer's minor classic, *The Black Cat* (1934), for Universal in Hollywood, made excellent use of the studio's contract actors, Boris Karloff and Bela Lugosi in a horror treatment that was far more "adult" in tone than any of Universal's other offerings of that decade. Then there was the equally strange, noir entry known as *Detour* (1945) starring Tom Neal and Ann Savage.

Ulmer was never an "in-demand" director, but he was clearly a competent auteur who could make the most of even very stringent production limitations. In a career that lasted over 40 years, he directed almost that many films.

As a kid, I was eager to see *Beyond the Time Barrier* and *The Amazing Transparent Man*. At age five I'd fallen in love with the *Hideous Sun Demon* (1959). I liked Robert Clarke's portrayal of a scientist whose exposure to radiation causes him to devolve into an ugly reptilian hungry for more than just insects. There was a creepy scene in which he squeezes blood out of a rodent the way others might squeeze their morning juice from an orange. It just seemed "right" in my five-year-old scheme of the world. A reptilian guy might really do something like that. Hell, some of the creepy kids in my neighborhood would've done it. Another thing I liked was that the transformations didn't happen at midnight like they always did in every other monster film. This guy became a monster in broad daylight. Not only was it original, but I could actually see everything in detail. Our old Monkey Wards TV set wasn't the best at reproducing scenes with a lot of darkness in the frame. With many old monster movies, I found myself guessing as to what the heck was actually happening on that little black and white screen.

The story behind the genesis of Ulmer's 1960 sci-fi double-bill is worth mentioning. Robert Clarke, who was originally from Oklahoma, had some backers in Texas who would finance a picture, but only if it was shot in the Lone Star State. He was a bit tired of wearing every hat in the production line-up, so instead of producing, directing and starring, he opted for handing off the directing duties to Ulmer. They had worked together in 1951 on *The Man from Planet X*. Clarke had learned the hard way on *Hideous Sun Demon*, that directing wasn't as easy as a man like Ulmer could make it seem. Shooting weekends only, Clarke and a team of college students, had filmed *Hideous Sun Demon* for $50,000. Exact figures are not available, but it's pretty certain that *Beyond the Time Barrier* was done for about half the money in half the time. As long as they were cranking cameras, Ulmer arranged to throw another film into the mix; *The Amazing Transparent Man*.

When production began to ramp up for indie features in Dallas in the mid-1980s, following the construction of the Dallas Communications Complex, a lot of individuals and organizations began holding events to acclimate potential investors to the idea of investing in film pro-

DVD Cover for MST3000's release of *The Amazing Transparent Man*.

ductions. One such event was a screening of Ulmer's original version of *Detour* at a gala featuring his widow, Shirley. I attended that screening.

During Mrs. Ulmer's address to the packed theater, she told of her experiences earlier in Dallas, when she served as script supervisor on *Beyond the Time Barrier* and *The Amazing Transparent Man*. She made it sound as if she and her husband had seen the futuristic settings in a display at one of the Texas State Fair exhibit halls and the exhibits had been the inspiration for the films. Hard to confirm, but who knows? Movie people are notorious for embellishing reminiscences and rewriting lackluster histories to infuse a bit of glamor.

Regardless how the films came to be produced, Edgar G. Ulmer framed the set pieces in the exhibit hall in such a way as to make them work as a setting in the underground Citadel in the year 2024.

Dazzling? No. But, certainly on a par with many of the pictures produced by poverty row and even some films the major studios had released in prior years. Ulmer's sensibilities were more suitable to an earlier era, so this double bill didn't exactly wow the largely teen audience.

After production, the filmmakers approached American International Pictures in search of a distribution deal. Clarke was looking to parlay the pictures into a recurring producer gig at AIP but was rebuffed by an uncooperative Sam Arkoff.

The sci-fi double bill ended up with a fledgling company called Miller-Consolidated Pictures, which went bankrupt in short order. Arkoff and Nicholson at AIP were then able to pick up the two films for the cost of the unpaid lab bills they had incurred. It was a lot like what happened with Larry Buchanan's *Free, White and 21* (1963). In 1960, under the AIP banner, the two films played the nation's drive-in theaters and a few walk-ins. But they continued in venues as second or third bills for close to a decade.

On January 25, 1960, Klamath, Oregon, marketers promoted a one-million-dollar contest where moviegoers were asked what they would do with the invisible ray featured in *The Amazing Transparent Man*. It's probably safe to assume that the contest never produced a winner. Perhaps AIP subjected the million-dollar check itself to the invisibility ray.

Both *Beyond the Time Barrier* and *The Amazing Transparent Man* have strong, thinly veiled anti-nuclear sentiments. Ulmer had begun a promising career in Europe during the silent film era, but had to flee to America when Adolf Hitler began his ascent in Germany. He had seen firsthand the destruction of war and the hubris of unbridled technological advances in the post-nuclear age. No doubt he'd heard the rumors of Project Paperclip and the new identities that were given to Nazi scientists when they were recruited to run research facilities in a variety of fields including NASA in post-war America. Ulmer had plenty of good reasons to preach against the military-industrial complex and his political leanings may account, at least in part, for his tepid success as a director. Anti-war stances were frowned upon in the 1950s and 1960s, especially when saber-rattling star John Wayne and conservative mouthpiece Senator Joe McCarthy were considered role models.

Twelve years later, on September 30, 1972, Edgar G. Ulmer passed away in Woodland Hills, California, after 45 prolific years during which he directed 37 feature films.

# PAT BOYETTE

## DUNGEON OF HARROW (1962)

In the opening sequence of the film, Aaron Fallon (Russ Harvey) stares for a good long while at the Fallon family crest hanging on the wall. He moves to a desk and, taking quill in hand, begins to draft a journal entry which promises to detail a descent into depravity. Lightning flashes through the window and as he writes his tale unfolds on the screen.

A late nineteenth century schooner is tossed on the waves of a ferocious storm. Fallon is called from his quarters by the captain of the ship (Lee Morgan.) The sets used in the ship scenes are notable in that they actually move. This attention to detail is usually abandoned in such a modest movie. As the Captain and Fallon try to make their way to the galley, their path is jammed with panicking passengers.

For many decades in Hollywood, miniature effects were less than convincing. The miniatures depicting the ship running aground are neither better nor worse that dozens of others from films of the era immediately preceding *Dungeon of Harrow*. The storm rages on.

"If I didn't know better, I'd swear *The Dungeon of Harrow* was one of the most influential films of all time, as it continually reminded me of films that actually came along later in time. But even if those other films HAD been inspired by Pat Boyette's opus, they all pretty much did it better, so that's fine."

--*horror-movie-a-day.blogspot.com*, May 11, 2011

"There was just enough cheesiness and fun to keep it from being painful, yet not enough to allow me, with any good conscience, to recommend it wholeheartedly. Even in saying that however, I feel myself a bit torn in my assessment of it."

--*bmoviecentral.com*

"*Dungeon of Harrow* bears a strong similarity to Jack H. Harris' *Equinox* (1970) in many respects, both in filmic style and creative use of no-budget special effects and awful, overemoting non-actors to build a surprisingly admirable and truly oneiric atmosphere the likes of which has been lost since the last true heyday of horror in the early 80s."

--*thirdeyecinema.wordpress.com*, April 27, 2011

The following morning, Fallon and the Captain wash up on the beach of an uncharted island. It appears there are no other survivors, but they find Fallon's family crest floating on the breaking waves.

*The Dungeon of Harrow* was remarkably ambitious for a no-budget Texas indie film from the early 1960s.

The castaways have made a rudimentary camp by the time night falls. The Captain roasts a fish on a stick over an open fire. Fallon's a rich kid and accustomed to having his way. He tells the Captain he's not fond of fish and prevails upon the man to find some game so he can eat real meat on the following day. Tactfully, the Captain tries to steer his charge toward more realistic concerns.

In the night, the two men hear the sounds of snarling dogs and a woman screaming. They are unarmed and unfamiliar with the terrain. The Captain insists they wait until daylight before investigating.

What the Captain and Fallon don't know is that there is a full-blown gothic castle on the island. The master of the castle, Count Lorente de Sade (William McNulty), berates his servant, a large black man he calls Mantis (Maurice Harris) for allowing the dogs to get out the night before. He splashes a beverage into his servant's face. His anger turns to hope when Mantis tells him the dogs killed a woman. A woman on the island? How? Perhaps, there are others? De Sade sends Mantis to search.

Once he's alone, the Count has a drink and proclaims, "There must be a way to keep the devils off my island." A disembodied spirit makes itself known to the Count and begins a dialog by saying, "This island was made for devils." Eventually, the unseen spirit becomes visible, claiming to be a nameless entity from another dimension, a product of the Count's madness. Though Count de Sade denies wishing evil on anyone, this demon from his unconscious mind begs to differ. The demon offers help with any sinister plans the Count may have. To prove his powers, he makes a cobra appear on the desk, threateningly close to the Count's hand. Thinking his new friend is unimpressed by the snake, the demon conjures a large bat and makes it land on de Sade's lap. This is followed by a gigantic black spider dropping from the ceiling. The spectral guest now has the Count's terrified attention.

The demon agrees to depart, but not before leaving a "calling card." An expansive spider web appears over the room, draping the frightened de Sade as well. He does not know what to make of these sinister omens. Is he mad? Was his wine drugged? He smashes the bottle on the floor.

Fallon and the ship's Captain wander through the heavily wooded terrain, tracing the tracks left by the dogs the night before. On the trail, they come across a piece of a woman's dress. Soon, they find the dead woman, her bare legs drenched in blood. Continuing their apprehensive exploration of the island, Fallon stumbles into a trap, causing the release of a large net that blankets him and the Captain.

Just as the two men manage to break free of the net, Mantis shows up, swinging a sling in his hand. Demonstrating deadly accuracy, Mantis beans the Captain with an egg-sized stone. Fallon tries to back away from the giant adversary unnoticed, but no dice. He trips and is knocked unconscious by Mantis. In a delirious state, he sees dogs and women and a castle as he is transported back to the master.

When Fallon wakes, he is lying on a bed somewhere in the castle. On the floor near his bed, he finds the Captain unconscious, with a bloodied face. A woman appears in his chamber. She is lovely, but aloof and commanding. The woman, Cassandra (Helen Hogan) informs Fallon he is invited to the Count's table, an offer he accepts; but not before putting the Captain on his bed. Half conscious, the Captain says, "They drugged me."

In a dark chamber, Count de Sade appears to be praying over a crypt. He leaves the crypt and enters the dining hall. There he is soon joined by Fallon and Cassandra. When Fallon expresses his gratitude to the Count, his host slams angry fists down on the table. Cassandra explains that the master doesn't allow conversation at the dinner table. Fallon tells the man he can go to hell.

They come to an uneasy truce. The meal progresses and Fallon arrives at the conclusion that his host is quite mad, either from a lifetime of dissipation, royal inbreeding or both.

After dismissing himself from the table, Fallon notices blood in the hallway. The bed where he had placed the Captain is now empty. He runs back to the dining hall and catches a glimpse of the Count disappearing through a doorway. He follows and finds himself in the crypt where the Count was praying earlier. There is no sign of de Sade. Fallon is about to open the crypt, but is interrupted by Cassandra.

She takes him to a misty balcony hanging with dead vines. Here he learns that de Sade's household is in exile. There are no boats. Fallon is trapped on the island.

Trying to sleep later that night, Fallon hears the sound of a whip and a woman weeping. He looks out his window catching a glimpse of the woman as she is beaten. Attempting to investigate, he finds he is locked in his quarters.

In the dungeon, the Captain is on a torture rack. Mantis sprinkles water on his face. At first this angers de Sade, but then he agrees with his servant's action. They must not let the Captain die. Not yet.

On the other hand, there is a beautiful mute girl in the dungeon. The Count suspects she tried to poison him by putting hemlock in his wine, so he forces her to drink it. The girl doesn't die as planned. Just another paranoid idea in the old coot's noggin?

Okay, so the girl's not an assassin, but he's convinced the Captain is a pirate. Seizing a torch from the wall, he presses it into the Captain's face, providing a gratuitous gross-out for drive-in movie patrons.

Later, when Fallon presses Cassandra for an explanation, she shows him a portrait of the (supposedly deceased) Countess. She explains the Count married the lovely young woman in spite of the knowledge that she had contracted leprosy. We learn that the Countess is not dead, but insane, obsessed with the memory of her wedding day, locked away somewhere in the bowels of the castle, wearing her wedding gown.[i]

---
[i] This angle in the plot definitely has the flavor of an Italian horror film, from Bava for instance, rather than a home-grown Texas flick!

Fallon has yet another tense encounter with the Count. He is told the Captain died. In reality, the Captain lingers on in the dungeon under the watchful eye of Mantis.

Certain he is being watched, Fallon pulls back a curtain in his room to find Anne, the mute servant. She tries to entice Fallon into some hanky panky, hoping to make him her ally. He asks her to show him to the dungeon where the Captain is being kept. She refuses, but makes him understand she will go herself.

Finding Mantis asleep in the dungeon, she breaks a board over his head. She unties the Captain, but he passes out. Unfortunately, for the brave girl, the master discovers her treachery. It appears the Captain is dead. Anne gets to take his place on the rack. They leave the mute girl alone, with water dripping on her forehead.

Stuck in his bedroom, Fallon waits anxiously. Someone knocks. "Anne?" he asks before opening the door. (I have no idea how he expected the poor mute to answer.) "No, it's Cassandra." He lets the woman in. They hatch a plot to assassinate the Count, but before they can seal their bargain with a kiss, the Count and Mantis burst in. As prisoners, they are to be taken to the crypt.

Meanwhile, in the dungeon, that old Captain is one tough son of a gun. He's not dead after all. Rising from the floor he goes to the rack to help Anne. He needs a key to set her free and goes in search of it, promising to return.

Promo art for Boyette's opus *Dungeon of Harrow*.

In the dining hall, the Captain catches up with the others. He engages in battle with Mantis, but the giant servant hurls a sword, impaling the Captain. There's no surviving this! Now, Mantis backs Fallon into the crypt. The open sepulcher is not a crypt at all, but camouflage for a stairway leading into the dungeon.

Down below the semi-conscious Fallon is chained to a dungeon wall. The Count informs him he will have the company of the demented Countess, who is locked away in the adjacent room. When Fallon is left alone, a dark leprous arm reaches through the bars of the door and works the latch. Clad in tattered finery, the Countess goes to him and tries to make love, mistaking him for her husband. At her touch, Fallon screams, knowing she is decomposing with the advanced symptoms of leprosy.

Cassandra cauterizes a wound Mantis received in his fight with the Captain. Then, Mantis drags the Captain's corpse from the dining hall.

The Countess hears a sweet voice calling to her. It is Cassandra. Glad to see her nurse, the Countess embraces her, but soon falls to the floor. Cassandra has stabbed her to death. Soon she has unlocked Fallon and led him into the woods outside the castle. He wants to rest until daylight, but this will not be possible. The Count and Mantis are tracking the two fugitives with the hounds.

Fallon and Cassandra fool the dogs by wading into a stream. De Sade and Mantis search through the night. By morning Mantis collapses, unable to continue. This angers the master, so he shoots the fallen servant. Fallon confronts the Count and the two gentlemen engage in a rolling bit of fisticuffs. At last Fallon manages to shoot de Sade.

He and Cassandra are happy for a time, but ever hopeful that a ship will arrive. When a vessel does finally appear,

Fallon rushes eagerly to greet the sailors rowing ashore. Seeing him, they flee in terror. He and Cassandra are now overcome with advanced leprosy.

In the final scene of the film, Fallon explains that Cassandra has become increasingly deranged. It is now time to put her away. As the film closes, he leads her into the dungeon to lock her in the chamber once occupied by the Countess de Sade.

By 1962, when Pat Boyette co-wrote and directed *Dungeon of Harrow*, Roger Corman had successfully tapped three Edgar Allan Poe titles to create highly successful B-movies. I cannot help but believe that Boyette was inspired by Corman's films when he embarked on his own period horror epic. It's remarkable that he attempted a story set in the 19th century on such a low budget and I have to say he gave the project a hell of a run for the money. Few indie film makers in the early 1960s displayed such aspirations. Needless to say, he did not match the production values of Roger Corman's Poe pictures, but he far surpassed the efforts of Staten Island's Andy Milligan; films like *The Naked Witch* (1967), *The Ghastly Ones* (1968), and *Torture Dungeon* (1970).

Other influences leading Boyette down the path of gothic horror could include Mario Bava (*Black Sunday* (1960), *Black Sabbath* (1963)) and the Hammer Films produc-

Pat Boyette was a local TV personality in San Antonio.

tions. Bava's horror classic *Black Sunday* had been released in 1960. It's scenes of torture were considered terribly gruesome for the time, leading it to be banned in some areas even though the movie was shot using black and white film. No screen drenched in crimson gore there. The plot of *Dungeon of Harrow* has the sorts of shocks and twists found in European horror films and, like the Hammer films, Boyette executed his cut-rate classic in color.

I have to admit a sort of awe at the aspirations inherent in *Dungeon of Harrow*. Here is a film with negligible funding, created in San Antonio, Texas (for god's sake!) with a castle, a shipwreck, period costuming and performances that were on a par with most cheapie horror flicks of the time. The specter of the Marquis de Sade (from whose name we derive our term "sadist") is thrown into the mix, lending the film historic and literary prestige. I think Pat Boyette was onto something. His was not a self-limiting perspective!

Despite all the great exploitation elements in the project, the movie does not seem to have made much of a splash. No doubt it played some theaters, at least regionally, if not nationally; but it's real appeal appears to have been as a late-night filler on television, where it was televised regularly until the early 1980s.

One thing Pat Boyette had going for him was his work experience in local radio and television. He knew the ropes of professional production on a shoestring budget. In the 1950s and early 1960s, locally produced children's shows and wrap-arounds for movies were common at TV stations all across the nation. A man with Boyette's experience knew how to put together sets and costumes that would be good enough to meet the audience's expectations and cheap enough to fit the budget.

Boyette is said to have completed two other features; *No Man's Land*, a 1964 war drama featuring the leading actor of *Dungeon of Harrow*, Russ Harvey, and a titillating black and white nudie/cutie, *The Weird Ones* (1962), about a couple of PR men who try to prevent a space alien from molesting naked Earth girls. As with many exploitation features over the years, Boyette's other two films seem to have vanished, leaving *Dungeon of Harrow* the only surviving example of his work. In those days, low-end exploitation titles, were believed to have only a very short window of opportunity in theaters. Future technologies had not yet been imagined and no one dreamed these movies would ever be allowed on television. Unfortunately, this meant minor efforts like *The Weird Ones* were simply discarded after a time.[ii] The few surviving posters and lobby cards from *The Weird Ones* definitely arouse the curiosity of the die-hard schlock enthusiast.

After trying his hand at indie film production, Boyette pitched himself as a comic illustrator to Charlton Comics (1945-1986). They were slow getting back to him, but within a couple of years he was a regular contributor. He had dabbled in comics back in the 1950s, creating a syndicated strip called *Captain Flame* that fizzled out pretty quickly. His first

---

[ii] Boyette claimed all existing elements for *The Weird Ones* were destroyed in an accidental fire in his garage.

notable gig with Charlton was a superhero known as the "Peacemaker." This quintessentially 1960s creation used a variety of non-lethal weapons to subdue warmongers and the like.

Pat Boyette worked at a whirlwind pace. Between 1966 and 1976 he illustrated and often wrote hundreds of stories for many Charlton titles, including my favorite; *The Many Ghosts of Dr. Graves*. He illustrated other titles I recall from my misspent youth: *Six Million Dollar Man*, *Korg: 70,000 BC*, *The Phantom* and *Ghostly Tales*.

In addition to his mountain of work at Charlton, Boyette did a few odd pieces for DC comics, Warren Publishing (*Eerie*, *Creepy*, etc.,) Archie Comics and Atlas Comics.

"Idiosyncratic" is the way Boyette, himself, described his style of illustration. His renderings seem to be either loved or disdainfully dismissed with not many comics fans on the fence regarding his talent. Certainly, his art did not have the overwhelming mass appeal of the greatest comics illustrators of his era. Still, devoted fans are not hard to find as many (like me) hold a special place in their hearts for the Boyette stories they read in their formative years.

The prolific, multi-talented Pat Boyette passed away in my own home town, Fort Worth, Texas in January of 2000.

Pat Boyette was a prolific comics artist.

# RUSS MARKER

## THE YESTERDAY MACHINE (1963)

Margie (Linda Jenkins) has got the moves, man. She can really shake it to the latest rock and roll on the radio while her boyfriend Howie (Jay Ramsey) tinkers with his fuel pump. And what's more, she's a maniac with a baton. What kid wouldn't totally dig seeing this flick at the drive-in circa 1963?

The fuel pump's shot and these two kids are going to miss the kick-off if they don't get some help. They decide to cut across a field and inquire at a farmhouse they passed earlier. Darkness falls and the farmhouse is nowhere in sight. They move toward a light flickering through the trees.

The light is a campfire, but no one's there. What's up here? The kids are accosted by a couple of rustic types. Howie tells Margie to run. He scuffles with one of the strangers, then makes a run for it himself. Two shots are fired. Twice Howie is hit! He makes it back to the car, but Margie's not there. Losing blood, he passes out on the road and is discovered by a motorist.

"This movie combines two of American cinema's favorite subjects; time travel and Nazis. You'd think that *The Yesterday Machine* would be a tasty stew, and you'd be kinda, sorta right. While it comes apart in the last reel, and all the female characters will give you a migraine, overall, it's not really bad. And yes, that is 'damning with faint praise.'"

--*millionmonkeytheater.com*, Nathan Decker, May 2011

"The Time Platform, or whatever it's meant to be, is merely a teeny raised stage bracketed by four poles adorned with strobing lights. As for the 'control' equipment, the ramshackle collection of electronic odds and ends seen here constitutes, perhaps, the most laughable example of Super Science since the assemblage of junkyard crap *Plan 9 from Outer Space*'s Eros had sitting on the dilapidated wooden table in his spaceship's 'command center.' There's also a Nazi flag hanging on the wall. You know, just so we 'get' it."

--*jabootu.net*, Ken Begg, July 15, 2007

At the Daily Sentinel in Dallas, Texas, reporter Jim Crandall (James Britton) is trying to collect his paycheck, so he can start a well-deserved vacation, his first in three years. The editor of the paper asks him to make a quick stop at the hospital on his way out of town, talk to the gunshot victim and phone in the facts. Reluctantly, he agrees.

> "*The Yesterday Machine* was a work of complete obscurity when it came out. I have dozens of books about science-fiction and fantastic cinema but this has never featured or been reviewed in any of them. Lead actor Tim Holt had appeared in a great many B Westerns throughout the 1940s, but was at the end of his career, while director/writer Russ Marker did subsequently write the equally cheap alien monster film *Night Fright* (1967)."
> --*moria.co.nz*, Richard Scheib

At the hospital, the attending physician informs Jim that he removed a Civil War era mini-ball from the college student's wound. Ah, those were the days; when reporters and doctors smoked cigarettes and drank whiskey in hospital offices!

Elsewhere in Dallas, a nightclub full of groovy cats and chicks are twisting their hearts out to some righteous tunes. Miss Sandra de Mar (Ann Pellegrino), the girl with the velvet voice, is the headliner. She also happens to be the older sister of

Russ Marker.

Margie, the baton twirler who never returned from the woods. Sandy delivers a sultry rendition of "Leave Me Alone," a song written by none other than the film's director, Russ Marker.

Police Lt. Partane (Tim Holt) and Detective Lasky (Robert Kelly) arrive at the nightclub just as Sandy is wrapping her performance. They are ushered into her dressing room. The reporter, Jim Crandall, arrives just as the cops are leaving. He tries to get a quick run-down so he can phone in his report and start his vacation. The cops are uncooperative, so he wangles an interview with Sandy by offering her a ride home.

It looks like that vacation is becoming a pipedream. Sandy begs Jim to take her to the place where her sister disappeared. He can't say no to a pretty blond, so even though it's nearly 1:00 am, they set off for the countryside.

The pipe-smoking Lt. Partane and a group of cops are scouring the area where Margie vanished, but so far, they've come up with diddly. When Jim and Sandy show up, Partane tells them to go home. Sandy's starting to freak and Jim's just the sort of manly dude to help her through a tough time. A budding romance? Perhaps. Jim tosses his cigarette down in the woods. We see a pair of military style boots. We know it's a bad guy wearing those boots when we hear the sinister chords playing on the movie's soundtrack. One of the boots stomps out the smoldering butt.

At headquarters the next morning the cops are trying to make sense of Margie's disappearance. Dallas B-movie perennial, Bill Thurman, puts in a fast-talking performance as a detective working the case. There's a break in their investigation when a cop comes in with some items found in the woods. The first is Margie's sweater. The second is a genuine Civil War era cap. Dogs were used to track the girl, but the trail ended abruptly and inexplicably.

The others clear out and Jim and Lt. Partane have a heart to heart. Jim throws out a theory of what may have happened, but his conjecture gets them no closer to finding the missing girl. Partane is reminded of a strange incident he witnessed while liberating a P.O.W. camp near the Alsatian border in 1945. It seems the Nazis may have been experimenting with time travel. He makes no claims, but he's not dismissing even the most outlandish possibilities until he has more facts.

Jim visits Howie at the hospital. The poor kid's distraught over the missing Margie. While Jim's there, Sandy shows up. She wants to go poking around that old farm again. Jim agrees to help her.

In the woods, Jim and Sandy pass through the underbrush and cross over an ancient cemetery before arriving at the dilapidated farm house. While Jim investigates the structure, Sandy peruses the headstones in the little graveyard. A sinister character leaps out from behind a tree and grabs her. Jim hears her crying out and dashes to help.

A good ol' B-movie fistfight with jazz music accompaniment ensues. Jim knocks the guy out cold. He and Sandy run away. That Sandy's quite a trooper, skittering across some pretty rough terrain in her tight-fitting skirt and high heels. They're headed back for the car, but as they race across an open field, the two simply vanish!

In another field somewhere…or sometime…they reappear. They know something strange has happened. Something they can't explain. When they arrive at the road their car has disappeared. What's

Bill Thurman, Tim Holt and others in *The Yesterday Machine*.

more, the barbed wire fence has been replaced by an old-fashioned wooden rail fence. Jim remembers Partane's crazy talk about Nazi time travel experiments and he's troubled. Sandy can't wrap her mind around the confusing details. The girl becomes frantic, forcing Jim to give her the cliché anti-hysteria slap.

They have no choice but to hoof it down the now unpaved road. Shortly, they happen upon a rider on horseback who seems to be from America's colonial era. When Jim uses a Zippo to light his cigarette, the stranger urges his horse to a gallop, shouting "Witchcraft!" as he flees.

Jim and Sandy are pretty sure they're time-tripping by now, but they don't know how to deal with the fact. They take a break near a tree. In an instant, they are transported to the secret laboratory of Professor Ernst von Hauser. They find themselves no longer leaning against a tree, but are crouched amid a strange array of high-tech equipment. We realize this von Hauser guy is the same Nazi Lt. Partane spoke of earlier in the film.

Jim asks what century they are now in. With a big smile, von Hauser cuts to the quantum physics chase. "What difference does it make? There really is no such thing as time, except as a relative measuring device in your own mind."

It turns out the professor has Sandy's sister, Margie. When Sandy demands to see her, von Hauser summons a woman who appears to be an ancient Egyptian (Olga Powell) telling her to take Margie to her sister. While Sandy goes to check on Margie, Jim and the prof have a little discussion. It seems Jim did some research this morning at the public library and he knows a good deal about the scientist, his accomplishments and incredible claims. Von Hauser is pleased that Jim's done his due diligence. For a moment, it appears they may become friends. Then, they fall into an angry disagreement over whether or not Adolf Hitler was a murdering psychopath.

The professor gets over his anger and begins to tell Jim about all the really cool toys of destruction he created for the Nazis just before the close of the war. If only they'd had a bit more time! (At this point I find myself thinking, 'If it's time you need, go for it dude! Your time machine seems to be able to take you to any point in history.')

In a dungeon, somewhere in von Hauser's complex, Sandy is reunited with Margie. They're happy to see one another, but distressed to find themselves locked away.

Jim's eyes begin to glaze over, back in the lab, when the professor uses a chalk board to explain his time travel procedure. He quit school and became a reporter to get away from this sort of thing. When Professor von Hauser is sure Jim understands him, he has his goons haul the reporter away.

DVD Art for *The Yesterday Machine*.

The thugs knock Jim out and toss him into the cell next to the one the girls are in. The professor may be a Nazi bent on world domination, but he's at least decent enough to provide separate quarters for men and women. It's only proper.

Later, one of the goons enters the women's cell, slaps Sandy and drags Margie away. Jim is powerless to help.

In the lab, von Hauser straps Margie into a chair and places her in the time

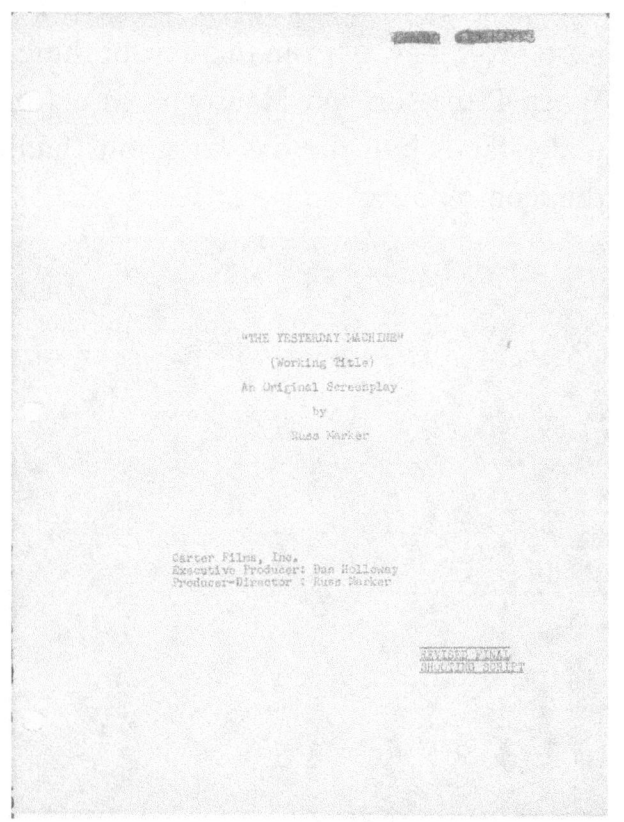

*The Yesterday Machine* script cover page.

travel apparatus. She will be his first subject to be sent into the future.

The Egyptian servant, Didiyama, delivers food to the prisoners. It's just deli sandwiches, but it's better than nothing. Jim tries to get the servant to help them escape, but the woman is afraid of the Nazis.

A guard shows up and throws Didiyama to the floor. Evidently, this is the final straw. She's had enough. Pulling a knife from her clothing, she slips up on the Nazi and stabs him in the back. The guy strangles her to death, before falling unconscious. The door to Sandy's cell is open. She grabs the guard's keys and releases Jim from the cell next door. Jim grabs a Luger off the dead Nazi and, together, he and Sandy return to the lab.

As they burst in, Margie is vanishing into the future. Jim shoots a guard and threatens to kill von Hauser if he doesn't return Margie pronto. The injured guard reaches for his gun while Sandy helps her sister out of the time machine. Jim dives to the floor and puts another bullet in the Nazi guard. He fires a couple of rounds into the professor's machinery and the trio go in search of an exit from this time fortress.

Lt. Partane and some cops are poking around the old house. One cop takes a smoke break in the cemetery. A trap door opens in the earth. Jim, Sandy and Margie appear to the cop's dismay.

Partane and Lasky descend into the lab and exchange gunfire with the professor. Von Hauser falls into the time machine and vanishes. Partane decides he's had enough of Nazis and time travel. Taking matters into his own hands, he smashes all the equipment.

Above ground, Partane suggests Jim take the ladies home. He admits destroying the time travel machinery. When Jim asks why, he explains the world's just not yet ready for such a device.

*The Yesterday Machine* may have received a lot of bad press, but I have to admit I like it. People say it's slow-moving, laughable and sub-par. Even so, I have a soft spot in my heart for stories and films dealing with time travel. I've had a voracious appetite for time travel tales all my life. I can't seem to get enough of them. Even the cheesy ones.

I think *The Yesterday Machine* is as good or better than any number of sci-fi pictures from the 1950s and 1960s. The premise is more creative than most time travel films of the era. I do not know exactly how much money was spent putting this thing together, but it obviously wasn't much. It covers all the bases for an exploitation film in 1963; it's got action, mystery, a recognizable film star (Tim Holt), a song for cross marketing and a respectable running time.

I'd say Russ Marker did a bang-up job.

Sometime in the early 1980s, a western movie town location was constructed near I-45, not far south of Dallas. This was during my tenure at Productions West Communications. One day, some of the other Productions West co-op members visited the western town. They wanted to check it out and see if there were any money-making opportunities there for us. Jess Sherman came back talking about an old Gabby Hayes-type character he'd met at the film location. He was the manager/caretaker of the western town and his name was Russ Marker. Jess told me the man said he had directed a time travel picture.

This got my attention.

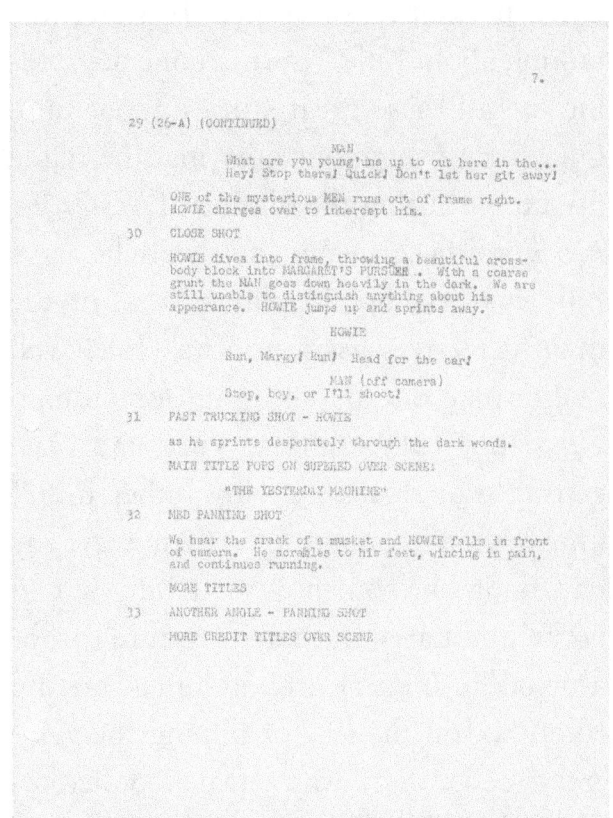

**The Yesterday Machine** script page 7.

I talked to Marker over the phone. He seemed a likable sort and he knew a lot about all the other films and film makers active in Dallas in the 1960s.

When I took a job at Allied film lab, I met and worked with a young man named Gary Kennamer. Gary, as it turns out, is Russ's son.

I told Gary Kennamer about the book I was writing and he was kind enough to share some anecdotes about his father's film career.

GK: I, too, enjoyed *The Yesterday Machine*. Imagine my shock when I discovered, as an adult, my father's movie!

An interesting side note: My father was talking about Billy Thurman one day, telling me all these great stories about him. One story was about how mad he made my father during the filming of *Yesterday Machine*, because my dad said he gave Billy his first break, playing one of the main detectives assisting Tim Holt. Well one day he doesn't show up for filming. No phone call, nothing. They had been getting along great, so my father didn't know what to make of it. Anyway, my dad finds out somehow that Billy left to go be in a Larry Buchanan picture (probably because Larry offered him a starring role). So, on the day of filming the cemetery scene, there was a Dallas police officer who'd been hanging around, I guess for security purposes, or to supply a police car -- I'm not sure. The officer's name was Jimmy Howe. Anyway, my father had him do Billy's part in the cemetery. It's when a trap door opens in the ground, at the end of the picture. Jimmy's leaning against the patrol car lighting a cigarette and does a comical double take.

Jim Sullivan (I think?) called my father one day and told him the Professor's laboratory was ready. My father drove excitedly over to the soundstage (I forget which one) but when he got there, to his horror, it was, in his words, "pathetic." First of all, there wasn't much to it, and the control panel had knobs that were obviously just toothpaste caps! My dad angrily paced the floor of the soundstage and chewed them out, demanding to know where all the money went. They were supposed to start shooting on that set the next day, and there was no more money for sets. There was no way to start over from scratch, so they had to use the set. My father left in a huff and went back home dejected.

The actor James Britton who plays the news reporter was actually my uncle James Kennamer. When my uncle and the leading lady, the singer from the night club, are accidentally sent back into the Revolutionary War period, and they are not on a paved, asphalted road anymore but a dirt road, and this character rides up on a horse, for some reason the sound wasn't working (maybe they were too close to a highway or something). Anyway, my uncle lights a cigarette which makes the guy think they are spirits or whatever, and he hollers "Witchcraft!" (or whatever it was -- it's been a long time since I've seen the movie), then gallops away on his horse. Well that's my father's voice dubbed onto the soundtrack, shouting "Witchcraft!"

One day when they were filming, out of curiosity, a crowd of people gathered to watch the proceedings. Tim Holt, who my father said always had a flask on him and was probably a tad tipsy that day, whispered, "Watch this." Tim then walked over to the crowd and politely addressed them, "Would you all please move

Tim Holt and Humphrey Bogart in *Treasure of the Sierra Madre*.

over there (pointing), you're standing on the sound track." The crowd obediently moved over!

It was during the making of this movie, that Tim Holt regaled the whole cast and crew with the actual story behind "Badges? We don't need no stinkin' badges!" They were shooting *Treasure of the Sierra Madre* (1948) in Mexico, when these thuggish-looking bandito types show up. Both Hustons, Bogart and Holt were nervous, as was the crew, who weren't armed. The leader of the gang approaches John Huston and says, in very bad English, "I want to be in movies. You put me in dees movie." Huston thought about it, and told the guy okay. So, Huston came up with the scene that's actually in the film, and that's the actual guy, and his gang, in their own clothing. Huston had written some lines for the gang leader to memorize. The guy goes off and studies his lines, comes back later & says, "Okay. I'm ready." So, they start filming. Bogart or somebody has a line wherein they ask the guy, "Where did you come from?" or "How did you get here?" Something like that. To which, the gang leader is supposed to reply, "We came on horseback." The guy's English was so bad, it came out sounding like, "We came on a whore's back." Well Holt said Bogart just came unglued, fell down laughing and was slapping his knee. Meanwhile, Huston is afraid the guy's going to be embarrassed and then get pissed off. So, Huston explains to him why Bogart is cracking up. The guy grins and starts chuckling as well. Huston coaches the guy on his line and they try another take, and another, and another, and the whole time Bogart keeps losing it, and before long the whole cast and crew is rolling around, laughing themselves silly. I'm not sure if they changed the line or it's in the finished movie or what, as it's been a long time since I've seen that film as well.

The old civil war soldier who shoots the kid, was Pat Cranshaw. My dad told me, like Billy Thurman, *Yesterday Machine* was his first movie. He would later be in *Bonnie & Clyde* (1967). Pat's the bank teller who informs Warren Beatty that there's no money. Beatty forces him to tell Faye Dunaway, and she cracks up laughing.

I just saw part of an old movie on TV yesterday, and it reminded me of one of my dad's stories. It happened sometime in

Russ Marker.

the mid-to-late 1960s, as we were still living in Mesquite at the time. My dad gets a phone call one day from some young man who is looking for someone to write a screenplay for a feature film -- a scary one. He explained that he'd been calling people in the local film industry, and someone had recommended my father. So, my dad drove to Grand Prairie to meet this person and discuss it. The guy's family was apparently wealthy and owned a successful hotel in Grand Prairie. Anyway, my father gets to the place where this person is living, to discover he's not a man at all, but a pimply-faced, long-haired teenager. The kid explains he's been making short horror films on 8mm or Super 8, maybe 16mm -- I'm not sure. He tells my father that he's only interested in the horror genre. Then he shows my dad this fantastic miniature set that he's built -- an underground tunnel that his camera can travel through. Anyway, they get to talking about the script, and the kid explains he can't pay much, and asks if my dad would be willing to write it on deferral, you know, for a percentage of whatever the film makes. My dad kindly turned him down, explaining he didn't have time to devote to writing a script if he was not going to be paid for it. So, the kid says, "That's fine."

My dad comes back home disappointed, because he was always desperate for income. He made a living, by the way, as a sign painter. Anyway, he gets back home and tells my mother, who's been waiting in quiet anticipation, that it was a bust. But he tells her, "But that kid's got real talent, and someday we're gonna be hearing about him."

The kid was Tobe Hooper, creator of *Texas Chain Saw Massacre*.

Before I sign off, let me share another funny incident from my father's life. Years ago, I'm guessing the 1980s or early 1990s, my dad was at some kind of convention, when this guy comes up to my father and excitedly tells him that he's a big fan of all my dad's films. Well my father is shocked and confused, because he only made *The Yesterday Machine*. Anyway, this guy is more and more enthused and my dad just thanks him. The guy leaves and someone explains to my father that the fellow had mistaken him for Russ Meyer!


Russ Marker (real name Hirom Monroe Kennamer) passed away in Dallas, Texas on February 22, 2010.

# HAL P. WARREN

## MANOS: THE HANDS OF FATE (1966)

The film opens with Michael (Hal P. Warren), Margaret (Diane Adelson) and Debbie (Jackey Neyman Jones) parked at the side of the road in a convertible. They're on their way to a vacation destination of some sort, but have incomplete instructions on how to get there (No GPS in 1966!). The little girl shares the back seat with a black poodle named Pepe. Her voice is dubbed by an adult female trying to sound like a kid. Little Debbie complains that she's cold and hungry. Then Mom and Dad have the traditional squabble about asking for directions (Thank you, GPS, for finally putting an end to that!). We're maybe thirty-five seconds into the film at this point and we're already having misgivings.

Perhaps, sensing that Michael will resist the idea of putting the top up on his snazzy convertible, Margaret suggests Debbie ride up front between them. The little family begins singing a round robin of "Row, row, row, your boat …' As the song states, life may be just a dream, but

"The story concerns a luckless young man with his underwear so bunched up he can hardly get around, and no time to straighten it out because he is beset by Fate in the form of a young couple with the family dog and the family child seeking shelter for the night, after having taken a wrong turn coming down off Scenic drive and getting lost in the wilds of Kern Place, or somewhere."

--*El Paso Herald-Post,* November 16, 1966

"Bad editing, worse directing, awful, soap opera-worthy acting, continuity errors galore, unexplained cat fights between gorgeous women in white tunics, human sacrifice, dogs with more acting talent than their human counterparts, blatant sexism, a hilariously inappropriate soundtrack… *Manos: The Hands of Fate* has it all! And it's only 74 minutes long, so you know it won't wear out its welcome."

--*screenanarchy.com,* Sebastian Zavala, January 7, 2017

there's also the possibility that it will become a nightmare.

The opening credits have just begun when the vacationers are pulled over by a pair of policemen. One of their tail lights is out. In a brief exchange, Michael talks the policeman into letting them off with a warning.

> "The title alone should warn people away. 'Manos' is Spanish for "hands" and that is about as clever as the film ever gets. Listening to the Master crowing about his deity's power or staring at ten minutes of women arguing is nothing to be proud of."
> --*badmovies.org*, Andrew Borntreger, March 30, 2003

An instrumental featuring a flute plays as the family continues on past mist-enshrouded mountains looming in the background. They turn off the main road toward Valley Lodge and the title theme's lyrics kick in. A female vocalist reminiscent of Dionne Warwick sings the jazzy number. The sound mix is a bit poor. Margaret speaks while the song is playing and we have difficulty making out what she's saying.

A couple of teenagers (Bernie Rosenblum and Joyce Mulleur) in a smaller, sportier convertible, are parked at the side of the country road making out. In addition to necking, they are swigging (presumably illegally) from a bottle of liquor. Some homegrown rock accompanies their interlude. We see the shadow of a car passing on the road behind the couple. After a long pause, and after looking at the camera as if she's receiving instructions on what to do, the girl says, "I wonder where they're going." Her boyfriend replies, "Man, like there's nothing up that road." They don't allow their momentary curiosity to put the brakes on their make-out session.

Over a lingering shot through the windshield we hear the couple discuss turning back to ask directions from the kissing teens. This "windshield cam" continues relentlessly, dissolving from one nondescript view to the next.

When we finally are treated to a different scene, we find ourselves back with the teens in the sportscar. In the opening frames of the sequence, we clearly see the slate being withdrawn on the right side of the frame. The cops who pulled Mike over earlier show up and tell the kids to move along. Enigmatically, the little sportscar tears off in the same direction that the boy earlier stated leads nowhere. Surely, local cops would know this, but I suppose viewers of the film were not expected to pay attention to this sort of thing.

The vacationing family are still trying to get their bearings. They happen onto a house which Michael swears wasn't there a few minutes before. Margaret still insists they should ask for directions. A strange man with a beard is perched near the entrance to the house. He twitches in a most peculiar, but unexplained fashion. When Mike and Margaret approach, he announces, "I am Torgo. I take care of the place when the Master is away." Torgo clings to a staff atop which is the symbol of a hand.

Before Margaret or Michael have said a word, Torgo begins to ramble about "the child and the dog." The Master would not approve of them. The married couple try to make it clear they just want directions to Valley Lodge. Margaret points out it's getting dark.

When Michael insists on directions out of the cul-de-sac, Torgo responds that there is no way out. Michael, against Margaret's wishes, browbeats the twitchy servant into agreeing to let them stay the night. This uncomfortable encounter is prolonged by interminable close-ups in which nothing happens. The soundtrack lets us know we should feel tense. Little Debbie is still cold and asks if they can go inside. By now, we're eleven and a half minutes into *Manos: The Hands of Fate* and we begin to wonder if the "Hands of Fate" aren't the hands of a torturously slow-moving clock.

As Torgo agrees to unload their luggage, we notice his legs are oddly deformed. His thighs bulge and his limbs seem to bend at unnatural angles. What is the intent of the film makers? Are we to assume he is a satyr? Another of the many enigmas associated with *Manos: The Hands of Fate*!

Hal P. Warren's epic schlock still garners fans even in Europe.

Torgo can barely walk, but he follows Michael to the trunk of their vehicle. Although he previously agreed, Torgo insists again that the family must leave. Michael demonstrates his empathy by loading the poor crippled man down with their luggage and ignoring his pleas.

Inside, Mom, Debbie and the poodle sit uncomfortably on a sofa. Margaret observes eerie art objects on the mantle above a fireplace that looks like a remnant from antiquity. Michael tries to put a happy spin on things. He directs Margaret's attention to a very dramatic painting of a glaring man and a large black hound. The painting is one of the nicer elements in the film, calling to mind the art featured on television's *Night Gallery* (TV series 1969 – 1973) hosted by Rod Serling. As they admire the painting, Torgo startles Mike by tapping his shoulder with the staff he carries.

When Michael asks Torgo where the Master has gone, the strange creature replies, "He has left this world. But, he is always with us." Again, Margaret voices her anxiety. Torgo informs her that the Master likes her and she need not fear. "I thought you said he was dead!" the confused Margaret blurts. "Not dead the way you know it. He is with us always," is Torgo's halting response. In keeping with the time-honored tradition of thick-headed macho leading men in cheesy sci-fi and horror films of the era, Mike assures her: "You have nothing to worry about. I'm sure it's all in your imagination."

Torgo, Margaret and Michael watch uneasily as Debbie gets the poodle to stand on its hind legs. Via one of the film's many jump-cuts, Torgo is in the doorway to the bedroom and announces he should show them their sleeping arrangements.

Though the creepy old house is adorned with strange and intriguing décor, we never have a real sense of the layout of the main room. Scenes here are delivered piecemeal, providing no reliable impression of where these objects are in the bigger scheme.

The howling of a wolf (or big black dog?) startles Margaret. Michael continues to spout reassuring quips of bravado. Debbie makes a rapid transition from playing with the dog, to sleeping on the sofa. In the very next shot she's sitting up as Michael goes out to investigate the howling in an effort to put his wife's mind to rest. The poodle follows him, dashing off into the darkness.

Michael tells Margaret to stay inside, then he runs to his car to retrieve a flashlight and revolver from the glove compartment. He dashes off in the direction of the pet's barking. Abruptly, we find him standing still, wincing at an unpleasant sight. There on the ground is a tangle of black fluff intended to represent the mangled body of poor Pepe.

Margaret rushes outside to see what's happening. Michael curses and orders her back inside. Apparently, profanity is rare in the couple's relationship. The swear word frightens Margaret even more.

Michael breaks the news that Pepe has gone on to the Big Kennel in the Sky. Jump-cuts abound, compounding the unsettling qualities the film already possesses in spades.

Promising to take care of everything, Michael sees Margaret safely inside, then goes to dispose of Pepe's remains.

Margaret insists they must leave once Mike's back inside. He agrees.

Instead of grabbing their stuff and throwing it in the car, he calls for Torgo. The strange servant stumbles in, hardly able to make it through the doorway.

Mike: *Would you mind putting the luggage back in the car?*

Torgo: (wearily) *As you wish.*

Mike: *Right now! Fast, dammit, fast!*

If we know anything about Torgo by this time, it's that he never, ever does anything fast.

We're 19 minutes and nine seconds into this adventure and still have almost 50 minutes to go.

"Reach a conclusion, film!" I shout. "Fast, dammit, fast!"

*When I originally saw the running time of 68 minutes, I'd thought this was going to be a breeze. How could I have been so wrong?*

Guess what . . . Mike's car won't start.

While he fiddles under the hood, Torgo explains to Margaret that it would be dangerous to try and leave. The master wants Margaret for his wife. Torgo twitches and reaches for Margaret's hair. She stands there, looking shocked, but saying nothing as Torgo's fingers caress her locks. Finally, as if someone flipped her anger switch, she begins shouting at him.

Torgo's worked himself up into a lustful frenzy. "The Master wants you, but he can't have you. I want you!"

Now, this guy Torgo has such a hitch in his get-along that even an old lady in a wheelchair could probably outrun him. The only chance he has of getting the upper hand with someone is if they remain absolutely immobile, which apparently is Margaret's plan of action. She swings a slap in Torgo's general direction and screams her husband's name.

Mike's still puttering with the car.

Torgo and Margaret come to a hasty and incomprehensible truce. She won't tell Mike what Torgo said.

Michael enters and informs everyone that the car won't start. Torgo volunteers this time to return the luggage to the bedroom. The couple are left to muse over the bizarre events that have transpired. Margaret wonders if Debbie will "understand" about Pepe. Certain his little girl is a chip off the old block, Mike assures her Debbie will take the news in stoic fashion.

Speaking of Debbie, where is she? While their backs were turned, she has slipped out.

They can't find their little girl inside, so they exit the house to search for her. Mike continues berating his wife for being a hysterical female.

With much less vigor than he displayed in his search for Pepe, Mike stands in one spot, waves a flashlight around and calls Debbie's name. They hear Debbie's voice and turn to see her rounding the house in the company of a monstrous black dog.

When they move toward Debbie, the dog bolts away.

Back inside, they question Debbie about where she's been. She describes a "big place" with a fireplace. She takes her parents there, a location they'd been unable to find without her guidance.

The scenes in the area I'll call "the temple" (for want of a better term), are photographed with a slightly more stylistic approach. There are braziers with flickering flames, pillars and swirling fog. A group of women in gauzy white robes appear to be sleeping in a standing position against the pillars. The black dog is chained to a sort of altar where the mysterious Master reclines.

Margaret (for maybe the twelfth time): *Mike, it's horrible! Let's get out of here!*

But their car is malfunctioning and it's the middle of the night. So, Mike secures his family in the bedroom.

Torgo hobbles into the temple. "I want her! She's mine!" he announces to the Master and his many sleeping wives, offering up a brief, miserable monolog. In the past, he's lusted after the Master's wives, but now he believes he will possess a wife of his own.

Torgo buries his face in the transparent clothing of one of the women. Is he sniffing her?

Energized, he announces he is finished with all of them and moves through the temple with greater speed and dexterity than had seemed possible for him in previous scenes.

Margaret undresses in the bedroom, while Torgo watches through a window. She feels his gaze, but whirling around, she finds no one there. Thankfully, Debbie is asleep on the bed, oblivious to her mother's turmoil.

Michael runs, presumably toward the temple? But, Torgo bushwhacks him with that staff he's been carrying around all night. Soon (well, not really soon, because nothing ever seems soon where Torgo's involved) the unconscious Michael is securely tied to a tree trunk.

The moon is full. Fires in the temple blaze. The Master (Tom Neyman) awakens. He looks a bit like the famous pop artist from the 1960s Peter Max and he's wearing this really groovy black robe with two enormous crimson hand appliques. He glares at the camera.

Remember those teens making out in the sports car? Well, they're still at it. Oops, here come the cops again. The boy asks why they don't go after that other couple. The cop tells them to "git!" Once more, the teens drive deeper into the dead-end desert road. The cops watch them go, evidently thinking nothing of it.

The Master says a prayer to Manos, "who dwells in the dark universe, in the chasms of night!" As the prayer is spoken we are shown a dark bust of a humanoid who resembles some extra-terrestrials we've seen in other films. Is this Manos? The Master bids his wives arise.

Abrupt cut to the Master sitting sullenly on the altar as the wives chatter in a circle around a temple flame. Does he regret waking them? It seems these vociferous female spirits are upset about the fact that there is a little female child among them. Who gets sacrificed and who gets to live? These wives of the Master debate in a rowdy fashion.

The Master says the child must die. He silences the wives and goes to find Torgo. In his absence, the females continue to argue, splitting into two opposing factions: those who would let the girl live and those who would kill her. The two teams face off in the sand outside the temple and stage a fight scene worthy of a *Three Stooges* episode or (if I'm being generous) a dance number from the 1960s TV show, *Hullaballoo*.

The Master finds Torgo sleeping on the floor with his head in a corner. He pokes Torgo in the belly with the staff. Torgo rises and argues with the Master. It is implied that Torgo has been "doing things" to the harem of wives while they were sleeping and unable to move. Waving the staff before Torgo's face the Master declares he must die. Then he says another prayer to Manos.

One of the wives discovers Mike tied to the tree. He's still unconscious. She kneels beside him. Is she going to release him? No, she wants to make out. Being unconscious, he's not a very good kisser, so she slaps him repeatedly to bring him around. The first slap has no sound effect, but the subsequent slaps resound like effects from a fist fight in a spaghetti western. No dice. Mike remains unconscious. I guess he's just not that into her.

The dissatisfied woman leaves in a huff.

The wild and crazy cat fight is still in full swing. Margaret wakes up on the bed with Debbie. She calls Mike's name. Still tied to the tree, he is oblivious.

One of the wives returns with the Master, Torgo and the black hound to the temple. The Master decides one of his wives is just a big trouble maker and ties her to a pillar to be sacrificed.

Now, Torgo is placed on the altar. The Master shouts the word, "Kill!" and two of the wives descend on poor Torgo with claw-like hands, fingers writhing. Perhaps they intend to tickle him to death?

Terrified Margaret calls out to Mike from the bedroom. Mike wakes up at last. With surprising ease, he unties himself and retrieves his handgun and flashlight.

Now, the angry wives are administering soundless slaps to the helpless Torgo.

Michael arrives at the bedroom door and cries out for her to open it. Maggie's in shock. She doesn't respond, just cradles Debbie on the bed. Mustering his strength, Mike breaks the door down. Well, more like scoots it open. Anyway, he gets in.

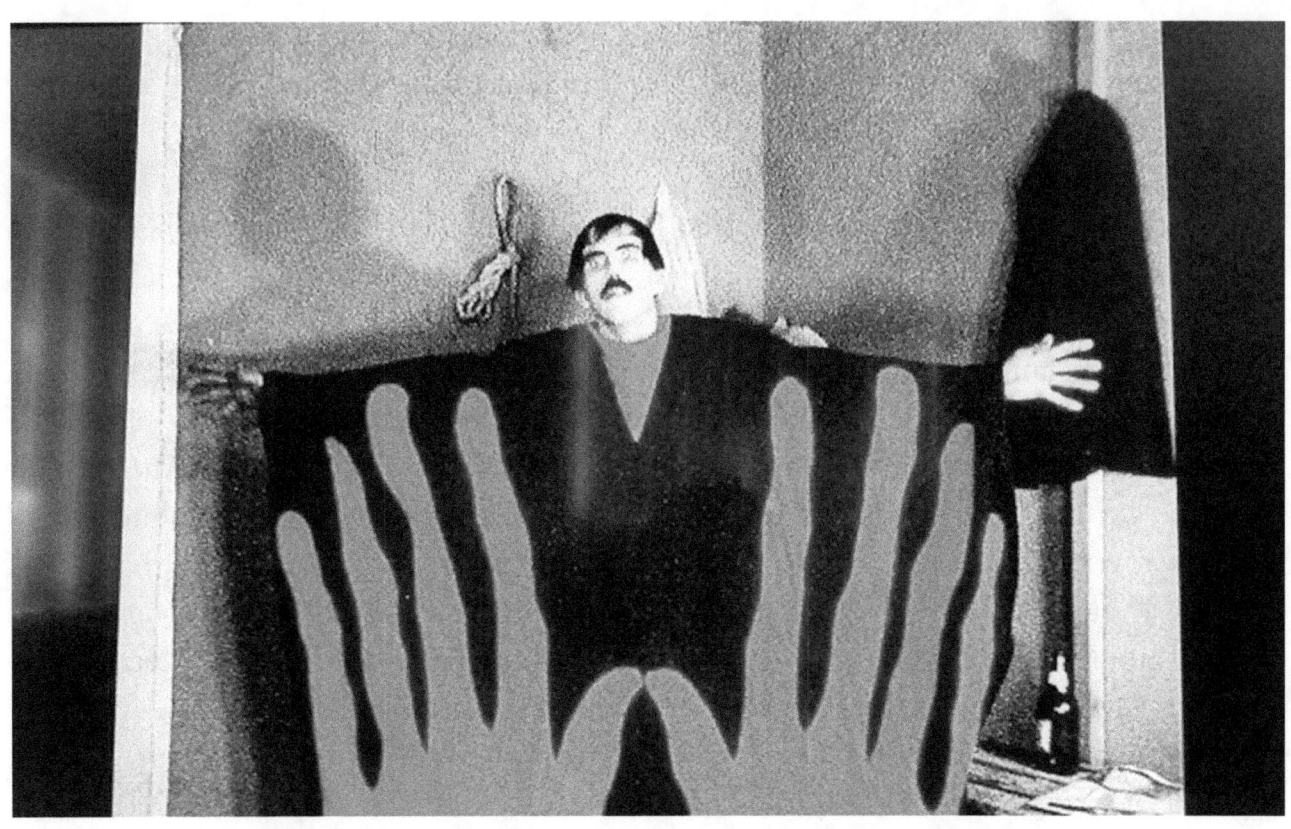
Tom Neyman as the Master wearing his famous ten finger muumuu.

The Master calls an end to the Torgo tickling ceremony. He is rolled off the altar. The Master focuses psychic power on Torgo, willing him to rise to his feet. He leads Torgo to the fire, pushing Torgo's hand into the flames. There is a flash, then the laughing Master holds a flaming hand and Torgo runs into the darkness with a flaming wrist.

The Master thinks this flaming hand is the funniest thing he's ever seen.

The wife tied to the pillar doesn't think much of it, though. She insults the Master, telling him he has lost all control and will soon be finished. Her insubordination leads the Master to slap her repeatedly.

These slaps have sound effects. They're a little more dramatic that way.

The Master slaps her until her face is bloody, but she continues saying she does not fear him. Has the guy lost his touch?

Mike leads his family through the rough countryside, stumbling and falling into a low spot. Margaret whines the whole time, but little Debbie takes it like a trooper. Manos and the wives spread out, searching for them. He can journey outside this world, but he can't find three mortals playing hide-and-seek? Yep, he's lost it.

A rattlesnake threatens Mike and his family, so he shoots it. Good news is, the makers of Manos could afford sound effects for the gun. Bad news, they weren't able to splurge for the rattlesnake's rattle. Cest la vie!

When Debbie finally voices her fear, Dad screams, "Please, Debbie! Not now!"

The cops probe the darkness with a spotlight, searching for signs of the folks the two teens had mentioned. They hear the gunshots, but talk themselves out of investigating.

The fugitive family returns to the house only to be confronted by an out-of-focus Manos and the hound. Michael, aiming a very in-focus revolver, fires two rounds into his adversary.

Fade to black.

Two women with big hair carry on the tradition established in the film by driving in a convertible. The problem is it's raining and their top is down. They turn off the main road at the sign that reads 'Valley Lodge.' Displaying wisdom, they pull over and raise the top.

We receive another dose of hypnotic through-the-windshield driving shots.

Their car does a very slow, muddy passby.

The teenagers have not lost their fondness for necking at the side of the road. They take a break from kissing long enough to notice the strangers.

The two women pull up to the Master's house and find Michael standing at the front door instead of Torgo. "Hello," he says, "I am Michael. I take care of the house when the Master is away."

The women exchange a worried glance. We see flashes of the Master and wives sleeping in the temple. Little Debbie, too, is among them. The end credits play over scenes from the film.

*Manos: The Hands of Fate* belongs to a cinematic fraternity shared by such films as *Plan 9 from Outer Space* (1959) and *Santa Claus Conquers the Martians* (1964). Both of these movies are frequently cited as "the worst film ever made." I seldom think or communicate in terms of absolutes, so I'll resist the temptation to apply that cliché. Still, *Manos* is a particularly inept Texas obscurity deserving a place of special honor in the annals of Schlock.

Most articles about this movie make mention of the fact that Hal P. Warren was a fertilizer salesman. I suppose that's the sort of *non-sequitur* that can get the ball rolling in the right direction when you're examining an enigma like this one. So, the guy sold fertilizer and was involved in an El Paso, Texas community theater clique. In 1966, he put together (some say) $16,000 to produce the movie *Manos: The Hands of Fate*. The film was shot over a period of five weeks or more, though watching it now, one wonders what the cast and crew were doing all that time.

Like many film fans of the 1980s, I first became aware of *Manos* by reading the brief mention Michael Weldon included in his ground-breaking book *Psychotronic Encyclopedia of Film* (1983). The damn thing sounded so obscure, so inane, that I was desperate to see it. This was the beginning of the home video era and no one had put the thing out on VHS yet. This was the case for years. Though I searched periodically, I always came up empty-handed. After a while I gave up.

In the late 1980s, I hired the multi-talented Benton Jennings to play a psychopath in my gritty action flick, *Highway to Hell* (1990). One day, just in conversation, Benton mentioned his dad had enjoyed acting which led to his own interest in the craft. I asked if his father had ever acted in movies.

"Just once, in some really terrible little film called *Manos: The Hands of Fate*," he answered.

I almost fell out of my chair.

It would be years before I finally witnessed *Manos* for myself. Be careful what you wish for. Once you've seen something like this, you can't 'unsee' it!

On May 22, 2017, I caught up with Benton Jennings by phone and he shared these thoughts on the bizarre movie in which his father appeared:

*BJ*: My dad played the cop, of course, but Jackie Neyman told me (after we began communicating) that she'd found some stuff in her father's papers indicating that Dad was also a silent producer and legal advisor on the project. Dad had the famous line, "Go do what you're not doing somewhere else" . . . or whatever it is.

I was at the premier in 1966 in El Paso. I don't remember a great deal. I was ten years old. I was barely aware that the production was happening. I'd be told my father was off making a film and I'd think, oh, okay. Because he also did community theater. He was often off doing rehearsals for the theater.

So, it was a big deal, this big premiere! We got to ride in a limo. Of course, it was the same limo everyone else rode in. It'd just go around the block and pick up everybody (*Laughs.*). But, I got to ride in a limousine for the first time. My first red carpet experience!

They had a big ceremony before the film. I guess the mayor was there. They presented Hal with some stuff. They presented my father with an honorary El Paso County deputy sheriff's badge. I think he helped getting the patrol car for the movie. I still have that badge. That's one memento that remains in my possession.

I remember wondering why, once the credits were rolling, my family was hurriedly getting up and exiting at the back of the theater. Everybody had been laughing and heckling the film. We got out of there and went to some sort of after party that Hal had set up. That's about all I remember about the screening. I think my photos of that are on Facebook.

I wasn't really aware enough at age ten to know what was happening. A lot of people were laughing and I'm just thinking, "Oh, I guess something funny's going on." I wasn't frightened by the film. My father was in it. No buttons in my brain were being pushed to trigger fear. Of course, nothing really scary happens in *Manos* (*Laughs*.). It's just strange, rather than scary. I was too young to make any judgments whether it was good or bad. I was just along for the ride.

I think the movie surfaced originally in some big catalog of cheesy movies, a very poor VHS copy of the film. After Mystery Science Theater got hold of it, then I was like, "Yeah, my Dad played the cop." Nobody believed me. Then there were all these pages dedicated to the film on the internet. Once a lot of people had actually seen it, these conspiracy theories sprang up. Like everyone involved with the film was dead and most of them had died violently or committed suicide. The only one who really committed suicide was the guy who played Torgo. Hal died back in

MST3000 VHS Release of ***Manos: The Hands of Fate***.

the 80s I believe from cancer. Other than that, everyone else at the time was pretty much alive!

All these evil legends had arisen, but everyone was doing fine for the most part. My father died about ten years ago I guess. From nothing horrible. Just old age.

Maybe 15 to 18 years ago, *Entertainment Weekly* ran an article about the film and its cult following. I wrote a short letter to the editor, explaining who I was and how strange it was, this resurgence.

They put the Mystery Science version out on DVD and somebody else put out a DVD of the movie without the robots. I bought copies of each for my parents, my brother and sister. When my mother unwrapped the package, and saw what it was, she just shook her head and said, "Oh, dear, I wish they'd just let that thing die."

Some people try to defend *Manos*. They say, "It's really not that bad" (*Laughs*.). Well, yes, it is! The whole thing was shot without sound. They used a little hand-cranked 16mm camera. Every line of dialog in the film was dubbed.

I can't say the apple fell too far from the tree. I've done my share of schlocky films as you know. Then again, I became a union actor and earn my living from it now. They attempted remakes followed the same route as *Manos* by being non-union productions. My brother, William Bryan Jennings III, was quite happy to be in the sequel. He's not a professional actor. I thought, that's fine, that's much better, you be in it!

Some guy named Rupert something, from El Paso, tried to get a sequel made, with himself playing Torgo. He kept after me to be in it, because of the connection with my father being in the original and the fact that I was a professional actor. It was non-union and I told him, "I can't do it. Bye bye!"

My brother flew to El Paso on his own dime to be in that film. Jackey Neyman and her father Tom appeared in it. Then the guy just disappears! We have no idea what happened to him, the film he shot or anything else.

I think that's when Jackey said, "Well, I'll just do it myself!" And she did. Hopefully, that one makes it out and is a worthy sequel to the original.

Hal P. Warren was involved in the Festival Theater which is where he met my dad and Tom Neyman. Everyone says he was a fertilizer salesman, but that was just one of the things he'd done in his professional life. I think he sold insurance and a couple of other things.

The reports always say that all the voices were done by three people. That's not quite right. My father did his own voice. Hal did his own voice. They had a woman from Dallas who was a well-known voice artist. I don't know if John Reynolds did his own voice or if he tried to do it and it didn't turn out well.

They had rented a sound studio to do the ADR [automatic dialog replacement] work on the film, because there was nothing like that in El Paso. I was in the station wagon we rode in to go to Dallas. I remember John was there, too. I told Jackey Neyman that John was in the car with us. She asked Tom and he said, "Maybe John did record his own lines, I don't remember." John had personal problems as well as drug problems. Maybe he was too high to do it. Who knows?

The little girl, Debbie, who so haplessly became involved in this fiasco, was Jackey Neyman, real-life daughter of Tom Neyman, The Master who appears clad in the Liberace-inspired 10-finger muumuu. B-movie aficionado and writer on all things schlocky, Greg Goodsell tracked Jackey Neyman down many years after the *Manos* debacle. Here are some highlights from Goodsell's interview with Neyman, used with his permission.

*Debbie from Manos: The Hands of Fate Speaks Out!*

NOTE: As of this writing, "Debbie" from Manos--Jackey Raye Neyman Jones--has appeared in two cinematic sequels: *Manos: The Rise of Torgo* (2015) and *Manos Returns* (2016).

*Manos: The Hands of Fate* (1966) is a notoriously bad film, in the annals of such epics as *The Creeping Terror* (1962) and *The Beast of Yucca Flats* (1959) in terms of ineptitude. Overly long at little more than 62 minutes, *Manos* has been described as an endurance test for even the most hardened cult film fan.

Jackey Raye Neyman Jones, who played *Manos*' little girl Debbie, has a different take on the experience. Six years old during the film's production, most of her experience with *Manos* is swathed in childhood nostalgia.

"It was a fun summer. What else was I going to do? There wasn't much to do in El Paso in the 1960s in the summertime," she says. "I was six years old. My father, Tom Neyman was the executive director at the Festival Theater, which is now known as the El Paso Playhouse in El Paso, Texas."

Her father, who would play the Master in *Manos*, used a little child psychology in order to secure his daughter for the role of Debbie:

"I remember my dad came home one day and said 'I'm doing a movie, and we need a little girl. Would you like to be that little girl?' I really didn't know, and he said, 'That's OK honey, you don't have to. We can always get another little girl!' That was all he had to say. 'I said, 'no way!' No other little girl can spend time with my dad. So that's why I said yes.

"I have a lot of memories about it, because to me it was the best summer of my life as a kid. I not only got to be with my dad, but I was the only kid on the set. I got a lot of attention from 'the wives.'"

As to *Manos*' production, Neyman Jones says that "It was mostly shot weekends and afternoon, evenings. Nobody knew what they were doing. It was just that Hal wanted to make a film and he talked people into helping him do that. There were people who actually thought the film might start a thing in El Paso as a destination point to film movies. That was of course, before anyone actually saw it."

Neyman Jones has mixed memories over auteur Hal Warren. "Warren didn't have any children at that time. He didn't know how to relate to children. I remember him saying, 'it's OK, we'll fix it in editing.' That was his main thing, 'we'll fix it in editing.'"

Even at that early age, Neyman Jones was skeptical that the fuzzy caterpillar project at hand would ever metamorphosis into a beautiful butterfly. "I remember being a little kid thinking, *I don't know how he's going to fix that!*"

There has been a cult of personality built around John Reynolds' character, Torgo. Fans of the film's appearance on *Mystery Science Theater 3000* airings dress up as Torgo at fan conventions, mimicking his spastic walk and manner.

"I just met him there on the set. I definitely remember him, as he was kind of a shy person. He spent a lot of time entertaining me. He was just silly, he did magic tricks. I thought he was a pretty cool guy. I found out later that most of the time he was pretty high."

Frank Zappa as the Master. Painting by Jackie Neyman Jones (Debbie in **Manos: The Hands of Fate**).

The Doberman pinscher or "Hellhound" seen in the film was the Neyman beloved family pet, Chanka, who according to Neyman Jones was ridiculously unthreatening. "That was my dog, Chanka! He was a sweetheart. He got the part because he was a Doberman. He was scary looking, but there was nothing scary about him."

As is the case with many regional, no-budget films, crew members wore many hats on the set. Neyman Jones has fond memories of the shoot, which to her was a real family affair. "My dad was the lead actor, plus all the artwork in the film is my dad's. He made John Reynolds' legs. The legs were made of mostly fencing wire, bailing wire and foam, more rigid than foam rubber, inside these really huge overalls."

"My mother made the robe. We're doing a sequel right now; the guy who is putting this thing together actually talked my dad into doing a cameo. The original robe was sent to us from Hal Warren's son. His son still has some of the props. It was pretty cool seeing that thing after 46 years. My mother was a pretty good seamstress!"

"I remember Diane Mahree, who played my mom. She and I just connected. I saw her last week, actually. I remember her, remember Hal, John Reynolds, the wives I remember just vaguely . . . these girls just flitting around."

Neyman Jones is still in contact with Diane Mahree, who is in Colorado. She went on to be a high-end model. She had an amazing modeling career in Europe for several years."

According to Neyman Jones, three people went to Dallas to do the voices. "There was this one woman they found in Dallas who dubbed all the female voices, including mine!" The fact that Neyman Jones' little girl voice is dubbed by an adult is all too obvious in the finished product.

Neyman Jones thinks that Torgo's voice is dubbed in by Tom Neyman. "I guess that's my dad. I think the other voice may have been William Bryan Jennings, who played the sheriff. Hal went too, so he may be the second male voice.

"None of us saw anything finished until we saw it on the screen. Nobody really knew that they were going to dub the voices, no one knew until they saw it in the theater. I was appalled, I was horrified . . ."

Another unpleasant shock that tainted the film's production was the October 16th suicide of actor John Reynolds, from a self-inflicted gunshot wound, a month before the film's premiere in El Paso. "My mom and I were driving to school, and it came out over the radio. He was kind of a tortured young man. He had a hard time in life. People liked him. I just remember that my mom just pulled over. She was shaking and sobbing, she was so upset. He missed the premiere by a couple of months, but I don't think that would have helped him any! The cast and crew were all so humiliated, had he made it that long, it would have been terrible. That would have been the one to push him over the edge . . ."

*Manos: The Hands of Fate* would have its notorious world premiere on November 15th, 1966 in downtown El Paso. Neyman Jones remembers the excitement that precipitated the disastrous reception the film would have.

"It was bad! People started laughing and from what I understand most of the crew snuck out and went to a bar. A lot of people didn't sit through the whole thing. It was pretty humiliating."

Her experience with *Manos* would drift off into the sands of time. She began to search for a copy of the film when she entered adulthood.

"I looked for it for years, just as a personal, nostalgic thing. Then, my dad called me one day and said that he'd been taking a nap in his easy chair when the *Sci-Fi Channel* was on. He was dozing in and out, and he heard something familiar. So, he called me, 'You'll never believe what I just saw!' he said."

*Manos* is widely seen and enjoyed, although Neyman Jones reports spotty success on sharing the title with close friends. "Few of my friends have been able to sit through it."

# JIM SULLIVAN

## NIGHT FRIGHT (1967)

It's a day-for-night evening in Satan's Hollow and a couple of nameless young folks are necking in a nice-looking convertible Camaro. The music they're listening to is suddenly interrupted by an announcer who reports that a strange object has fallen from the sky in the general vicinity.

Nothing that would concern two romantically inclined teens.

Moments later the young woman looks up and screams at something looming over the car.

The following day, Chris[i] (Ralph Baker, Jr.) and his jealous girlfriend, Judy (Dorothy Davis) banter before heading out on an afternoon date. They park in the woods, noting this is where the mysterious object fell from the sky. As Chris waxes philosophical, some friends show up and invite them to come along to the beach. Judy and Chris politely decline, wishing to be alone.

[i] In some of the scenes his last name is Jordan, in others it's Johnson.

"Sometimes you just need to watch a bad monster movie from the 60s. There's nothing particularly good about *Night Fright*. It works as a relic of a time long since passed; when all you needed for a monster movie was any sort of suit, a down-on-his-luck actor (in this case John Agar) and a few bland kids."
  --*horror-movie-a-day.blogspot.com*, September 5, 2008

"To start with, this movie was like a huge collection of the various things that irritate me in a movie. One of the biggest things is that you never really get a good look at the monster."
  --*bmoviecentral.com*

"Much like the monster it presents, *Night Fright* is far too lumbering for its own good."
  --*horrorandsons.com*, August 28, 2017

The two kids frolic in the woods to a soundtrack of canned music that would be more appropriate for a doomed TV sitcom. Then Judy sees something so terrifying she cannot help but scream.

A police squad car races to the scene,

siren blaring, as the opening credits play. The credits are full of names we recognize from various Larry Buchanan productions. The screenplay was written by Russ Marker and John Agar is given top billing.

Deputy Ben Whitfield (Billy Thurman) and Sheriff Clint Crawford (John Agar) are the stalwart law enforcement officers tasked with investigating the goings-on in the woods. The problem is the Federal boys won't let the locals anywhere near the crash site. Is it a secret military project?

Professor Alan Clayton (Roger Ready) arrives at the scene. Seems the Feds want an egg-head in on the party. About this time, the Sheriff and his deputy get a call. It's murder…in Satan's Hollow!

Wes Blau (Gary McLain) is a reporter from the local paper. The Feds are keeping him at arm's length too. He complains to Sheriff Crawford. We learn that the boy from the opening scene is alive, but his girlfriend had her face so badly mutilated she was unidentifiable. Blau is enlisted by the sheriff to help search the woods for any clues the killer may have left behind.

While searching the area, the sheriff hears a threatening grunt. Weapon in hand, he prepares to defend himself. False alarm. It's just some wild pigs. At this point we realize any intended dramatic impact in *Night Fright* is being seriously undermined by preposterously inappropriate music cues.

**Night Fright** was Jim Sullivan's directorial debut.

Blau discovers a clue; a muddy footprint that seems reptilian, but is too large to be a gator. When Crawford follows the tracks, he finds a tuft of hair clinging to a twig.

The carload of kids who were headed for the beach in an earlier scene happen upon the area and are stopped by Sheriff Crawford. He tells them to go home. The driver of the car calls Crawford "fuzz" and the sheriff has to use a little force to make his point to the disrespectful young ruffian.

Deputy Whitfield notes that the tracks seem to come from the area where the strange object fell from the sky. *Could there be a connection? Naw!*

In the local burger joint, the ruffian and his teen cohorts are complaining about Sheriff Crawford spoiling their plans. In his office, Crawford is visibly frustrated. He needs help from the state troopers and he's intent on keeping Blau from blabbing about the weirdness in the woods.

In spite of Sheriff Crawford's warning, the rowdy teens go out to the lake for a "dance-in." They don't realize how much trouble they could be getting into. It's up to Chris and Judy to warn them.

While the kids are out at the lake, wagging their fannies, Sheriff Crawford is showing Professor Clayton the cast he made of the strange, three-toed footprint. Meanwhile, Crawford's steady gal, Joan (Carol Gilley) comes home to find a note from her younger sister, Darlene. It mentions the party at the lake. Joan tries to reach Crawford, but of course, he's not available. Because she can't reach him, she must take charge of the situation. She hops in her Mustang and sets out for the lake to bring her sister home.

Deputy Whitfield runs into a monster on a country road. Trying to escape, he gets his car stuck in a ditch. Frantically, he radios for help. But his fellow deputy is busy making himself a cup of coffee, so he doesn't hear Whitfield's screams as the beast breaks into the car and kills him.

Later, the monster is attracted to the rock and roll music. He lumbers through the woods, thinking he'll crash the party. Meanwhile, Chris and Judy approach their dancing friends to deliver their warning. The leader of the group, Rex (Frank Jolly) gets aggressive and Chris has to beat some sense into him. Their civic duty performed, Chris and Judy split.

The party fizzles. All the kids depart except for Rex and Darlene. Rex is still nursing his injured pride and Darlene wants to help. They make out in Rex's car, but the monster arrives and seems to be mightily aggrieved that someone's turned off the music. The beast kills Rex, then lumbers after Darlene.

John Agar as Sheriff Crawford in **Night Fright**.

Joan arrives at the lake and hears her sister screaming. Darlene and Joan seek refuge in a cabin as the monster advances. Sheriff Crawford arrives and cuts off the creature's pursuit of the girls. He orders the ladies to take off in the Mustang, while he empties his pistol into the thing. The bullets have no effect.

Crawford tears through the woods on foot with the monster in hot pursuit. This thing may have feet like a reptile, but it's got a body like a gorilla and a hairless demonic-looking head. The bullets didn't harm the beast, but Crawford wonders if maybe a piece of dead wood from the trail will do the trick.

Naw, that doesn't work either.

Picking himself up, the sheriff runs on. Chris and Judy happen upon Deputy

Whitfield's abandoned vehicle, finding his mutilated body. Sheriff Crawford comes running out of the woods and the three of them pile into Chris's car.

Safely back at the station, the sheriff is visited by Professor Clayton. Clayton confides that the thing that fell in the woods was a craft NASA launched as part of a secret project known as Operation Noah's Ark. As a possible hedge against nuclear annihilation, many animal species were sent into space. Exposed to cosmic rays, several of the native Earth creatures mutated into a single beast – the thing that's stalking the woods.

The sheriff gets a wild idea and sends Chris on a scavenger hunt.

Later, Sheriff Crawford and a large group of men lay in wait in the woods, planning to stop the creature. Chris and Judy arrive to deliver the secret items Crawford had asked for.

While the lawmen set a trap, the young couple wait in their car. After falling asleep, they are surprised by the monster. Yet another epic chase through the woods ensues.

The mutant creature is lured into a clearing occupied by the rigid Joan. The lawmen have the place staked out for an ambush. It turns out one of the items on Sheriff Crawford's mysterious list was a cache of dynamite, which they detonate, destroying the beast. But, the sheriff's girlfriend, Joan, is caught up in the blast!

Naw, that was just a mannequin. Unfortunately, Joan had to sacrifice her favorite uniform in the ruse. The sheriff promises to buy her all the uniforms she wants. They seal the bargain with a kiss, upbeat music plays and that's a wrap!

Judging from Larry Buchanan's *Curse of the Swamp Creature* just a year or so before, one might have assumed that John Agar was old, infirm, short of breath, unable to do much more than sit in chairs or stand for a while, occasionally mustering a disgusted expression. In *Night Fright*, Agar runs through the woods and does real low-budget action stuff like a regular leading man. I'm guessing Jim Sullivan had a larger budget and could keep Agar around long enough to stage and shoot these things.

Back in those early days, when I'd just returned to Texas from film school, Jim Sullivan was one of the guys I spoke with. He seemed a likable, down-to-earth sort, neither bragging about nor condemning his monster flick. But, Jack Bennett who did special effects on the project was pretty vocal about his complaints.

"I've got opinions on everything," Bennett told me, at the start of our phone conversation. "Some are justified, some are unqualified, but since you're asking I'll tell you."

Bennett's first complaint was that the wayward, mutated monster was a mindless beast. "How can you have any real horror when it's just a mindless brute? Brutes do what they do. If you have a psychopath, a thinking human who's culpable, for me that's where the horror begins."

John Agar has his hands full when a monster from space lands in his jurisdiction.

Second, Bennett said the music cues used in the film were often so inappropriate that they created a sense of incongruity that rendered the action laughable. At the time of that conversation, I had not yet seen the movie. When I did finally watch *Night Fright*, I had to agree with Jack.

The third problem, from Mr. Bennett's perspective, was the choice of shooting day-for-night. "I made a pretty good monster costume for the guy. To save money, he shot everything in daylight, then timed the print to make it look like darkness. The picture was so murky, you never really got a good view of the beast. What's the point of having a monster, if the audience can't even get a good look at it?"

I also spoke with Gary Kennamer, son of Russ Marker who wrote the screenplay and played Mitch in *Night Fright*.

GK: I knew about *Night Fright* because I have two distinct memories from childhood, concerning that film. One, was my father carrying me into somebody's house -- I can still picture the entryway and adjacent dining room vividly -- my father and some man greeted each other and started talking. Then the man led us into the dining room, where a hideous monster mask was sitting in the middle of the circular dining table. The mask must have been on a Styrofoam head meant to support wigs, because it wasn't lying flat on the table, but was upright. I remember being more fascinated than frightened by it, because it wasn't attached to a body, and there were no eyes. I'm guessing this must have been Jack Bennett's[ii] house, but not sure. It was definitely the guy who created the mask for the mutant creature in *Night Fright*, because many years later (when I was a teenager) my father brought home a 16mm print of the movie, that Jim Sullivan or someone let him borrow, and he threaded up the projector and screened it for us on a fold-out, pull-down screen we owned. I think my mother made us popcorn. Anyway, the moment I saw the creature I immediately recalled seeing its head years earlier.

[ii] Jack Bennett was the premier effects artist in Dallas, Texas who worked on all the Buchanan films and a host of other projects.

The other memory from the making of that film, was going to some outdoor setting and my father introducing me to John Agar. I remember standing on the ground and tilting my head way back to look up at this very tall man in a sheriff's uniform. He smiled and said something kind and reached down to shake my hand. I can still picture his face and his smile, but at the time I didn't know who he was.

A year or two later I would, because I saw three of my favorite monster films at that age, *The Mole People* (1956), *Revenge of the Creature* (1955) and *Tarantula* (1955), not to mention one of my favorite war films, *Sands of Iwo Jima* (1949). Come to think of it, he was the first film star I ever met.

John Agar and Bill Thurman inspect one of the creature's victims.

Billy Thurman, in my opinion, gave the greatest, most realistic death scene I've ever watched in *Night Fright*. Am I right? I even told him so one day there at Allied Film. He was playing a projectionist in some indie feature film. I noticed him by the projector we used for sound mixing and recognized him right away, as I was a huge fan of his. He was leaning against the projector, waiting for a set-up to be ready, and I walked up and said, "You're Billy Thurman!" He looked at me surprised, and I introduced myself as Russ Marker's son. Well, his face lit up. We had a nice chat. I'm happy to say that I think I made his day.

My father didn't stay mad at Billy[iii] and they remained friends. And my father told me another humorous story about Billy. When they were shooting *Night Fright*, apparently, a gay actor was playing the monster, and Billy was never afraid to say what was on his mind. One day the gay guy, wearing the monster suit, but not the mask, walked past Billy and my dad. Billy turned to the guy and said out loud, "Well that's just what this picture needs -- a homosexual monster!" My father stifled his laughter, but others couldn't keep from it. My dad actually felt sorry for the guy.

I think I only met Jim once, very briefly. Regrettably, I wasn't there for the filming of the *Horseman of Heth* (an unfinished Russ Marker project) promo film because I couldn't get off work, but a friend of mine was. My friend told me that my father and Jim disagreed about a lot of the filming. I have the storyboards, and

[iii]Russ Marker had a falling out with Bill Thurman during the production of *The Yesterday Machine*. See the chapter on Russ Marker for details.

I saw the finished film, so I know they shot it pretty much the way my father drew the storyboards. But my friend said Jim fought my dad on almost everything, and my friend couldn't figure out why my dad didn't just fire him. I explained that my dad and Jim went way back together, and it was Jim's equipment and crew they were using, so it wouldn't have behooved my father to fire him. My friend said a lot of valuable shooting time was wasted that way, and that it was kind of like Jim was rushing things. I know my father always spoke highly of Jim, so it came as a shock to me when I heard this. They got along well enough to finish the promo film, even edited it together. I remember when I watched it, I recognized the music -- it was the same music Jim used in *Night Fright*.

I never heard anything negative about Jim from my father. I think it was just that they were both highly creative perfectionists, who pushed each other to do their best efforts. Kind of the way John Lennon and Paul McCartney were when they were working together in The Beatles. As to whether or not they got along the same way on all their earlier collaborations, I honestly couldn't tell you. I suspect not.

I *do* know that when my father couldn't get *Demon of Devil's Lake* finished he shelved the script, and a few years later Jim came to my dad, asking if he would write a low budget horror film for him. Jim had come into some funding and was ready to direct his first feature. My dad said "yes" on one condition, that Jim let him have a part in the film. Jim agreed. So, my dad took *Demon of Devil's Lake* off the shelf, dusted it off, and basically just changed all the characters' names & retitled it, *Night Fright*, and sold it to Jim! So, when you're watching *Night Fright*, you're watching a revamped *Demon of Devil's Lake*. I'm not sure Jim was ever aware of that.

Jim Sullivan was a crew member on many of the down and dirty indie flicks that came out of Dallas in the 1960s and 1970s. He directed a forgettable TV western called *Fair Play* in Dallas in 1972. He shot *A Matter of Honor* (a *Dead Poet's Society* (1989) knock-off) also in Dallas in 1995. Jim passed away in Irving, Texas on October 13, 2004 and is fondly remembered by most who knew and worked with him.

# TOM MOORE

## MARK OF THE WITCH (1970)

The 1960s were a time of shifting moral attitudes. Witchcraft, a topic previously viewed as an archaic novelty by mainstream Christian America, came vividly to the forefront of mass-consciousness along with rock music, hippies, astrology, psychedelics and other signs of the "dawning of Aquarius." Even good, moral folk who would never dream of having a Tarot reading were curious and titillated by the subject of witchcraft. Dozens of films with plots revolving around witches were produced. Titles like *The Naked Witch* (1961), *Burn, Witch, Burn* (1962) and *Simon, King of the Witches* (1971) produced really good box office numbers. Witches were a solid bet for the low-budget producer looking to cash in on the fad. Little wonder that Tom Moore chose this sub-genre for his directorial debut.

In the opening sequence, the Witch, (portrayed with flair by Marie Santel) is led barefoot through a muddy bog to the gallows where she is to be put to death. In keeping with tradition, she pronounces a

> "While schlock guru, Larry Buchanan, was the king of Texas drive-in fare in the 1960s, the following decade saw a significant uptick in the Lone Star State's horror output, most notably with a certain chainsaw-oriented classic by Tobe Hooper. Sandwiched somewhere in between is the mostly forgotten oddity, *Mark of the Witch*, a Dallas-shot cheapie obviously inspired by *Black Sunday* and *Horror Hotel*. Right down to imitating their opening scenes with a nasty witch cursing the descendants of her persecutors."
> --*mondo-digital.com*, September 28, 2016

curse on the "good men of Lancashire," foretelling their doom and her revenge. Her curse is aimed in particular at MacIntire Stewart (Robert Elston) for the usual reason; sleeping with a witch, then ratting her out to the authorities. Two years prior, on Walpurgis night[i], Stewart had sold his soul to the devil in exchange for wealth. Talk about an expository lump! The witch lays it on thick, nearly frothing at the mouth as she carries on for a lot

---
[i] In German Folklore, Walpurgis Night occurs on April 30th and is the time when witches engage in revelry with the Devil on Brocken Mountain.

longer than most lynch mobs would've allowed.

> "In the late sixties, two Dallas women named Martha Peters and Mary Davis noticed that, although the horror genre was exploding, very few films were being made by or for women. Since both women had an academic interest in the occult, they composed a draft of *Mark of the Witch*, in which a young co-ed is possessed by the spirit of a centuries-dead witch. The film was shot with a cast and crew comprised mostly of local Texan amateurs: Peters seems to have never written anything else, while Mary Davis's sole other screenwriting credit was for 1974's *Scum of the Earth*."
>
> --swampflix.com, Mark "Boomer" Redmond, January 31, 2017

> "Made in Texas in 1969 and released in 1970, *Mark of the Witch* starts with a tightly shot (hiding budget limitations) pre-credit sequence that takes us back to a 17th Century outdoor execution. A dark-haired woman accused of witchcraft named Margery of Jourdemain (Marie Santell, who displays the expected overly-hammy antics) is hung after ranting and raving revenge in what resembles a dime-store recreation of the opening of Mario Bava's *Black Sunday*. After that, we are treated to an absurd hymn ('sung' by Trella Hart and written by the lead actress) which is performed over the opening credits."
>
> --dvddrive-in.com, George R. Reis

Finally, they spring the trapdoor on her and we find ourselves in modern-day America on what seems an awful lot like the Texas Christian University campus in Fort Worth, Texas. These opening sequences establish that the cinematography of Robert E. Bethard is a lot cleaner than the usual no-budget horror flick of the era. *Mark of the Witch* strives for the visual clarity of Roger Corman's Poe films, in spite of budgetary limitations. As the opening credits play, what the filmmakers chose to call *The Title Rune* (written by Anitra Walsh and sung by Trella Hart) is sung acapella. It's a nice touch and lends an eerie feel to what would otherwise have been mundane visuals.

There's a huge used book sale going on at the campus bookstore. We hear some stereotypical male/female banter, common to films of the late 1960s, before we're introduced to some of the characters. Alan (Darryl Wells) seems to be buying out all the titles dealing with witchcraft. When the cashier questions his choices, he explains that he's in a class studying the psychology of superstition. The professor has the students meeting once a week at his house to delve into the topic. The professor's name? Mac Stewart, as in MacIntire Stewart. I think we can see where this is going.

Cute little Jill (Anitra Walsh) is Alan's steady girl. Walsh is very much cut from the same cloth as Yvonne Craig, TV's Batgirl. They exchange more nonsensical wordplay in the back room of the bookstore, and make plans to meet at the witch discussion

Promo art for Tom Moore's 1970 horror flick **Mark of the Witch**.

group later that night. Alan departs and Jill's eye and imagination are captured by a moldy old book bound in red cloth.

At the party that night we see the eager young minds of the university engaging in dangerous things like astrology, palm-reading and Ouija boards. What are these cleancut youngsters getting themselves into?

The party is well underway when Jill shows up with her book. She insists on working a spell and Mac Stewart gives her permission. With some candles, a cup of wine and substituting powdered rosemary for a sprig, they launch into the dark arts. Professor Stewart puts his German shepherd outside. We know they are treading on thin ice when they put away all the Christian symbols of protection, because, as one students puts it, "Witches don't go for crucifixes."

Professor Stewart already knows the words to the Witch's Rune that Jill reads from the book. He silently mouths the words as she speaks them aloud. When the spell is done and the lights have been restored, no one seems to notice, but a new personality is peering out at the world through Jill's eyes. Exploring, glad to be once more in flesh, the witch occupying Jill's body wanders outside, but the professor's dog doesn't like her. Thunder and lightning play in the sky.

There is a scream, but it's just one of the partygoers who has had ice dropped down her back by an immature male student.

When Alan takes Jill home from the party, he's confused and offended by her strange behavior.

Later, Professor Stewart is cleaning up after the party and he is surprised to find Jill back at his house. She taunts him and is completely forthcoming about who she is and why she's returned. He dismisses her as drunk and playful, until she tells him his dog, Sam, is dead, "near the roses." Mac Stewart is enraged and slaps the girl, but the witch within overwhelms him with her powers of sorcery.

She outlines her history and agenda, revealing to him that they share the same mark. Each has a "birthmark" on the wrist, a mark that looks suspiciously like an "S" drawn with a sharpie marker.

As a dutiful slave, the professor teaches her about telephones and the benefits of coffee. He skips his morning class at the university and Alan comes looking for him. When Alan finds Jill at the professor's apartment, he naturally suspects the worst. Mac tries to tell him the truth, but we know how these things always work out in films like this one. To prove the whole "witch thing" is real, Jill zaps a helpless parakeet with her powers. Poor bird didn't have a chance. Don't worry, no parakeets (or dogs) were harmed in the production of this film.

Alan and Professor Stewart provide Jill with all the info she needs to continue her charade as a student. When she leaves to explore her new turf, the professor explains to Alan that he deliberately placed the spell book where he knew Jill would find it. It was a psychological experiment that backfired. The book, we learn, has been in Stewart's family for generations. Mac tells Alan about the matching birthmarks.

Jill makes herself at home in a place the locals call "the Grove," builds a fire and starts on her witchly agenda. Summoning demons from another realm, she bares her breasts and rolls in the leaves.

Later, Alan and Professor Mac Stewart hold a pow-wow in a cocktail lounge. They reason that the only way to fight a witch is with witchcraft. Mac gets an idea and slips off to Jill's apartment. There he finds black candles burning and a seductive Jill expecting him. He seems to fall for her ploy, but then pushes her away, begging her to finish her plan, whatever that may be, and release him.

At the on-going book sale at the university, Jill recognizes the buffoon who puts ice down girls' dresses as one of the souls she's come back to capture. She makes an advance and he takes the bait. Her intended prey, Harry (Jack Gardner), has a groovy convertible and they make plans to meet at the Grove.

Their breath is frosty and fog swirls in the air at their rendezvous. Harry has brought a blanket. Jill offers him a small flask. Evidently, the contents of the flask have an off-putting flavor, but Harry doesn't have much time to consider this as he quickly falls into an altered state of consciousness.

Jill forces Harry to make an oath to the Dark One, then brands him with a dagger handle she's heated in a fire she conjured into existence.

Alan and Professor Stewart figure out the missing pair may have gone to the Grove and set out to intervene.

Meanwhile, Jill is drawing some of Harry's blood with the dagger to complete the ritual. As the scene proceeds, the film makers employ a simple, but effective technique of superimposing the Witch's features over Jill's. It's surprisingly eerie. Harry screams as his soul is carried away by unseen forces.

At the Grove, the professor and Alan find Harry's blood-drenched corpse. Stewart notices the burn mark on Harry's wrist. It resembles his own serpentine birthmark.

Over coffee the next morning, Jill, Mac and Alan have a surprisingly civil discussion about the whole affair. After all, that's what grown-ups do.

In the next scene, Sharon, Harry's erstwhile girlfriend shows up at Jill's apartment and accuses Jill of killing Harry. The gullible Sharon is taken in by Jill's lies and soon the hapless girl imbibes the same potion that placed Harry in a trance.

The professor and Alan have another conference, trying to gain the knowledge they need to expel the witch from Jill's body. Stewart reads an ancient potion recipe and comments that someone transcribed it wrong. His past life memories are coming forward.

Jill is up to her old tricks. In the Grove, she goes through the same ritual she used on Harry, except this time her victim is Sharon.

While poring over old books on magic, Professor Stewart falls asleep. Alan finds something promising. He sees that his teacher is snoozing, but is shocked when the unconscious professor begins to scribble out a message.

Quite a crowd has gathered at the crime scene after a second body is found at the Grove. A local journalist phones in a report to be recorded for broadcast.

The following morning the groggy student and professor are trying to anticipate the witch's next move when they receive a phone call informing them of Sharon's death. The men tell the witch the jig is up and they're calling the cops regardless of the consequences. She tells them in order to get Jill back they'll have to reverse the spell. The men follow her instructions, using tokens to represent all the members of the circle who were present when the spell was cast. But, they've got a little surprise in store for her.

Jill gives the men the potion and invokes

the spirits, dripping her own blood on the table and in the candle flame. She seems about to plunge the dagger into Professor Stewart when the timer the men have set kicks in, projecting a cross of white light on the witch. She is trapped. Jill falls to the floor, but the image of the witch remains there, a separate fleshly form. The professor presses a crucifix against her breast causing her to hemorrhage from mouth and eyes. She kisses Stewart and draws him into the darkness along with her. Professor MacIntire Stewart finds himself standing on the gallows in an ancient land. There is a rope around his neck and next to him hangs the lifeless corpse of the witch. The trapdoor opens and he is executed.

In the late 1980s and into the early 1990s, I was a scheduler in the Post Production department at Allied + WBS in Las Colinas. It was there that I first met Tom Moore. We spoke in passing, but it wasn't until I interviewed him for *Guerilla Cinema*[ii] that I really got to know him.

Sometime in 1991 I was approached by a company whose business it was to promote the artist Thomas Kinkade. They wanted me to produce a marketing program to entice art buyers. I asked Tom Moore to come on-board as director and we made a pretty good pitch to the company's media department. I was really looking forward to

[ii] *Guerilla Cinema* was a no-budget video program produced with minimal funding for the Irving Community Television Network in 1991. It was my attempt to preserve a bit of Dallas filmmaking history.

Jill tries to convince Sharon she meant no harm by killing Harry in **Mark of the Witch**.

working with the man. Of the Dallas-based directors I knew personally, he was by far the slickest. There was a bit of in-house political intrigue at the Kinkade company and our project fell through. Such is the life of the indie producer.

Chris Jenkins, the man I shared the scheduling office with at Allied, was a huge fan of Linda Blair. When we heard that she was going to be a guest on the *Joe Bob Briggs Drive-In Theater*, he begged me to get us in to see her. Tom Moore was directing the show for The Movie Channel on a soundstage at Dallas-based Channel 33, so I called him up and put in the request. "No problem," he said. "Come on over."

We slipped away from work that afternoon and had a great time watching Joe Bob interview Linda on the lawn chairs outside his mobile home set. Chris got to shake hands with Linda and I got to watch Tom Moore and Joe Bob Briggs (John Bloom) two of my favorite media personalities work together.

The following is a transcription of an interview with Tom Moore I conducted in 1991 for the Irving Community Television Network documentary program, *Guerilla Cinema*.

TM: I directed *Mark of the Witch* (1970). I produced *Horror High* (1973). I produced *The Town that Dreaded Sundown* (1976), but that's not really a Dallas film, is it? It's an American International, Hollywood, stroke, slash Texarkana picture, I suppose, with a lot of Dallas people involved.

I didn't want to waste time going to school. It was silly to go to school, I barely finished high school. I didn't go to college. I already had a job. But, I was from the south and one doesn't just automatically go to the motion picture business if you're from the deep south. There were no channels at that time in the early fifties.

I think it's important for a director's first picture to be a horror picture. I think you learn a lot from them, you get a lot from them and you have a lot of license. You can do a lot of different things and still stay within the format. It would be nice to make *Batman* as your first picture, but you can't really do that, can you? I mean, you've only got one of those and lots of horror pictures! So, you get your turn more quickly.

TS: Do you enjoy horror films?

TM: I enjoy the work. I know what's going to happen. I don't get scared. I'm not sure horror pictures are supposed to scare you. Hmm, I'm not sure. Suspense pictures I love. Hitchcock. Horror pictures I enjoy. Yeah, I guess I do enjoy seeing them. I don't wallow in them. Not quite like Joe Bob Briggs might. I know what's going to happen. Now, if someone shows me something new, that's kind of interesting.

I'm not sure I like terror films very much. Terror films do scare me. I don't like violence very much. "Toon violence" is fine. In horror pictures, the sort of things we did, it was toon violence. You know, everybody got up. (laughs) I know Brownie Brownrigg made some pictures here and you're going to be talking with him. I know in his pictures people didn't get up necessarily.

Well, we killed some people in *Horror High* (1973). Oh, we really did kill some people, didn't we? We cut off a teacher's head with a paper cutter. That was fun. We stomped the track coach to death with track shoes. That's violent, isn't it?

Gee, I guess when I think of violence, I think of it as being real. When someone gets hurt. If someone gets their head cut off they're not really hurt, are they? It's kind of toon violence. I don't know, so, I accept that. I find a rape scene in a film very difficult to watch. I don't want to watch it. I *won't* watch it! I don't want to see someone cut up with a razor blade by a sneaky person in an elevator. I don't want to see that. That does not entertain me. But, sneaking around a dark corner where a paper cutter might be and the music's going *Dah duh dyah dun dun dun!* I like that. Yeah! That's fun. That's *toon violence*, if there is such a thing. We can coin that phrase, can't we? *Toon violence*. They get up! And they do it again. If a refrigerator falls on them, it's okay. Just kind of makes them flat a little bit. Then, they get up and 'Take two!' (laughs)

But, yeah, I can watch horror pictures. I like them.

I think probably the finest American film, thank goodness for the rental places now where we can go and see these wonderful films we couldn't get our hands on before. And the foreign pictures. Which I do wallow in! I watch four or five a weekend sometimes. I've seen every foreign picture Blockbuster offers. I'm starting on other rental stores in the hopes they have something new and different. I watch them by countries. I'll have a Japanese month. Well, a Japanese week. It doesn't take a month to see all the Japanese pictures. An Israeli weekend. A French month. An Italian year! I love French pictures and I love Italian pictures. I like American pictures, but we haven't made the kind I really like until just recently.

I think the finest American film is *The Godfather* (1972). Both films together, the work, *Godfather*. So, Francis Ford Coppola, I believe, is probably one of our finest. I enjoy the comic book films very much. Steven Spielberg's things that he's done. And George Lucas and the wonderful things they're doing. The revitalization into American film, of course is storybook now. It's so important.

But, my favorite filmmakers, I like very complicated love stories. So, I like Claude Lelouch very much. I love the way he can intertwine stories and weave them around to where you're not sure who's who and what's going to happen next. French films.

*Jean de Florette* (1986) and *Manon of the Spring* (1986) (both directed by Claude Berri). These are wonderful pictures.

The titular witch gets trapped and sent back to the gallows.

The Italians, I still love Frederico Fellini, of course, the wonderful, surreal things that he did with film. My film likes are very eclectic.

**TS**: What's the biggest drawback to working with a small budget?

**TM**: The compromise. Time vis a vis money. You don't have time for the close ups. And if you really are a director and you really do care about the story. Well, I used to do an interesting thing when I'd go on location. When I would check into the motel or hotel, wherever we were going to be staying for a picture. If I were the producer I'd call the maid for my floor and tell her not to erase what I had written on the mirror. Sometimes we'd be there for months. I made a picture, *The Norseman* (1978), in Florida for five months. I write on my mirror in the bathroom at the hotel, this message to myself, so I see it first thing every morning. If I am the producer, I take this pentel or marks-a-lot and write on there, "You are the producer. Make it possible for the director to tell the story." And I see that first thing every morning. On pictures that I directed, I would write on my bathroom mirror, "You are the director. Tell the story." Exclamation point!

If you want to tell the story, if you feel you understand the characters and if there is indeed a story to tell, even if it's a silly story, like a bunch of kids getting together at a professor's house to call back a witch, still, it's a film! You have a responsibility to the film! As a filmmaker, you have a responsibility to use the tools of the trade to tell that story. That is, you introduce the situation and you show close ups. That's what you miss in the low-budget film. The close-ups. There's no time. There's no time to get that other little shot you improvised while you were making the master shot. You say, ah, golly, wouldn't it be great if we could just take the camera, put it up here and have it move around here and come back in, because that business you just did was wonderful. That was great. You did that really well. Then someone says, 'But we don't have time for that. I'll have to get the dolly track from there, I'll have to relight this, we'll have to change the key to over here, we'll have to gel those windows' because we're always filming on location. It's cheaper. We use real places. Then, all of a sudden, the sadness comes over you and you say to yourself, 'Okay,

I'll remember I wanted to do that shot.' So, you sit and you watch these pictures and you say, 'There's where I wanted to do the shot with the staircase. There's where we wanted to do the unmanned cameras for the car chase to run over it. There's where we wanted to do this.'

You were asking me earlier; do I enjoy watching horror pictures? Usually, that is to say, do I enjoy seeing low-budget pictures? I think one of the reasons I do not enjoy them as much as other people, is that I feel for the director and for the filmmakers there. I know they didn't want that reflector to move from the wind in that shot, but they couldn't do another shot.

I'm told people like Spielberg storyboard every little thing, down to the two ants on the tree branch. Wonderful. It'd be nice to have forty million dollars, then you could think about your two ants on your limb up front. You wouldn't have to worry about improvising with a second unit probably.

All of that's out the window when you're making your first picture. You don't know about the pad. You don't know about the dialog with the editor. You don't know anything. You don't know what you're doing. You're making a movie! (laughs) 'We're making a movie!' That's the reward in itself. You're making your movie! It's what you've always wanted to do. Doesn't mean you know how to do it. So, you do the best you can.

Now, that's an ingredient you're seeing when you watch horror pictures. And first time horror pictures. Not like after a guy like Roger Corman has decided to do that, who makes a living doing it. There's nothing fresh there. His every action's deliberate (slams hand into his palm) Boom, boom, kill that one, (laughs) blow up that outfit! (laughs) You know, we're going around saying, 'Whose fingers can we cut off next?' Because it was fun! If we found a prop that worked, we had to use it twice, three times! 'The finger scene! It worked! We cut off her fingers! What do we do now? Let's cut her head off! Oh, okay!'

See, when you make your first picture, your slip is showing. Whether you want it to, or not. Whether you know it is, or not. It is. And there are flaws. The flaws are always in tying the story together and keeping the pace of the thing going.

**TS**: How might your career have been different if your first horror film had been a big success?

**TM**: I don't know how it would've been different. I suppose you might be stuck with that. If your first picture was a horror picture and you made it for American International. Or you made it for whomever, and it went to Sam Arkoff to be released and it was a success, they'd make you an offer you couldn't refuse, to make another. And another. And another. And another. And you would never make your love story. Of course, I haven't made mine, either, have I?

I did recently rent and watch *The Town that Dreaded Sundown*, which was based on a true story. I produced that picture. It was a Charles Pierce production and Charlie directed it. I was just Associate Producer.[iii] Charles produces, writes, directs and stars in everything he does. But, he has people around him, who have lesser titles, who do all the work. Not true. He's a hard-working filmmaker!

Anyway, that picture, is fun to watch. It holds up well. It's based on a true story about a phantom killer in Texarkana. It involved 'Lone Wolf' Gonzaullus, a Texas Ranger, who lived in Dallas and, I think, just passed away a few years ago. He retired here and was an old man when Charlie spoke with him before we made the picture. His part was played by Ben Johnson in the film.

That picture has some silly parts in it, that Charlie wanted to do for comic relief. That was part of what one did in drive-in pictures of that time. So, it was very *apropos* and it was fun. Now, it's a little bit silly. You have a sort of a Barney Fife character; which Charlie does play himself. But, it's good for comic relief, because the murders were dreadful things. We played it as a sort of camp old thing.

We spent a lot of time getting the proper cars for the era. We were very meticulous in the costumes, the wardrobing. We took the old train station in downtown Texarkana and completely renovated it. We put it back to how it was in 1947, with the little vending kiosks and things like that, that were a part of that period of time. So, the picture's very watchable. I enjoyed it. Dawn Wells is in it. I made four pictures with Dawn. She's one of my favorite people. She was Mary Ann on *Gilligan's Island* (TV series 1964-1967). She does a very heavy-duty dramatic role and she was quite good. But it holds up.

I think *Mark of the Witch* would hold up. If it…I don't know why it's not in distribution, come to think of it. It's better than a lot of things that I've seen. There are one or two other pictures I made that probably shouldn't be in distribution. (laughs) But, *Mark of the Witch* could be.[iv]

The last picture that I made was *The Norseman*, with Lee Majors and Cornel Wilde, Chris Connelly. Lots of people. That was 1978. In 1979, I was one of three people who started Spindletop Productions. Spindletop manufactured television commercials. We never made any pictures, so for a full decade, I've been out of any contact with making features.

Now, I'm no longer connected with Spindletop, as a matter of fact, I've been

---

[iii] Tom Moore had a bit part in *The Town that Dreaded Sundown*, playing a law officer. I recall (as a teen) watching the film in a theater and noticing that bit player had a presence. I remember thinking he was too good for the part, probably too good for the movie.

[iv] *Mark of the Witch* does indeed hold up well. Compared to horror films with similar budgets from the same era, it holds up surprisingly well. Despite the sometimes-corny dialog (which was a staple of such films then) the story is above average, the performances competent and execution professional.

doing some writing. I have a script that I've written, based on a series of short stories I've been working on. It's being looked at by Ron Howard Productions. Something else is being looked at by Ted Turner, the Family Channel Network. I am directing the *Joe Bob Briggs' Drive-In Theater* for the Movie Channel now. Which keeps me in contact with drive-in movies vicariously through Joe Bob. It's a lot of fun to reminisce about some of the pictures I've seen. He certainly has seen a lot more of those pictures than I have. He's seen them all. Every last one ever made. He really has.

I do that. I make TV commercials. I'm a fan and I still need to make my love story.

I've never been able to figure the trends in filmmaking. Therein lies the secret to one's success. All films are good. All films have some redeeming value. The success or failure of that film, is fate. It's the luck of the draw. It's when it was put out.

There was one year when there were no G-rated pictures. And I decided, 'I'm going to make one.' Purely as a commercial venture. We made *Return to Boggy Creek* (1977). And it was good. It's a good little kid's picture. I made it for five-year-olds. I was stupid! Five-year-olds can't go to the movies. Their mommies have to take them. You've got to make something that will hit a time when adults will have some interest in it. You can't make a movie for five-year-old kids, because they don't have any money, they haven't got a car and their mommies won't let them cross the street. They can't go to the movies! So, if you're going to make those kinds of pictures, you have to make them for television. That's where the five-year-old can turn on and watch.

Marie Santel prepares to be hanged in ***Mark of the Witch***.

The year that I made that picture, we thought, 'This'll work!' We bought a hundred release prints. That's a lot for a low-budget picture. And there were nine G-rated pictures that came out that year. The big opening date then was June 2nd. That's the weekend after school's out. Kids have nothing to do. That's the big hit for all the G-rated pictures and all the PGs. I'm not sure what the release dates are now, that was a decade ago. We decided to get the jump a week. So, we went back into May and we opened. We did good business! We opened 80 theaters in the Houston umbrella. We opened 54 theaters in the Dallas umbrella, the following weekend. Did good business in both towns. Then, motion picture history was made.

On June 2nd, a picture called *Star Wars* (1977) came out. And all other pictures died. There was our picture that was doing well in our own little territory and we were ready to branch out. We had lots of bookings all over the country. Joe Camp released *For the Love of Benji* (1977), which is the one he made in Greece I believe. John Wayne's son, Patrick Wayne, made *Eye of the Tiger* (1977). Walt Disney had some kind of a giant fluffy dog picture. I don't recall all the others, but there were nine G-rated pictures that came out that year, because everyone had seen that gap. All the distributors had said, 'Give us G-rated product.' We all went out and made these things. Nobody told us about this guy named Lucas.

Then, *Star Wars* hit. *Stars Wars* was a motion picture experience! Not only was the picture superb, our pictures were nothing in comparison with that film, but it was an experience! If you recall, the theaters were open 24 hours a day to take care of the crowd. You had to stand in line one day for the ticket and go see the picture at 2 o'clock in the morning the next day. That's a motion picture experience. You're through with movies for two or three weeks after that. It's like if you went to Woodstock. You're not going to take off the next weekend and go to another rock and roll concert in a field somewhere. You are through with movies for a week. That was your movie going experience. And you experienced it. It's over. Little pictures like we made, die on the vine in one week. If you're not held over on Tuesday, it's over. And if it's over, then all those other bookings that you had were just pencil on a piece of paper and they're cancelled.

So, this happened to every one of those pictures. I later met Patrick Wayne and talked to him about it. We were comparing notes about this. Joe Camp and I talked about it, too. It absolutely killed them all.

Now, will there ever be a market for little pictures again? I bet there will be. I'll bet there will even be a four-wall market again.[v] Where a film maker will make a modest little film, with a lot of love and a lot of care and a lot of fun. It'll play somewhere. And he'll say, 'That was my picture.' He will have had his dream come true. And that's really what it's all about. Yeah, as Joe Bob would say, 'The drive-in will never die.' It probably won't.

[v] 'Four-walling' was a practice used by indie filmmakers from the early days of Hollywood into the 1970s. An indie producer would rent a theater for given dates, paying the theater a flat rate and pocketing anything ticket sales earned over and above the rental fee. Many very modest films earned big box office by utilizing this strategy, especially with small town theaters and drive-ins. Often the producer/promoter would saturate the local media with lurid radio and TV ads the week preceding a play date.

# S.F. BROWNRIGG

## DON'T LOOK IN THE BASEMENT (AKA THE FORGOTTEN, BEYOND HELP AND DEATH WARD 13) (1973)

Drive-in horror flicks were, for me, an entirely separate genre from the films that played in the classy theaters of downtown Fort Worth; venues like the Seventh Street, the Palace and the Worth. Roger Corman's slick, low-budget Poe movies and the Victorian horrors from Hammer Productions in the UK might make it to those screens, but Crown International pictures and the odd indies that wound up in the hands of Sam Arkoff over at American International Pictures couldn't hope for such lofty aspirations. If you wanted to see a film like *Don't Look in the Basement*, you went to the Fort Worth Twin, the Southside Twin, the Meadowbrook Drive-In or one of the other nine drive-in theaters that encircled the city during the heyday of exploitation cinema.

The films were grainy, their colors either pale or over-saturated. The prints were speckled with dirt and scratches and there was a steady crackle of noise interwoven with the soundtrack. To the young, undiscriminating mind, these seemed like stylistic decisions consciously made by the film makers. The grit, glare and noise

> "When it comes to unorthodox pictures, *Don't Look in the Basement* ranks quite high on the list. However, for fans of outlandish vintage fare, it's a film that should win masses over. There isn't much of an actual story to absorb, but there's a charm here that works well. If it were still 1973, I'd have no qualms with hitting a drive-in to check this quirky little film out."
> --*horrorfreaknews.com*, Matt Molgaard, June 6, 2016

> "For the time period the film was made, which was 1973, the characters are pretty colorful and if for no other reason, make it worth watching. The crazed Vietnam veteran, the big galoot, the sex addict, the screeching madman, prophetic old lady, and the list goes on. Each have their moment to torment poor Nurse Beale."
> --*horrornews.net,* Corey Danna, November 22, 2010

made these films more frightening. The visual quality of these bottom-of-the-barrel feature films seemed painted from the same palette as the savage 16mm news footage depicting the horrors of the Vietnam War, which continued to claim lives daily.

In 1972, S.F. Brownrigg, who'd worked in many capacities on films at Jamieson Film Company[i] and on the indie features of mavericks like Larry Buchanan, with the help of financing from an "insurance man" named Walter Krusz, finally helmed his own exploitation opus. The film, written by Tim Pope[ii], was produced under the title, *The Forgotten*.[iii]

A regional chain of roughly one hundred theaters, headquartered in Boston, known as Esquire Theaters, wielded some heavy box office clout when it came to envelope-pushing violence in cinema. The company was owned by Steve Minasian, Phil Scuderi and Robert Barsamain. The trio had an enormous success with the release of *Mark of the Devil* (1970), a German import which was so gory, it was claimed to necessitate the distribution of barf bags to theater patrons. It was not a subtle promotional campaign, but one that worked on thousands of morbid movie-goers. The name chosen for the regional distribution arm of Esquire Theaters was Hallmark Releasing. These were the first guys to get their hands on Wes Craven's *Last House on the Left* (1972) and a little picture from Texas that eventually came to be known as *Don't Look in the Basement*.

> "Consider the curious case of S.F. Brownrigg, a resourceful independent filmmaker who's become something of an enigmatic auteur of this era, having cut an odd little trail during a three-year span that saw him release a handful of horror oddities before retreating to further obscurity. Each of these films is a singularly strange and idiosyncratic experience teeming with grime, oddballs, and outlandish plots delivered with a hint of Texas twang. However, one truly rises above the gore-soaked din as his definitive dispatch: *Don't Look in the Basement* (aka *The Forgotten*), a delirious 1973 treasure trove that introduced audiences to Brownrigg's signature blend of slack-jawed dopiness and frenetic insanity."
> --*oh-the-horror.com*, Brett Gallman, December 31, 2014

In the early days of its release, the movie was also seen under the title *Death Ward 13* and *Beyond Help*. Three titles for one movie? This sounds a little crazy. Actually, the practice was common in the days of the drive-in theater. Indy filmmakers often would work their way across the

---

[i] Founded by Hugh Jamieson in 1916, Jamieson Film Company became known for innovation and was largely responsible for Dallas becoming a major hub of commercial film production.

[ii] Later, Tim Pope would become well-known as a producer/director of music-related shorts and MTV videos, for bands like Ministry and The Cure.

[iii] The premise of the film, like others before and after, borrows from Poe's short story, *The System of Dr. Tarr and Professor Fether*.

country with their low-budget product, playing theaters in first one region, then another. If their film was getting poor reviews, they'd just change the title in the next town. If they knew the picture was a stinker from the get-go, they would sometimes make up three different titles with complete ad campaigns for each and play them one by one in rotation as they shuttled their prints slowly across the country.

The guys at Hallmark were doing good business in their limited region and when they wanted to expand their reach to the entire United States, they relied on the resources of American International Pictures. Sam Arkoff and Jim Nicholson were widely recognized as B-movie gurus. They had been the purveyors of over-the-top exploitation flicks since the early 1950s. These guys had written the book on getting the public to buy tickets for garish, inferior productions. If anyone knew how to spin straw into gold, it was AIP's dynamic duo. They were the ones who came up with the infinitely more attention-grabbing title, *Don't Look in the Basement*.[iv]

From the opening shot of leaves dancing in the hot Texas sunlight to the final scene of Sam comforting himself with a grape popsicle, the movie screams drive-in classic. So, what if the plot was episodic and not particularly logical? So, what if the dialog was inane? These shortcomings were part and parcel of the drive-in horror movie experience. The movie delivered where it counted; bright red scenes of visceral violence. Perhaps the film's unintended gaffes even softened the psychological blow of the gore.

Brownrigg's first and best known film, *Don't Look in the Basement*.

Walter Krusz put up the money for Brownie's maiden voyage as a horror film director and naturally he wanted the quickest return on his money that he could get. When AIP realized the picture could gain some serious drive-in theater traction, they made Krusz an offer for a buyout of all rights. To the insurance man who liked to dabble in film production, the deal made perfect sense.

During the years I was a friend and business associate of S.F. 'Brownie' Brownrigg, he only swore me to secrecy on two matters of confidence. The first was the truth of what his initials 'S.F.' stood for. I've never violated that promise, though I think his first and middle

---

[iv] Arkoff and Nicholson were geniuses at hitting the nerve at the center of audience motivations. This title was particularly appropriate because it evoked Freudian associations with repression and the unconscious and the story revolved around mental illness.

name have been reported elsewhere. The second was the actual budget of *The Forgotten*. I kept that quiet for a long time, but these many years after his death, I see no harm in revealing the secret. Brownie told me they shot the picture in 1972 for $25,000. When Arkoff offered them a buyout for $50,000, Krusz jumped on it. Sure, it had been a lot of work and no one was getting rich off such a deal, but they were enthusiastic and thought they could just keep shooting little pictures. If they doubled their money on every film they made, then surely, they were ahead of the game.

Once Arkoff owned *Basement* outright it became a drive-in box office legend. I don't know how well it did in other parts of the country, but in Fort Worth, Texas it played several times a year for over a decade, sometimes on a double-bill with *Last House on the Left*, sometimes paired with whatever new indie horror flick AIP was promoting. Attendance held up for *Basement*, perhaps better than any ultra-cheapie horror film ever.

This led to a touch of bitterness on Brownie's part. What if they'd held out for a "piece of the pie" as he liked to put it? Collecting royalties from an outfit like AIP was a whole 'nother can of worms. My thought is that Krusz made the right decision in taking the upfront money. Successful distribution companies have always had a slew of methods for holding onto the receipts generated by films. I'm of the opinion that the exposure AIP gave the movie created a strong platform from which Brownie could have established himself as an exploitation auteur to be reckoned with.

The first face in *Basement* that really grabbed my attention was that of Camilla Carr. She had the 'look' of a horror film diva, she had a cool name and her performance was head-and-shoulders above most of the others in the film. Her portrayal of Harriet, the schizophrenic who will defend her baby doll at all costs is one of the highlights of this terrorfest. In my opinion, Carr rivals Ingrid Pitt and Barbara Steele for having unforgettable facial features and delivering a compelling performance despite budgetary limitations. Camilla became one of the mainstays of Brownie's repertory company.

The second stand-out is Gene Ross, another perennial Brownrigg performer, who plays the axe-wielding Judge in the film's initial burst of gore. Michael Harvey, as Dr. Stephens, exercises questionable judgment in placing an axe in the hands of the demented judge and encouraging him to chop away his frustrations on a convenient log. 'Axe therapy' has since been discredited and is no longer used in legitimate mental institutions. Little wonder the Judge turns on his doctor and opens him up like a can of tomato soup.

Bill McGhee as Sam in *Don't Look in the Basement*.

A regular in Larry Buchanan's movies, Annabelle Weenick (as Annabelle MacAdams) puts in a notable performance playing Dr. Geraldine Masters. Weenick's aunt, Rhea MacAdams as Mrs. Callingham provides a creepy cameo as the verse-quoting whacko with a "fear of little men." Brownie credited Weenick with direction of the actors' performances. He was the technical guy and she was the acting expert. When he and I were making plans to do a sequel (in 1992), he told me with great excitement that Weenick had agreed to return to Texas from California and coach the actors for our proposed sequel. By all accounts, Weenick was a sharp business woman with a keen instinct for survival. Rumors abounded that she was the brains behind a few porno productions funded by Walter Krusz. I couldn't help but think of Annabelle and Rhea as the tough sort of women who might have operated a brothel in the old west. Brownie clearly enjoyed the fun, the fame and the prestige, though he wanted to make a buck. I had the distinct impression that money was Annabelle Weenick's only motivator. She was in this game to make it pay.

A little over nine minutes into *Don't Look in the Basement*, the second murder occurs. This time Harriet does the killing because she thinks a poor nurse who just wants to get the hell away from this loony bin has stolen her baby. Janie, the nurse is innocent, but that doesn't stop Harriet from smashing her head with the suitcase she was in the process of packing.

Then another surprise follows – the opening credits. Credits? WTF? Didn't that happen two murders ago? I guess not. While curiously inappropriate canned music plays, like something from an educational film you'd watch in school, we are treated to the pretty features of former Playboy model, Rosie Holotik, in a montage depicting her arrival at the sanitarium amid a rain shower.

Holotik, as Charlotte Beale, receives a cool reception from Dr. Masters who was unaware that she had been hired. Realizing there are no locks on any of the doors, she settles nervously into her quarters. After a shower, she's surprised on the stairway by Rhea MacAdams in one of my favorite scenes of the film. MacAdams is a patient, obviously suffering from dementia, named Mrs. Callingham. In an extreme close-up, sans teeth, she slyly declares, "Up the airy mountain, down the rushing glen, we can never go a-hunting, for fear of little men."[v] This is not exactly the sort of greeting Charlotte Beale had expected, but she does her best to take it in stride.

As Dr. Masters explains the background of a patient called Allison to Beale, we are treated to a tense encounter between the Judge and the young woman. Heavily made up, Allison comes to the Judge's room. She wants desperately to be loved, by anyone, everyone. Her perfume smells of strawberries. Judge Cameron notes that ripe strawberries are the color of blood. When Allison flaunts herself, the he throws her onto he bed, admonishing her carnal ways. She tears her blouse open, giving the male members of the audience a nice view of her breasts and begs the Judge to love her.

All is not well in the Stephens Sanitarium. An unseen culprit snips the telephone wires, eliminating contact with the outside world. Beale reports the phone service disruption to Masters. After which the demented Mrs. Callingham warns Beale to get out and never return. The next morning, someone has cut out poor Mrs. Callingham's tongue! Dr. Masters tries to convince Miss Beale that Mrs. Callingham did this to herself. Beale doesn't seem to buy this explanation and the audience certainly doesn't.

When a phone repair guy shows up, he has a tense encounter with the Judge and the tongue-less Mrs. Callingham, who seems very spry for someone who just had her tongue cut out. Dr. Masters is angered to discover his presence in the building, but grudgingly directs him to the closet where the phone connections are. While he's poking around in the closet Allison shows up, eager for love.

Memorable ad for **Don't Look in the Basement** that ran for years in newspapers across the country.

Charlotte Beale irons her uniform and when she tries to hang it in her closet, out springs a previously unresponsive patient named Jennifer, wielding a large knife. The two fall onto the bed in a struggle. Dr. Masters arrives and slaps the attacker into submission.

A patient known as the sergeant, who suffers from PTSD stays up past his bed-

---

[v] This eerie proclamation is lifted from a 19th century poem, *The Fairies*, by William Allingham.

time and Dr. Masters doesn't like it. The first real evidence we have that Masters might be the malignant source of violence in the sanitarium is when she forces the sergeant to hold a burning piece of paper in the palm of his hand.

Charlotte's routine inventory of the medicine cabinet reveals missing drugs. In an angry search of Jennifer's room, Dr. Masters finds the vials of drugs and a syringe. Jennifer discovers her room in disarray and rushes to the cabinet to try to steal more drugs. In this day of computers and electronic files, many viewers may not be aware of paper spikes. Something like an ice pick with a base, so it would stand upright on a desk top, the paper spike was used to prevent receipts and other paper items from fluttering off one's desk. There is a paper spike on the desk near the medicine cabinet and from the ominous light falling on it in the darkened room, we instantly know some bad shit's about to go down. Jennifer reaches for the vials of drugs that Masters took from her room. The hand of an unseen assailant, shoves her head downward and the spike pierces Jennifer's eye, penetrating her brain. Gross!

After sweeping up the kitchen, the big, childlike Sam grabs himself a popsicle, then opens a door and is disturbed by what he sees. He manages to get Allison to take a look. She screams when it's revealed the phone repair guy has had his throat cut. Upset that the only man who really loved her is dead, Allison spills the beans to Charlotte that Dr. Masters is no doctor at all, but a schizophrenic patient who cannot control her emotions.

Charlotte freaks and tries to escape, but evidently the windows are barred and the doors locked. She rushes from one loony tune scenario to another. The lunatics are riled and the judge tells Masters she's been found guilty and must be punished.

Sam delivers a note to Charlotte from Dr. Stephens who is supposed to be dead. She goes into the dark basement and after everything she's been through, completely snaps when someone grabs her ankle. Using Sam's heavy model boat, she beats the unseen assailant. Unfortunately, it was Dr. Stephens and now he's dead for real.

Masters and Sam enter the basement. Sam is instructed to carry the kicking and screaming Charlotte upstairs for treatment. Sam views Masters as a mother figure and follows her every command until she explains she's going to lobotomize Charlotte and make her childlike again, "like you, Sam." The infantile man flashes back to his own lobotomy and rebels. He carries Charlotte to an escape route through the basement that only he knows about.

The patients have had enough. They converge on Masters. The judge gets in the first blow with his axe, then it's a frenzied free-for-all as they tear the woman apart.

Once Charlotte is safely out of the building, Sam returns and is infuriated to see what the others have done to his mommy. Seizing the axe, he lays waste to the entire army of maniacs.

The hysterical Charlotte wanders off in a rain storm while Sam comforts himself with another grape popsicle from the sanitarium's antiquated fridge.

## POOR WHITE TRASH PART 2 (AKA SCUM OF THE EARTH AND DEATH IS A FAMILY AFFAIR) (1974)

As noted elsewhere in this book, it was fairly common for low-budget indie films to be released under more than one title, often for a variety of reasons. A producer/director named M.A. Ripps, who had some exploitation clout in the southern states, produced a lackluster movie called *Bayou* for United Artists in 1957. The film starred Peter Graves and infamous movie bad guy, Timothy Carey. Box office for *Bayou* was less than impressive.

Sometime around 1960, Ripps bought the film back from UA, shot a couple of exploitation scenes, including female nudity and retitled the project *Poor White Trash*. The lurid title and the addition of breasts, turned the film into a drive-in hit. For years, the movie played throughout the south on double bills with movies like, *I Hate Your Guts* (1962) and other Hixploitation fare.

About the time the original *Poor White Trash* had run out of steam, Brownrigg and Krusz had finished their second psycho cinema feature under the title *Scum of the Earth*[vi]. Trailers and promo art for *Scum* made it clear the film makers were

> "Alternately billed as *Poor White Trash Part II* for reasons that seem iffy at best — the original *Poor White Trash* having come out all the way back in 1957 and being much more widely known (to the extent that it was even known at all) by its "proper" title of *Bayou* — Brownrigg's complete lack of taste or subtlety oozes through every celluloid pore of this astonishingly over the top take on life, as its poster says, "below Tobacco Road," and the end result is enough to make even the proudest resident of Dixie either blush, howl with anger, or who knows — maybe both."
> --*trashfilmguru.wordpress.com*, February 12, 2014

"The first time I had moonshine, I was 10 years old. I hated it. It burned my throat and made my eyes water. As an adult, I've learned to appreciate things that are homemade and get you fucked up. This same learning curve applies to redneck exploitation movies. The performances and the genre blending in this one push it into the upper echelon of the subgenre."
--*letterboxd.com*, laird

---

[vi] Playing off of, or even duplicating, titles with proven exploitation clout was quite common. In the case of *Scum of the Earth*, Brownrigg and Krusz were "borrowing" from another well-known schlockmeister, H.G. Lewis who had released a film with that title in 1963.

not just selling horror, but a sleazy sexual component as well. This was right up the alley of impresario M.A. Ripps. He took the film on a regional basis and retitled it to cash in on the success of the previous movie.

> "Seemingly encouraged by the unexpected grassroots success of *Don't Look in the Basement*, Brownrigg promptly delivered more eclectic low budget backwoods horror featuring much of the same cast, starting with *Scum of the Earth* – a grim story of marauding psychopaths, women in peril and incestuous familial insanity in the sweltering darkness of the Louisiana bayou. Regrettably *Scum of the Earth* would not repeat the success of *Don't Look in the Basement* and perhaps even more unfortunately Brownrigg's distinctive brand of exploitatively driven "southern gothic" would only be seen in two more seventies horror efforts, those being the somewhat less memorable *Don't Open the Door!* (1975) and the offbeat yet engrossing southern fried psychodrama *Keep My Grave Open* (1976)."
> --*cultmovieforums.com*, jacksmith1983, February 25, 2009

All of this may seem absurd in the day of the internet when information travels with near lightspeed all over the world. In the early seventies, there were a lot of very backward communities lingering in rural Dixie. People still did their laundry on the front porch in old machines with ringers. Things moved slow for these folks and they certainly remembered old Mike Ripps' *Poor White Trash* movie! It was a humdinger!

Though *Scum of the Earth* was certainly a more lurid title, the renaming proved to be a wise move. *Poor White Trash Part 2* struck pay-dirt at the drive-ins. This time Krusz and Brownrigg were a little more determined to ride the wave, take a share of the gross and see how the thing played out.

Brownie was not one to mess with a winning combination, so Hugh Feagin, Camilla Carr and Gene Ross were brought back to play parts in this backwoods imbroglio. The screenplay was written by Mary Davis who was the author of Tom Moore's *Mark of the Witch* (1970), four years earlier. Creepy Gene Ross contributed additional dialogue to the project and I'll wager some of the sleaziest lines in the picture were conjured up by old Gene.

A young couple, Helen and Paul Fraser, are in the woods to enjoy a romantic getaway at an isolated cabin. They haven't been there long, when Paul is murdered by an unseen axe-slinging assailant. The terrified Helen dashes into the dense woods, fleeing the killer.

Coming upon Odis Pickett, a grimy hillbilly, she fears he's the killer. The guy's rough around the edges, but he's carrying a shotgun, not an axe. He tells her he's got a telephone and offers the safety of his home. Reluctantly, without a decent alternative Helen goes with Odis.

No matter what you call it, this is one creepy film.

The scene at the Pickett residence is like an episode of *Green Acres* (TV series 1965-1971) on a bad acid trip. The place is a pigsty. Odis has a mean-spirited, slutty daughter named Sarah (Camilla Carr) and a mentally challenged son called Bo (Charlie Dell). Sarah torments Bo relentlessly and Bo does his best to defend himself. To make matters even less savory, Odis has a new bride, Emmy, played by Ann Stafford. The new Mrs. Pickett is about six or seven months pregnant and may be younger than her step-daughter, Sarah.

Helen soon learns there is no telephone. She's stuck spending the night in this hell-hole. When daylight comes perhaps she can safely leave the hovel. But, will the morning ever come? Odis settles in to drinking some moonshine, while the women folk tend to dinner, a freshly skinned bloody possum Bo has provided. It's clear the shine is arousing ol' Odis's prurient interest.

The only truly sane member of the Pickett clan, the pregnant Emmy realizes Odis will try to rape their houseguest once he's got enough booze in his belly. Pulling the half-wit Bo aside, she sends him on a secret errand for help. Reluctantly, Bo sets off into the dark woods and soon becomes the killer's next victim.

Always looking for creative ways to dispatch folks from this mortal coil, Brownie came up with a nice gruesome demise for poor Bo. The hillbilly boy is shoved onto a spiked iron fence, forcing a sharp barb through his throat and out the backside of his neck.

Odis and his kin find poor dead Bo on the porch and Odis goes ballistic, blaming everything on Helen. He sends Sarah this time to go to the neighbors' house and make a call to the police. On her way, she encounters the killer and tries to get on his good side by using her slutty wiles. The murderer's having none of it. He soon dispatches her by strangling her with a piece of barbed wire.

Things continue to simmer at the house. There's plenty of raunchy dialog and tension. Finally, when Sarah doesn't return, Odis sets out for the neighbors' place. He finds his dead daughter and encounters the killer. The unseen assassin wrestles the gun from Odis and shoots him in the face. That's four, count 'em, four grisly murders drenched in blood!

As good-hearted Emmy tries to explain to Helen how she can escape by taking a circuitous route around the lake, a stranger enters the house. Its Jim, played by Hugh Feagin. As it turns out, Jim is a former husband of Helen's who was reported missing in action in Vietnam. He finally managed to escape the VC and he's pissed that she married some other guy while he was out there suffering in the Vietnamese jungle. Using the skills he learned in Uncle Sam's military, he has killed all the people who got in his way and now he wants to kill Helen.

This, of course, breaks all the rules of screenwriting. You don't introduce a key character in the final reel of the movie. Soap operas might do that sort of thing, but serious artists frown on it.

Before Jim can kill his faithless wife, Sarah drags herself in through the door and shoots him with her father's shotgun. There! Everything's tied up in a nice, neat almost happy ending. But wait, this is a horror film. We can't end on a happy note. What can we do?

The final scene shows Emmy and Helen on the porch of the house. Helen's evidently lost her mind after experiencing the horrors of the night before. Emmy's pregnant and has no other family now, so she's decided to adopt Helen. She explains they'll live happily together.

For all its failings, *Poor White Trash Part 2* is a powerful piece of exploitation cinema. The characters, especially Camilla Carr and Gene Ross, are classic exploitation bravura. The first time I saw this film, I had to rewind the cassette and watch it again. It was just too wild, too out there to warrant a single viewing. I liked this film even better than *Don't Look in the Basement* and it became my favorite Brownrigg movie until I saw *Don't Open the Door* (1974).

During the writing of *Texas Schlock*, I got to know David Szulkin, an exploitation film enthusiast and author, presently involved in restoring *Poor White Trash Part 2* for re-release.

"You mentioned the dolls at the beginning of *Don't Open the Door*. Mark Hundahl shot that.

He's the one who gave me a real behind-the-scenes account of making *Poor White Trash Part 2*, because he was a young SMU student at the time and worked on all three of those movies. He worked on *Poor White Trash 2, Don't Open the*

*Door* and *Keep My Grave Open* in a row. He gave me all sorts of stuff. He explained how Century Studios worked, everything that was going on around these productions. A lot of the information I had on those movies was wrong, you know, because looking into it, all four of the movies were made like in the span of a year and a half."
--From a phone conversation with David Szulkin, 01/18/2017

As David Szulkin[vii] pointed out to me, even though most people think Brownie's movies were made over a period of years, because of the release dates associated with the various titles, they were in fact all produced in a relatively short span of time. One of the reasons for the span of release dates on the films was the fact that the last two pictures, *Don't Open the Door* and *Keep My Grave Open* have a very prominent executive producer; Martin Jurow. That's right, the same Martin Jurow who brought you such well-known films as *Breakfast at Tiffany's* (1961). Jurow retired from Hollywood and in 1971 moved to Dallas. It was there he approached Brownrigg about directing a couple of drive-in style horror flicks. Initially, Brownie was ecstatic at the prospect of working with the great Martin Ju-

row. His enthusiasm turned to bitterness when he learned the two films were never intended to be released. They'd been created solely for the tax benefits allowed investors at the time. They were meant to lose money. Brownie eventually reworked both pictures enough to consider them "new" works and released them. This explains the range of release dates from 1973 to 1979 on the four pictures.

## DON'T OPEN THE DOOR (AKA DON'T HANG UP AND HOUSE OF THE FOUR SEASONS) (1974)

From its opening sequence showing Annabelle Weenick (as Annie) walking down the narrow corridor of an antique railway car to its unsettling ending, *Don't Open the Door* has a different feel than the other Brownrigg movies. There's a European flavor to the film. The bizarre characters and situations seem more like a Jesus Franco or Dario Argento flick than another Texas-based terror-fest.

Annie finds Judge Stemple (Gene Ross) seated at a table reading a newspaper. Their conversation rambles, alluding to sinister mysteries, reminiscent of dialog from Tennessee Williams' stage plays. As the scene unfolds we hear a constant clickety clack, leading us to imagine that these two are on a moving train, until we see a car pass by one of the windows. The

[vii]David Szulkin is the author of the popular nonfiction title Wes Craven's *Last House on the Left: The Making of a Cult Classic* (FAB Press, 2000). Szulkin is currently working on an encyclopedic examination of S.F. Brownrigg's career.

"While most of the action takes place in a rambling old house, the camera is allowed a few surprising flights of fancy. One might even wonder if Brownrigg (or cinematographer Robert Alcott) was influenced by the more adventurous camerawork found in Italian horror (after all, Mario Bava's *Blood and Black Lace* (1964) and Dario Argento's *The Bird with the Crystal Plumage* (1970) passed through Southern drive-ins in the early 1970s)."

--*horrorpedia.com*, Stephen Thrower, January 14, 2014

"We shot the film in The House of the Seasons in Jefferson, Texas. When the guys on the West Coast saw it, they wanted to know where the set was. This was because of the shot where Susan Bracken climbs the stairs all the way to the top. We accomplished that by putting a 16mm camera on a wooden platform and hoisting it up the stairwell with a rope and pulleys."

--S.F. Brownrigg in a 1992 conversation with the author

"When the bodies do start dropping, Brownrigg turns up the sensory overload with crashing cymbals and cross-dressing, giving sleaze fans what they came for while still crafting something very weird and unique. The budget is low and the pace is deliberate, but *Don't Open the Door* pays off big with a demented aura and an artful display of small town savagery."

--*allmovie.com*, Fred Beldin

judge asserts himself with a sudden slap to the woman's face. When the shamed Annie departs, we see they were in a train car, but one that has been parked permanently. So, what was up with the railroad sound effects? We are treated to a scene of the judge fiddling with a cassette player. With a demented gleam in his eye, he says to himself, "All aboard." Does he imagine himself to be a robber baron of bygone days, riding the rails across a newly tamed frontier? Just one of the unsettling mysteries of this unusual film.

Immediately after leaving the judge, Annie drops a dime and phones the granddaughter of the woman they were speaking of in such an enigmatic fashion. Amanda Post (played by Susan Bracken, daughter of the well-known comedic actor, Eddie Bracken) plays Annie's message back on an early model answering machine the size of my father's brief case. Her grandmother is in some sort of danger.

Disturbed by the vague warning, Amanda begins packing her bags. The doorbell rings and Nick (Hugh Feagin) blusters in. The two have been an item, but Amanda is fed up with his controlling behavior and no longer thinks of him as her "ol' man." The fact is introduced that Nick is a doctor. After being rebuffed, his ego bruised, Nick starts to leave, but Amanda's heart softens a bit and she begins to explain that it's been thirteen years since she's been home and her grandmother may be dying. As the lovely young woman provides a hefty lump of exposition, the visually intriguing opening credit sequence, featuring dolls in darkness unfolds. This title montage and the unmistakable 1970s-style music by Bob Farrar contribute to the European flavor mentioned earlier.

When the story continues, we learn that Amanda's aversion to the home town and Grannie's house is the understandable result of her mother's murder in 1962. After she receives an obscene phone call, she is stabbed to death in her own bed.

When Amanda wheels her car into town, a creepy guy named Claude Kearn (Larry O'Dwyer) notices and notifies Judge Stemple. Who is this fellow, why is he keeping tabs on Amanda and how come he's so damn creepy?

Amanda finds her grandmother (played by Rhea MacAdams) asleep in her bed. Seemingly in her sleep, Grannie whispers "Go away." This is virtually a reprisal of MacAdams' role as Mrs. Callingham in *Don't Look in the Basement*, except she doesn't get her tongue cut out this time. An addle-brained Dr. Crawther (James Harrell) who may be sampling the same drugs he's giving Grannie, wanders into the room and interrogates the young woman in a laconic fashion. As they speak, Claude and the judge come down the stairway from the floor above.

In the ensuing conversation, Amanda learns that Dr. Crawther refuses to admit her grandmother to a hospital, Claude Kearn wishes to have the estate bequeathed to the local museum and though Judge Stemple's angle is not spelled out, it's clear he's used to having his way and considers the town his domain. The young woman tells them all to get lost. When she's alone, she calls ex-ol' man, Nick and asks him to come and help her. He tells her he'll be there that night. Exploring the house, Amanda climbs to the tower where the windows on each wall are tinted with a different color of glass.[viii] After her ramble through the mansion, Amanda receives a "heavy breather" sort of phone call. She is mildly amused.

In the following scene, she takes a trip down memory lane, looking through old photographs. She runs across a copy of the Allerton Newspaper with a story about her mother's murder. The bloody memory returns to her consciousness, bringing an abrupt end to her reverie.

Upstairs, she settles in and indulges in a bubble bath. What she doesn't know is she is being watched by someone through a small crack in the bathroom wall. The phone rings. It's the heavy breather calling to tell her how much he misses her. This time we see more than the caller's lips and it seems the caller is creepy Claude. We know it, but Amanda does not yet.

[viii]Scenes for this film were shot in a historic home in Jefferson, Texas known as "the House of the Seasons." Though little mention is made of this in the final cut, it explains the movie's original title.

House of the Seasons in Jefferson, Texas

There's a sound downstairs.

Armed with a deadly vase, the nearly naked young woman goes to investigate. Happily, it's just Dr. Nick arriving as promised. Doc checks out Grannie and (big shock!) comes to the conclusion that something's not kosher. He promises to put the old woman in a hospital in the morning and Amanda allows him to sleep over – in a separate bed. But, as she sleeps, someone explores her bedroom, lifts her nighty with a walking stick to investigate her supple young flesh. Surely, it's not the doctor. She wakes in time to see someone departing and gives Nick a tongue-lashing, but he's been busy taking Grannie's blood pressure and such. If it wasn't Nick, then who? Someone moves in the shadows in the tower.

The next morning Nick requests an ambulance. Dr. Crawther shows up and the two physicians clash.

Amanda visits the local museum and finds that many of her grandmother's belongings are on display. Then creepy Claude show's her a representation of her mother. Amanda finds the whole thing in poor taste and insists that he return all of her family's belongings immediately, or she'll take legal action.

Upset, Claude visits Judge Stemple in his private railroad car. He's impressed. He likes old things. He asks for the judge's help in keeping Amanda's stuff in the museum. The judge threatens to send Dr. Crawther around to administer some of whatever he's been giving Grannie. Unable to strike a deal, Claude returns to the museum and has a conversation with the mannequin representing Amanda's mom.

Judge Stemple offers to buy the old house from Amanda. After her angry refusal, he threatens her.

When darkness has fallen over the town, Dr. Crawther shows up at the museum, thinking the judge has sent for him. He calls out and is told by a voice that doesn't quite sound like Judge Stemple to come upstairs. He searches the abandoned building and is preparing to leave when the mannequin of Amanda's mother comes to life. It's Claude, all dolled up, with murder on his mind. He bludgeons the doctor repeatedly with an antique hammer.

All excited by the murder, Claude calls Amanda and proclaims his amorous intentions toward her. As the conversation progresses, he threatens Amanda and her grandmother, then reveals he murdered her mother. Unfortunately, our heroine does not yet realize its Claude who's been calling. Running from the house, Amanda encounters Annie. The older woman is merely concerned, but in her frightened state of mind Amanda misunderstands Annie's intentions and comes to believe she's behind the threatening phone calls. Terrified, she runs back into the house.

It seems the phone is always ringing. Amanda answers and Claude has a lingering conversation with her in which he tells her what to do while he watches from his hiding place and, you know, gets his jollies. After the caller signs off, Amanda sweeps through the house, locking doors and grabbing a large knife from the kitchen. Claude slips a mickey into her water glass. She frantically tries to explain everything to Nick who's at the hospital, but her doctor pal dismisses her fear and tells her he'll check in later. She drinks the water. The drug begins to take effect about the same time Judge Stemple shows up to force another offer to purchase the house.

Bang, bang, Maxwell's ... make that Claude's ... hammer comes down on the judge's head. It's a newer, more modern hammer than the one he used on Crawther, but its effect is just as deadly.

While Amanda is under the effects of the drug, Claude gropes her. When she wakes from her drug-induced slumber she finds Nick in his bed. All is well at last, until she finds a photo of Dr. Crawther's dead body taped to a wall in the kitchen. She runs screaming to Nick, but finds it's a mannequin in his bed.

The phone rings. You'd think by now Amanda would know better, but she answers. As the caller asks her for a kiss, the judge stumbles into the room, accusing her of nearly killing him. She thinks the judge is her tormentor, but then the phone rings. Judge Stemple takes control of the situation, talking to the caller and agreeing to meet him upstairs. While Amanda waits, he climbs the stairs, but soon returns. It seems all he got for his troubles was a knife in the back.

Amanda loses it. She goes upstairs. Why? We can only guess. Dr. Nick arrives and calls to her, but by now she's gone 'round the bend, snapped. She doesn't know which end is up. She screams for Nick to stay away from her. Berserk, she bludgeons her boyfriend who falls down the central stairwell to his death.

Wandering the house, in shock, she falls into a rocking chair. The phone rings. At the sound of Claude's voice, she descends into an insane laughing fit.

## KEEP MY GRAVE OPEN (1977)

The sun is low on an autumn day, casting long shadows from the oak trees lining the road. A solitary man rides on the tailgate of a pickup truck travelling down the isolated country highway. The driver of the truck pulls to the side and lets the man off in the middle of nowhere. As the hitch-hiker walks along carrying his duffle bag we realize his face is familiar. It's Billy Thurman from the Academy Award-winning film, *The Last Picture Show* (1971) and scads of Larry Buchanan movies.

Hitchhiker (who is apparently homeless) comes to an opulent ranch house and mulls over the prospect of getting a decent hand-out. This location is not nearly as visually interesting as the locales chosen by Brownrigg for earlier endeavors; it's a bit too clean, too upscale. By the time the man arrives at the house, it is dark outside. He calls out, but receives no response. As he checks out the seemingly abandoned house, a couple of names in the opening credits catch our eyes; Larry Stouffer and Doug Smith.[ix]

Finding an open door, Hitchhiker makes his way to the kitchen where he loots the fridge, stuffing his duffle bag with edibles. Somewhere in the woods near the home, the Hitchhiker settles in for the night, frying a pork chop in an iron skillet over a small camp fire. A shadowy figure creeps through the woods toward the man. He notices too late and screams something as the wraith brings a saber down on his head.

There's a match-cut to a cleaver chopping raw meat in a butcher shop. Lesley Fontaine (Camilla Carr) is doing her grocery shopping. Before leaving the General

[ix] Stouffer, credited as assistant director was the director of *Horror High*. Doug Smith is perhaps better known as the Reverend Ivan Stang, founder of the Church of the SubGenius.

Store, Lesley lovingly selects a new pipe. Apparently, the pipe is a gift for someone she loves. When she picks up her mail from the rural Post Office, she is informed she's received a package. When Lesley returns to her home, we realize it is the ranch house where the homeless man was murdered. Pulling in, she calls to someone named Kevin, announcing her arrival. Placing the new pipe on a tray with coffee, she goes upstairs.

Lesley comes to a bedroom door. Someone (presumably Kevin) is inside typing. He does not respond or open the door when Lesley urges him to forget about last night. She promises she will not let anything happen to him. The typing continues. A frustrated Lesley returns downstairs.

A local high school student named Robert who cares for Lesley's livestock knocks on the door. The woman insists the boy have a cup of coffee even though he's late for school. Things turn tense when Robert asks if he can ride her horse, Caesar in a calf-roping event. When Lesley realizes Robert has been training the horse behind her back, she is not happy. She says she'll speak to her "husband" about it. At the word husband, Robert behaves in a peculiar fashion and quickly exits.

After the boy leaves, Lesley tries to talk with Kevin again, but is interrupted by a ringing telephone. The caller is our old friend, Gene Ross as Dr. Emerson. It seems Lesley has missed an appointment.

"*Keep My Grave Open* may not be the best movie of the genre, but it served very much as the boilerplate for many films that would come after. As for Brownrigg, he may have screened 1971's *Play Misty for Me* and from there gone off the deep end with his own twisted, knotted version. Worth checking out once or twice."
--*axs.com*, Octavio Ramos, August 27, 2015

"In Brownrigg's first three films there's a compromise – the narratives follow the trajectory of outsiders who must enter tightly-knit groups far removed from 'mainstream' society. A new nurse at a run-down asylum, a woman fleeing into the bayou to elude a murderer, a relative called back to her rambling childhood home – these women are audience identification figures as they enter disturbing new environments. The tension between their innocence and the situations they encounter keeps the narrative engine ticking. What makes *Keep My Grave Open* different and less commercial, is that the lead character is no longer someone who gets tangled up in other people's craziness – she embodies it herself."
--*horrorpedia.com*, Stephen Thrower, January 16, 2014

"*Repulsion* (1965) seems to be an influence here, but obviously we're dealing with a completely different level of quality. Director S.F. Brownrigg (who directed the superior *Don't Look in the Basement*) isn't exactly Roman Polanski, but it's a fairly competent film all the same."
--*horror-movie-a-day.blogspot.com*, April 8, 2011

He's worried about her state of mind and her headaches. We realize Lesley may have a mental problem when she reminds the doctor that he is not a psychiatrist.

Later, when Robert feeds the animals, his girlfriend Suzie shows up unexpectedly. He is annoyed because Lesley doesn't like others coming onto the property without her permission. Suzie is clearly in aggressive pursuit of her young boyfriend. The two do not realize Lesley is watching them from her balcony. When Suzie tries to lure Robert into a "roll in the hay," he insists they leave. And it's a good thing, because a booted individual is stalking the young couple. Is this Kevin? Perhaps, but it's certainly the same person who hacked the homeless man to death. We are treated to scenes of this person riding the horse, Caesar, but we're kept at a distance, the figure in soft-focus so we're unable to make a positive identification. Still, we suspect the rider may be a woman dressed as a man.

Lesley continues to carry on an emotionally distraught interaction with Kevin. But, we never see Kevin. Is he really there? Is he a figment of Lesley's imagination?

Suzie sneaks out of her home and goes to the ranch, hoping for a rendezvous with Robert because he told her he could not see her as he would be working late. Someone locks her in the tack room of the barn and taunts her with noises. Gradually, Suzie freaks out and pleads to be released from the room. The saber slides through the crack in the door and impales her.

Brownrigg's final opus, **Keep My Grave Open**.

When Dr. Emerson visits, we learn that Lesley was tormented as a child by the adults in charge of caring for her. Consequently, she developed an "abnormally close" relationship with her brother, Kevin. Their conversation hints at mental illness, that Kevin may now be a personality inhabiting Lesley's mind.

Lesley refuses to let Robert do his chores, sending him home. She feeds Caesar herself, then goes into the house and spends a great deal of time and effort dolling herself up. What follows is a bewildering, even ludicrous, scene in which Lesley tries to seduce the unseen Kevin.

Robert arrives, upset because he's learned Lesley has no intention of allowing him to ride Caesar in the calf-roping event. Lesley says she may change her mind and proceeds to seduce the teenager. Robert plays along in hopes of riding Caesar in the competition. She sends him to the bathroom, saying she wants to take a shower with him. The poor lad is confronted there by Lesley, dressed as a man and armed with the saber. This time there is no doubt that Lesley is Kevin. When she chooses to be.

Just to confuse us, we next see Lesley shouting to Kevin on the stairway in the throes of another of her powerful headaches. She goes to the medicine cabinet for her pills.[x] Examining her reflection in the mirror, she says, "No wonder you don't want me."

Abruptly, we are in the bar of a whore house. An inebriated patron is haggling with one of the ladies of the evening over the price.[xi] The madam behind the bar is Annabelle Weenick playing a minor role rather than her usual substantial character bit. Lesley enters and negotiates to take one of the girls home for Kevin's pleasure.

A working gal who goes by the name Twinkle accepts the assignment. While Lesley quizzes her on the ins and outs of prostitution, Twinkle smokes a joint to put her in the right mindset for the work ahead of her. Afterwards, Twinkle's clothes come off while Kevin's clothes go on … Lesley.

Kevin has the sword in hand. The prostitute makes a mad dash, slicing Lesley/Kevin with a switchblade knife as she passes. Twinkle flees the house while the sword-wielding maniac pursues like a relentless zombie.

It seems both Lesley and Twinkle have gotten more than they bargained for. Twinkle is under attack and to Lesley's surprise the prostitute fights back more aggressively than her previous victims. When Twinkle tries to hide in a vintage car in the barn, she finds she has company; the corpses of the Hitchhiker, Robert and Suzie have been tucked away in the back seat of the vehicle. Understandably, she freaks. Lesley plunges the saber through the car window and into the throat of the terrified woman. After this fourth murder, she quivers and recalls the faces of each of her victims.

Back at the house, she calls Dr. Emerson, telling him Kevin's arm has been cut. It is her own arm that is bleeding, from the wound inflicted by her guest's switchblade. Waiting for the doctor, she uses Kevin's typewriter to complete her last will and testament.

The doctor arrives. Lesley tells him she's made him the executor of her will

---

[x]If you watch the movie on a device that offers frame-by-frame advance, you can catch a glimpse of the camera crew in the medicine cabinet mirror.
[xi]That customer is none other than the illustrious Larry Stouffer.

and offers to have sex with him. Then, she tells a story about her overbearing aunt who misunderstood an intimate moment between Lesley and Kevin when they were teens. The doctor leaves, saying he'll be back soon. We get the distinct impression he's going to make arrangements to have her committed.

Lesley claims defiantly that she will never leave this house. She swallows a handful of pills and just before losing consciousness on the front porch, a male figure comes into view on the balcony above. Kevin?

The doctor and the storekeeper depart Lesley's funeral, each expressing regrets. Then familiar boots and pants enter the scene. Kevin? This time it's a real man, not Lesley pretending. He comments what a beautiful place this cemetery is to be dead. Next, we're in the house. Kevin announces that they'll have coffee in a few minutes. Lesley laughs with pleasure from the second floor.

Kevin goes outside, grabs a shovel and says, "The least you could've done is bury them for me." As he walks toward the barn, the end credits roll.

As if we didn't have enough nagging questions, Brownrigg seems intent on piling on a few more before the close of the film. Are both Kevin and Lesley now dead and enjoying an afterlife together? Is Kevin alive and returning home from a long absence? Why does a ghost need to bury bodies? And, ghost or not, does Kevin really believe he can bury the four bodies in the barn and be back in a couple minutes for coffee with Lesley?

In 1983 I was in the midst of my tenure at Productions West Communications, the media and entertainment "co-op" I was part of along with Jess Sherman, Mike Minton, Jerry Leggio, Adam Steinfeld and a juggler named Dropsen. In a little over a year, I had written three screenplays, produced a pilot for a proposed cable TV program on short indie films, toyed around with animation and had played Santa Claus at a hot Dallas night spot where I was relentlessly groped by the drunken female patrons. I'm not complaining. All of this was fun, but none of it seemed to be moving me any closer to my ultimate goal; making a horror film.

I knew there were several men who'd made exactly the sort of films I wanted to make and some of them were still living in the Dallas area. Repeatedly, I broached the subject of establishing contact with these experienced film makers, but my cohorts at PWC weren't interested. They voiced concerns that these guys had done a bunch of schlocky movies of low repute. I didn't have a problem with that. It was my position that if we hooked up with men like Brownrigg, Stouffer and Buchanan, we might be able to benefit from their experience, not have to reinvent the wheel.

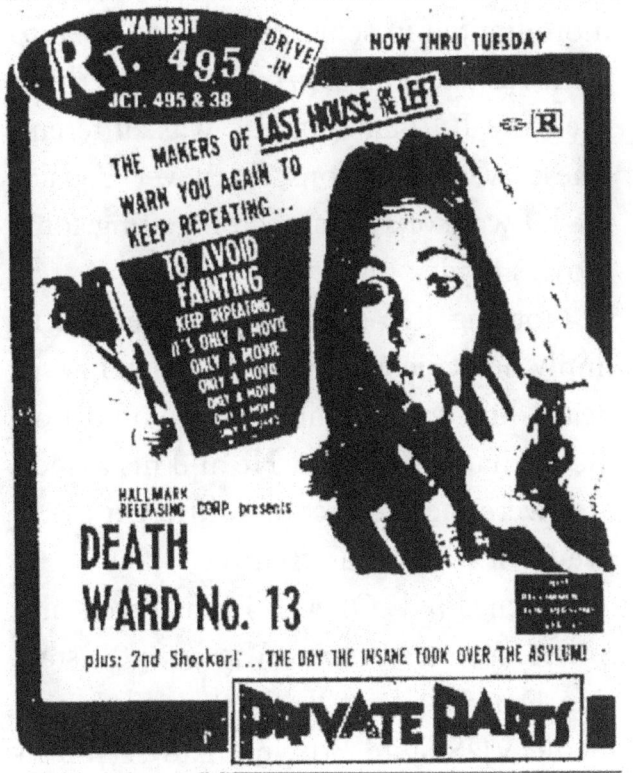

Rare ad featuring the **Death Ward 13** title.

One day in the fall of 1983 I took it upon myself to ring S.F. Brownrigg's home phone number. I left a message with his wife, stating that I was a young film maker just getting started in Dallas, a fan of his work and I'd like to buy him a drink and discuss future production possibilities. It wasn't long before Brownie called me back. We arranged to meet for happy hour at a bar (the name of which I do not recall) somewhere in the vicinity of Video Post and Transfer.

I found Brownie to be friendly and entertaining. We drank a few beers and he let me bombard him with questions. For the most part he was an open book, readily telling me what I wanted to know. He was guarded on a few topics, like exact budget figures. After spending almost two hours with the man, I felt I'd tapped into a goldmine of B-movie production information. This was a man I wanted to maintain a relationship with, maybe even work with someday.

The meeting drew to a close, I said goodbye and went to my car. In the parking lot, I had second thoughts, returned to the bar and asked if he'd like to see our place on Commerce Street. "Sure!" he responded.

I gave him the tour of PWC. He was polite, but not too impressed. Our band of rag-tag wannabes was nothing if not a diamond in the rough. Actually, more rough than diamond. We visited for a few minutes, then he went on his way. I hoped I had not destroyed any chance I had of working with the guy.

For some reason, Jess Sherman was annoyed that I'd brought Brownie to see the place and he let me know.

It wasn't long before I left PWC for good. I stayed in touch with Brownie. Over the next ten years I saw him on a semi-regular basis, meeting for drinks, asking advice, renting equipment from him and eventually collaborating on a couple of screenplays with him; one for a sequel to *Don't Look in the Basement* and another called *The Dark Mirror* involving cannibalistic Karankawa Indians and a Mayan obsidian mirror used to communicate with dark forces. Neither of these ever became movies.

I became aware of a definite generational, ideological gap between us one day after I'd submitted my first outline for *The Dark Mirror*. As usual, we were meeting for drinks, this time at The Wild Turkey on Walnut Hill, one of Brownie's favorite haunts.

"It's not bad. I think it's got potential," he said, waving the thin stack of pages over the table. "But we need to be aware of the marketing angle from the beginning. I ran it past one of my contacts in distribution and he said we need to change the title."

"Really?" I asked, "Why's that?"

"The word 'dark' could give viewers the wrong idea."

"Hmmm?"

"They might think it's a black movie, intended for black audiences."

This seemed highly unlikely to me. The heyday of so-called blaxploitation films was already long past. I pointed out to him that the movie *The Dark Crystal* (1982) had been a huge success.

"That was a big-budget Hollywood movie. It was Jim Henson and the Muppets. We don't have all that going for us. It's different with low-budget films."

There may have been something to what he was saying, but it wasn't what I wanted to hear. The concern that Brownie's distributor friend had voiced made me realize that we were not yet living in a post-racial society, even if I thought we were. Certainly, the venues available to the sort of film we had in mind were more limited in scope than those open to a movie like *The Dark Crystal*. Perhaps even the IQ demographic was different. These were questions I'd never considered. I was solely focused on getting some movies made.

Nothing I've said here is intended to imply Brownie was an overt racist. I never heard him say anything that would lead me to that conclusion. He and his associates were the product of a different era, a pre-Civil Rights mindset.

When Fred Olen Ray financed my movie, *Macon County War* (1990), starring Dan Haggerty, I did the offline edit in the VHS suite Brownie had set up in the cabana next to the swimming pool in his backyard. I was under a great deal of stress, working my regular customer service job at Allied, editing in any free time I had, all while trying to be a good husband and father. I was spread pretty thin. One night I was working into the wee hours, editing away, when I heard a rap on the sliding glass door of the cabana. What I saw, when I looked up, still brings a smile to my face. There was a soaking wet Brownie, clad only in swim trunks. He'd had a few drinks and was enjoying a midnight swim. "Want to take a dip?" he offered. It was all I could do to withhold my laughter. I declined as politely as possible and went back to piecing together my cheesy action epic.

Brownie's son, Tony, did special effects on *Macon County War*.

During the time when we were writing the screenplay for *Don't Look in the Basement 2*, Brownie hosted a barbeque at his home. Some local actors were invited to audition for roles in the film. One of the auditioning actors was Jerry Lentz, the morning voice of the Edge, Dallas' most popular alternative radio station at the time. This was the first time I met, Jerry. Eventually, we became good friends and worked on a few projects together.

While I was going through my divorce and other violent disruptions in my life, I sort of lost touch with Brownie for a while. When things were beginning to settle back into something approximating a normal state, one day he crossed my mind. I called his house and spoke with Tony. "We lost Dad a while back," he told me. I was stunned.

Brownie passed away on September 20, 1996. At the time, I was in the midst of shooting *The Protector* (1997) for Roger Corman. I felt a sense of guilt for having neglected contact with my friend and for being completely unaware of his death.

Here is an interview I did with Brownrigg, originally published in *Draculina Magazine* issue# 13, 1992.

In 1973, S.F. Brownrigg produced and directed a strange little horror film entitled *The Forgotten*. Brownrigg had worked in the Dallas, Texas commercial film industry for twenty years before taking the plunge into feature film production. In addition to directing hundreds of commercials and industrial films, he served on the crews of several of Larry Buchanan's Dallas-based productions. The 1958 film, *The Naked Witch* was the first horror film Buchanan ever produced and directed. Brownrigg was the sound man and his wife, Libby, played the lead. That's right! Libby Brownrigg was *The Naked Witch* (but, to tell the truth, she wasn't actually naked. She was wearing a full-body, flesh-colored suit.) It was fifteen years after *The Naked Witch* that Brownrigg decided he was ready to produce and direct his own horror feature.

*The Forgotten* is the story of an out-of-the-way private sanitarium where the patients, not the doctors, are in control of the facility. Horror fans the world over know this film as *Don't Look in the Basement*. Brownrigg's drive-in classic was first distributed by Hallmark – the same company that distributed Wes Craven's first film, *Last House on the Left*. Both films utilized the now-famous ad campaign, "To avoid fainting, keep telling yourself, it's only a movie...only a movie...only a movie..." When Hallmark filed for bankruptcy, these two horror classics ended up in the hands of Sam Arkoff at American International Pictures. Arkoff's decision to pair the off-beat, shockers on a double bill, created a box-office dynamo that continued to play drive-in theaters for ten years! This record-breaking double bill inspired a host of imitators.

Both Craven and Brownrigg had opportunities to move up in the feature film business as a result of the attention this sick double-feature received. Craven moved to California, and went on to direct a long list of well-known horror films. These include *The Hills Have Eyes*, *Nightmare on Elm Street* and *The People Under the Stairs*. Brownrigg journeyed to Hollywood to check out job offers, but shortly returned to Dallas, because as he put it, he "Couldn't handle the bullshit."

Brownie went on to produce three more drive-in horror epics; *Poor White Trash Part 2*, *Don't Hang Up* (aka *Don't Open the Door*) and *Keep My Grave Open*. After a number of financial disappointments, Brownie decided to hang it up and go back to directing Lone Star Beer commercials.

The following interview was conducted by Bret McCormick in 1992, at a time when he and Brownrigg were contemplating the production of a sequel to *Don't Look in the Basement*.

BB: I became involved in film production the same way a lot of other people did in Dallas; Jamieson Film Company in 1955...I started out as an audio engineer, designing some audio systems for a company called Carver Sound Equipment. My father had an electrical contracting business, but I got pretty bored connecting a speaker to an amplifier and a microphone to the other end...so I was trying to expand my horizons a little bit in audio, and in the paper, there was an ad for a sound engineer for Jamieson Film Company. I went to work there in 1955 as a sound man...so that's how I got started. I went from there into some editing, started shooting and directing. It just kind of grew from that.

Promo art for ***Don't Look in the Basement***.

TS: Why do you think so many horror films are produced?

*BB*: Obviously, there's a market for them or there wouldn't be so many horror films made. I can't explain why the market is as large as it is…I guess the same reason people still sit around the campfire and tell ghost stories and not stories about happy things. I don't understand it myself, but that is the way it is. There is another thing that comes into play here and that is the fact that the horror film may be the easiest to make. It's less gamble to an investor, less need to have the perfect script or the perfect actor or the perfect performance each time. There's a lot of room for mistakes in a horror film.

*TS*: Do you think Dallas will ever become a major hub of film production?

*BB*: Obviously, we are not where we want to be in Dallas. I sure hope we get there before I have to get out of the business. I've been waiting on it for a long time. I'm like some of the others, I've held off on throwing in and moving out to Hollywood several times, because I still think it's going to happen here. By all means, we're not there yet and I don't know what it's going to take. I really don't. I think if one of the smaller networks, like Fox, moves into Dallas and starts operating their headquarters out of here, that might be a good thing to kick it off really well. Of course, from the television projects would come the talent to support the movie end of it. Movies used to lead to television, now I guess television leads to movies.

*TS*: Who kicked off feature film production in Dallas?

*BB*: Larry Buchanan. As far as I can tell, Larry was one of the first pioneers. If anybody said, "No, you can't do that!" Larry would just go ahead and do it. I was fortunate enough to work with Larry on a lot of his features, in various capacities. Larry was a dreamer and it takes a dreamer to get it done! There were a lot of other movies made in and around Dallas of course, but I think Larry was the first to do it all right here from start to finish.

*TS*: What made you pick horror as a genre for your first film?

*BB*: I became involved in horror films specifically because there is less chance for an investor to lose their money in a horror film. And obviously, the first picture I did I didn't want to fail. We had a friend named Walter L. Krusz who believed in us. A friend like that is tough to find when you've never done a film before. I had worked on a lot of films, but had never produced and directed one. He said, "Let's go!" So, we did it. And it worked out well enough that we did another one after that. We didn't have our marketing skills honed, though, so we weren't in too good of shape profit-wise, but the pictures themselves made a lot of money.

*TS*: Do you enjoy watching horror films?

*BB*: I like watching horror films. I must admit, though, that it's primarily to see what everybody else is doing, compared to ideas I may have. Unfortunately, I feel like the horror films today are getting into a "Let's see who can spend the most money on special effects" or who can boil the biggest pot of blood or who can make the longest gash, which I don't think is really necessary. I hope that maybe there is going to come a circle in the trend, where we try to go back to some of the suspense or Hitchcock type horror. Not so much blood. Although, gore has been the name of the game for a long time, so we're not going to get rid of it.

*TS*: Weren't you pushing the envelope with the gore in *Don't Look in the Basement*?

*BB*: I certainly was. When we did *Don't Look in the Basement*, we were trying to out-do everybody in blood and everything else. Exactly the same thing. You're right. However, I think today, with the amount of money that can be spent on special effects, they almost get in the way of the story. For example, Freddie Krueger; the first couple of pictures were great, now it's just how much more blood can we stick in? How much more horrible can we make it? That's what's become of the genre of the horror film. I'm not against that, but still, I think we're going off and leaving some of the story.

I enjoyed making the films I've done. I was fortunate to work with a lot of good friends...used up a lot of favors, of course, on the first ones. We enjoyed it a lot. Especially *Don't Look in the Basement*. It was an absolute joy. We nearly killed ourselves working on it. It was twelve days. I don't think I really remember the last couple of days, but we got it out. And it was extremely successful money-wise for such a small film. No budget at all, hardly.

I'd like to do all sorts of films. Being realistic, I'm going to have to do a couple more horror films, since I quit doing them for so long... I think before we can get enough confidence back for investors to do other types of films. But, by all means, I'd like to do some action/adventure, even some G-rated ones. I'm not really hung up on any one type.

I was influenced by Hitchcock, if anybody, but unfortunately, I've never felt like I had enough budget or the right situations to really utilize the things I'd like to do.

*TS*: What were your biggest drawbacks in production?

*BB*: Just not having enough money to do what we needed to do. That's the plight of the indie film maker. Personally, in my own personal situation, we had a lot of friends and a lot of help. I had the equipment at the studio there that I had access to. We couldn't get into too much trouble there. That helped a lot. We really didn't encounter a lot of problems once we'd raised enough money to get started. It became obvious that when you think you've got enough money raised, you don't. So, you have to add a little more

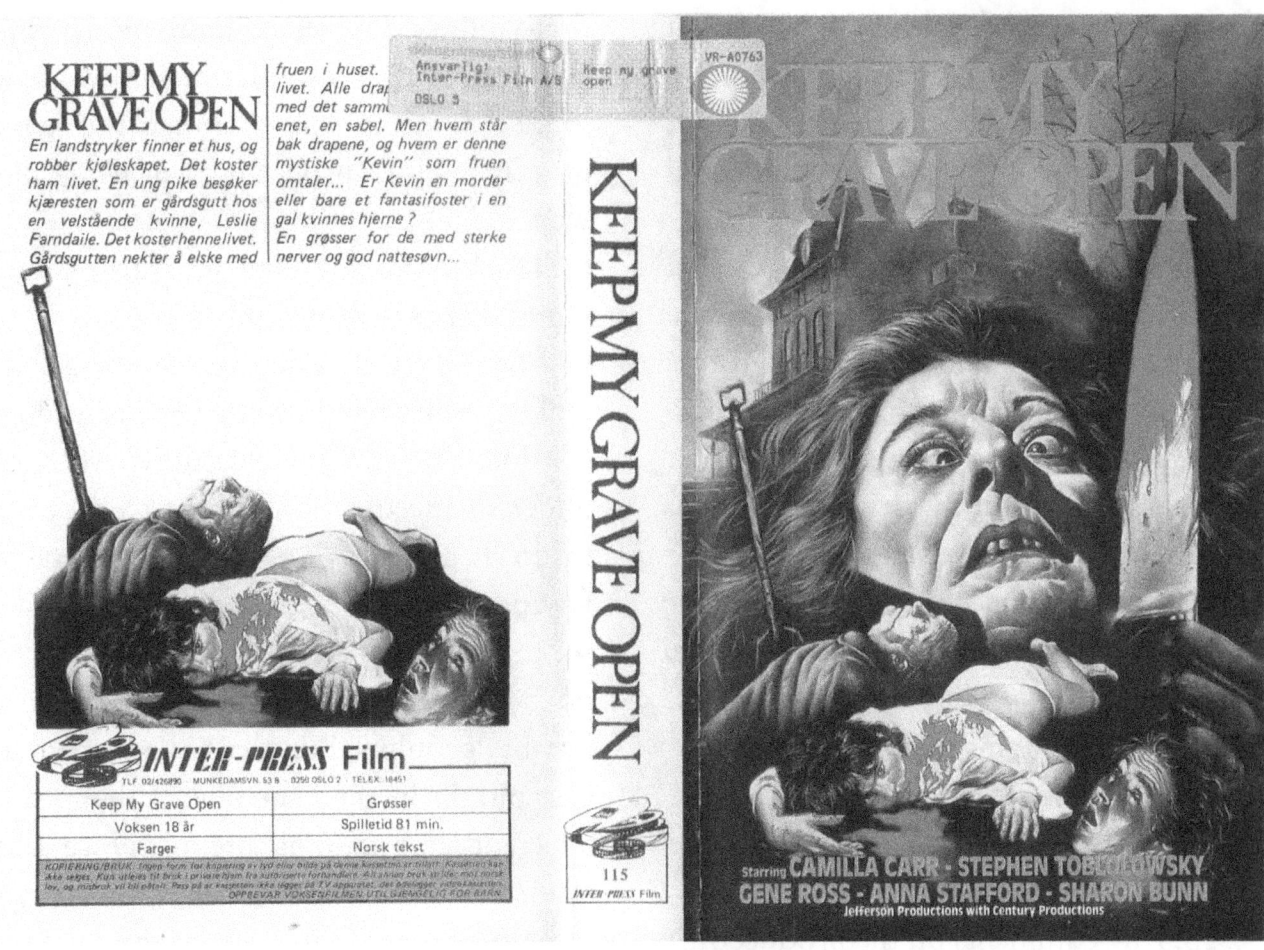

Cover Art for **Keep My Grave Open**.

to it, which we learned to do. Especially for the marketing. We enjoyed making films, and that's what you primarily do. It's kind of difficult to worry about the marketing. But, those pictures, no matter how good they are when you finish them, they are no good sitting on a shelf. You can't put ketchup on them and eat them for breakfast! You have to have some way to go out there and get them into the marketplace. That costs money, too. And it's just as big a cost and just as important an expense as buying the film. You've got to be able to go out there and get your film into the marketplace. That takes money.

*TS*: What do you feel was your biggest mistake?

*BB*: My biggest mistake was that I quit after four pictures that were relatively successful. The first two were extremely successful, for the distributors. I personally did not make the sort of money I should've made. In fact, I made almost nothing out of them. And I just got dejected to the point that I decided I'd do something else. I'm just concentrating my efforts into the same old things I've been doing all along, which is commercials, documentaries and sales films. At that time, I was producing an outdoor hunting and fishing show for Star Sportsman. So, I'm putting myself back in that hot and heavy, too.

Before I knew it, time got away from me. We talked to some folks who were interested in doing movies, but the drive-in market was disappearing. Let's face it, the original movies that I did in '73, '74, '75 and '78 were for the drive-in theaters. That was our primary market and those went away. When they went away, it took a little while before the new market, which of course is video cassette rentals... and it's the same market, the same audience we used to do the pictures for at the drive-ins, but now they're going to the video store and renting movies.

TS: Any comments on the producer/investor relationship with directors?

BB: I can't really speak for any other producers and investors. I can tell you about my specific relationship with an investor and that is, he made the final decisions until he got his money back in that particular case. He was able to do that. We weren't able to make too much profit, because again, you've got to put aside enough money to market the picture. You don't just set aside enough to make the picture, because when you're sitting there, with a finished film, you're at the mercy of anybody. Especially, if you tell them how much you've got in it and that you don't have any more money and you need to turn it fast...which is what we did. I'll admit it. And of course, they gave us a little bit of profit and sent us on our way.

TS: Would you like to warn young filmmakers about any pitfalls?

BB: The pitfalls I'd warn beginning filmmakers about would be under the heading of: don't be under financed! We've been under financed on everything we've tried to do. It gets better as we go. We have a few projects now working that looks like we're finally going to get enough budget to do it right, even though they are still very low budget films. But, that's the single biggest pitfall. In the beginning, I thought if we could ever get a picture made, we'd be in the clear, but that's not true. You've got to be able to have the time and the patience and the clout to go out and market it after you edit it.

The first picture we produced, *Don't Look in the Basement*, was put together rather hurriedly. And we did put it together along the lines that I try to do the low budget pictures; and that is we try to keep the script, until after we get the thing financed, kind of loose so we can go to the actual location and write the script around the location where we're going to shoot. It's about a sanitarium where there are crazy people running loose, as it were, in an isolated area. One of the doctors, we find out at the end of the picture, is also a patient. Of course, he's done away with the real doctor. Very simple, but it followed all the rules and regulations for a good horror film; keep it isolated. Lots of boobs and blood!

*TS*: Did any of the folks you worked with on your films go on to bigger things in Hollywood?

*BB*: A guy named John Thomas Lenox worked with us at Century Studios for a while. John produced some *Laverne and Shirley* (TV series 1976-1983) and some *Happy Days* (1974-1984). He did quite a bit of work out in Hollywood. In fact, I guess he still is. One of our actresses, Camilla Carr, has a best-selling book out; *Topsy Dingo Wild Dog* (Birch Lane Press 1989). Annabelle Weenick is presently in Hollywood. I believe she just finished working on a picture with Bernadette Peters. Gene Ross is touring and has been for the last five or six years I guess, with Debbie Reynolds. So, everybody's doing pretty well. We stay in touch fairly often.

*TS*: Now that Hollywood is producing really big budget horror films, what's the prognosis for the indie/cheapie?

*BB*: I think the new high-tech, high-budget horror films have definitely hurt the low budget films, because they've just got an awful lot of wonderful special effects available today, and these just have to get your attention. But, I also think there's a section of the market that the low budget films will always be able to garner. There's enough people out there who just sit and watch the laid-back pictures, to make it worthwhile to keep doing it. There are quite a few folks out there doing these types of pictures right now.

Brownrigg's perennial horror diva, Camilla Carr.

*TS*: Anyone ever call you a schlock-meister?

*BB*: I've been called lots of different names. I think one of the recent articles in *Fangoria* labeled me as a "splatter-meister," and that's okay, you know? Again, it's being a good teller of a good ghost story around the campfire. That's the name of the game. The better the story you tell, the more you'll be noticed.

I must admit, until they called me from *Fangoria* magazine, I didn't know they existed. I had never seen one before. A lot of my so-called fans knew about it. In fact, I got a few phone calls after that magazine article came out and they were telling me they still get letters asking when Brownrigg was going to do another movie. I even picked up one magazine from Europe, which had the information about the same thing; "Coming out of the tomb," as it were. For that market, if they want their own magazine, that's great.

I would love to know the reason why people still rent *Don't Look in the Basement*, or any of the other horror films that have been collected over the years. Boy, if I knew the answer to that question, you and I both could make a lot of money! (laughs) As I understand it, whoever currently owns *Don't Look in the Basement*, just released it to video again. And I'm just amazed that it's still going on. Another picture I did, *Poor White Trash Part 2*, is still in the video stores. I wish I could bottle the reasoning. I could sell it for a lot, I bet you!

TS: What do you think of your fans?

BB: To be honest, I have not met many of my fans, as it were. I've gotten a lot of letters, but I really haven't met too many fans. I'm sure they're mostly fans for short, limited terms, while they're there looking at the picture. But, there are some that have written me three or four times, wanting to know when we're going to do another picture.

I think most of the people doing horror films, again, it's like almost wearing a protective covering to keep you from losing your shirt. It lets you get out there and get your feet wet. Get a picture out there and see if it will sell. Because, you know there's a market there. It's not a small market. It's a large market. So, I

Rare ad featuring the title **The Forgotten**.

don't see anything wrong with young film makers producing their own. The market is certainly changing. The same teenager who had an appetite for one film a week at the drive-in theater, is now going to the video store and renting six in a weekend. They're consuming the product a lot faster. So, why not more product? And that's a good way to get your feet wet. Again, you have to go back to the reason for horror films for a producer is not just the money...it's the lack of money. You don't have a lot to spend and it's no huge loss if you lose a little bit. You don't have to worry too much about it not being a great script, great talent, great location. You can always cut to the blood!

*TS*: Do you think the ultra-cheapie horror flick has evolved into its own genre?

*BB*: I think I probably do agree with the assessment that those types of pictures now have their own little niche, their own little magazine that follows them. I wish it weren't that way so much anymore, but the market is so divided now. It's just hard to do one of those types of movies for film, to actually get it in a theater, because there are so many other good movies being made that have bigger budgets. I think the smaller, "schlock film" as you call it, they're just trying to find a spot on a shelf in the video stores. Maybe some art houses, college movies, but that market has always been a segmented one and I think it will continue to be more so. Because today, if you spend some money on a film, you can get some special effects that again, whether you like the movie or not, you have to just stand in awe of the effects and how many gallons of blood they can spill.

There's a genre of filmmaker today, just coming into being, that has a challenge as great as that of the high budget filmmaker who can spend as much money as they want on special effects. The challenge for these new filmmakers is to make their movies on the least amount of money possible. It's a challenge. It's like the computer hacker. Can they get into the big computers? They are not going to give up until they do. And I think there's another genre of filmmaker that can make it as bad as they want to. I don't know if it's because the market is wanting it, but I think that they too are going to be challenged to get as much notice as the folks who are spending lots of money. It'll be interesting to see how this manifests in the movies. I'm trying to align myself now with a couple of young folks so I can hang onto the business, too. Because I'm out to see how little I can do it for and how much attention I can get for the least amount of money. But, I do believe there's a separate breed of film maker. It's going to be exciting. Like MTV. I don't enjoy watching MTV personally, but boy have they come up with some effects! Some creative concepts that have crept into every type of audio/visual presentation that exists today. I guess you'd say they're expanding the vocabulary of cinema.

*TS*: When was your last feature production?

*BB*: The last feature I did was in 1978. I worked with Martin Jurow. We didn't quite put enough blood in that one. I don't think it was a big seller. I don't think it lost any money, but again, that was a specific situation where I didn't have much to say about what was done with the film after it was completed. Since that time, I've continued with sales films and documentaries. I kind of went ahead and bowed to the "video booger bear" that's out there. A lot of us have been fighting to continue shooting film, but video's here to stay. We have to use that, too. But, I always prefer to shoot film if I get the chance. I'd like to try some new stuff. I'd like to do some G-rated films. I'd like to work on soap operas. I think there's plenty of room for improvement in soap operas, and still keep them soap operas. We'll just have to see how it goes.

In the last five or six months, for several reasons, because of some attention I've been getting in Europe and here, some fans have asked why I'm not doing movies. Some investors have said, "If they're that interested, let's talk about it." So, yeah, we're planning on doing some films. I have a pet project I'd like to do. *Freaks 2*. Another *Freaks* picture, very much like the first one that was done back in the 1930s. And I have some other projects, too. They're not all horror films. I'm looking forward to getting a couple of those cranked up this year.

I think the future for the small, independent horror film is as good as it ever was. It's a way to get started and there's an audience out there that can't wait to see more of them. I think there will always be. I think we'll always need another ghost story around the campfire.

When I began writing *Texas Schlock*, I reached out to Brownie's wife Libby and his son, Tony requesting interviews. On 12/20/2016 I spoke with Libby by phone. Known to me as Libby Brownrigg, the lady performed under the names Libby Booth and Libby Hall.

TS: Libby, the film (*The Naked Witch*) is listed on imdb.com with a release date of 1961. What year did you shoot it?[xii]

LB: I don't remember exactly. If you have Buchanan's book, you'll probably find the dates in there.

TS: How did you come to be cast in that role?

LB: I did a lot of stage work, but when I was home in Dallas, I'd do commercials at Jamieson Film Company. That's where I met Buchanan. He was getting ready to do *The Luckenbach Witch*. One day he stopped me in the hallway and asked if I'd ever done a movie. I told him, no, but I'd done a lot of stage work. He said he wanted me to try out for a part in this film he was getting ready to do. He told me all about it. I said, yes, that sounds very interesting. I'd never done film work before. It was a whole different ball game for me.

[xii]Buchanan states in his book that he received the phone call from Claude Alexander in 1957. On-Line sources indicate the film was completed in 1961, but not released until 1964. Libby Brownrigg suggested to me that the film was released as *The Luckenbach Witch*, then re-released in 1964 as *The Naked Witch*. In any case, it should not be confused with Andy Milligan's schlockfest of the same title released in 1967.

We threw all our stuff together and tripped down to Luckenbach. It was very exciting to be making a movie. When the movie was finally finished, and put out, it was apparently very popular. After a while, they changed the title from *The Luckenbach Witch* to *The Naked Witch*. Which…it wasn't and I wasn't.[xiii] They thought it would be more exciting.[xiv]

Then, I don't know, maybe six years ago, they decided to put it out on DVD.[xv]

So, a while after that Larry moved to California. I went out to California and did some work. Then when I came back home I ran into Brownie Brownrigg. He was the sound man on *The Luckenbach Witch*. I married Brownie and decided to stop acting and raise my children.

A couple of years ago, my son Tony decided to do a sequel to *Don't Look in The Basement*, after all these years. Tony asked me to come out of retirement and do a cameo part. He had me play a 95-year-old Alzheimer's patient. I told him, sure, I'd like to do that! It came out I guess the year before last and was very well-received. It got some awards. It's available on DVD.

*TS*: Let's get a bit on your background. Were you raised in the Dallas area?

*LB*: I was born and raised in Dallas. A friend and I did Spike Jones records.[xvi] We were constantly being pulled out of school to perform for civic clubs. We'd come running out and perform to Spike Jones records. They loved that.

SF Brownrigg's son Tony finally created a sequel to ***Don't Look in the Basement*** in 2015.
Image courtesy Daniel Redd and Dave Rennke, the film's producers.

[xiii]Libby wore a stretchy, flesh-colored body suit for the scenes in which she was supposed to run about in the nude.

[xiv]On the original one sheet, a naked woman is seen from behind as she lunges with a knife in her fist. This was before the days of the MPAA rating system, but the poster features a banner reading: An Adult Picture.

[xv]Something Weird Video released a double-bill DVD of *The Naked Witch* and *Crypt of Dark Secrets* (1976) in October of 2012.

[xvi]In a follow-up phone call, I asked Libby to elaborate on "doing Spike Jones records." She explained that she and her friend Sheila would dress up in funny costumes and pantomime routines to various Spike Jones recordings. They began doing it in junior high school and the bits were so popular they continued to perform them for about ten years. They were frequently recommended as entertainment for groups like the Lion's Club and allowed to miss school to perform for these civic organizations, which was a perk the girls really enjoyed.

I was six years old when my Aunt Olive decided I needed to act. She began training me. She knew so many people in California and was anxious to get me out there. I started doing stage work with Elizabeth Peabody and the Young People's Theater Group. I went away to school in Virginia. When I went back home I won a contest for beauty and glasses and was on the Steve Allen Show. Neiman Marcus outfitted me

A young man from SMU asked me to marry him. My mother was excited. My father was excited. So, I said okay. After about five years, the marriage just didn't work. I had a young daughter. I let her stay with my mother while I went back out to California. I did some film work, but I didn't feel I could raise my daughter out there in California. It was not as rough as it is now, but it was pretty rough. So, I came back home.

I ran into Brownie Brownrigg again, the sound guy from *The Luckenbach Witch*. And I married him. We had a son who's still active in film.

TS: There's some history there, isn't there? Aren't you related to John Wilkes Booth?

LB: Yes, my family is related to John Wilkes Booth and General William Booth founder of the Salvation Army. After I learned in school about the assassination of Lincoln, I went home hysterical, wanting to know if one of our relatives had killed the president. My father said, "No, girls, you are not related to John Wilkes Booth. You're only related to Edwin Booth…which of course was his brother. But, that made us feel a whole lot better. We had a lot of relatives in show business, a very colorful background.

TS: Were you in any of Buchanan's other films?

LB: I was in *Beauty and the Cave* (1961). And this other one…I can't recall the name.[xvii]

TS: *Beauty and the Cave*? That was a film Buchanan did?

LB: Yes.

TS: Can you tell us anything about that one?

LB: It was about this man who went out into the woods, exploring, and he ran across this cave. Exploring the cave, he discovers a woman. He brought her out into the open and talked to her, tried to bring her around. Apparently, she'd been there for many years. That's about the essence of it.

TS: Did this film play in any theaters?

LB: I know Larry's films usually played to drive-ins. I don't know how many indoor theaters those films showed in. I hated watching myself. So, I just never saw

[xvii]The film she could not recall the title of was *Common Law Wife* (1963). Oddly, Beauty and the Cave (1961) is not mentioned in Buchanan's autobiography. There is an imdb.com listing for the film, but no mention is made of Buchanan's involvement. The only names associated with it are Max Anderson, Dale Berry and Libby Hall. Dale Berry is a fairly well-known schlockmeister in his own right, though I don't believe he made any horror or sci-fi flicks.

those films. I saw some still photos and so forth, but I never sat down and watched them.

TS: What year was it you married Brownie?

LB: Let me see. Very close to 1960. But, now we made the movie (*The Naked Witch*) much earlier than that. Brownie was such a nice person. When I'd bring my daughter onto the sets he was so nice to her and made sure she stayed out of everybody's way while I worked.

He was married at the time. And I was married at the time. He got divorced first. I ran into him and he found out I was in the process of getting a divorce. We consoled one another over coffee. After some time passed; he had a son and I had a daughter; and we decided we needed to get together and make a family. Which we did. Then about four years later, he and I had a son.

Stacey, Brownie's son by his first marriage, is still in the business. He's a brilliant sound man. California calls him out all the time to work. So, between him and Tony they're still in the film business.

On 02/28/2017 I followed up with a second call to Libby to get more details regarding her comment about "doing Spike Jones records."

After I recalled some of my fond memories of visiting the Brownriggs in their home, Libby told me she missed Brownie. I echoed her sentiment and told her he was my greatest mentor and had a huge impact on my experience as a film maker. Then, she told me in the final days of his life, when he was lying in bed, waiting to die, he received a call from someone in London who wanted to fly him to the UK and host a lecture on his career. He politely declined. Two days later another similar offer came from someone in San Francisco. "I'm glad those offers came when they did," Libby said, "they made him very happy."

# ROBERT A. BURNS

## MONGREL (1982)

Something or someone moves down the misty, dimly lit corridor of an old boarding house. A silhouetted figure in a doorway, upstairs the playful laughter of young women, in the darkness a guttural growl.

After the opening credits, Ken (Andy Tiennan) approaches his new home for the first time. The place is gothic, almost like a castle. He doesn't notice the large black dog chained near the entrance and is startled when the animal barks at him. An older man, Bouchard (Aldo Ray) pushes past him at the door. Ken rings the bell, knocks, then lets himself into the imposing old house.

The place is decorated in unique fashion, including a rare *Deep Throat* pinball machine in the living room. Jerry (Terry Evans) calls from the stairway. Ken introduces himself and Jerry suggests he close the front door so the dog will shut up. Jerry shows Ken to his room. This really is an ancient house. The bedroom has its own wood burning fireplace.

"In many ways, *Mongrel* is a concentrated and intelligently filtered artistic catharsis that exists to both entertain, but also act as an artifact of therapy. Upon viewing the sheer ugliness of the film – which is designed and painted with a sleazy sensibility – you can sense a lot of who Robert A. Burns was, as his personality and attempts at communicating his dynamic ideas pulsate within the makeup of the film."
--*comingsoon.net*, Lee Gambin, April 29, 2017

"Those huge video boxes you run across are usually a no-no, but still I pick them up, when will I ever learn? In my defense the case, with its slide out plastic tray that smacks of so many low budget porn films, had a rendition of Cerberus on the cover. Seems like a killer dog movie, right?"
--*badmovies.org*, Andrew Borntreger

When Jerry opens a closet the two young men receive a shock. The closet's been booby trapped with metal hubcaps that clatter to the floor unexpectedly. Jerry guesses the prank must have been executed by someone named Woody (Mitch Pileggi) who gets his kicks that way.

Robert A. Burns.

of collapse. Turquoise mentions the "new guy" is really cute, so Woody goes to check this possible threat.

Everyone hates Woody and Ken is no exception. Woody launches into an attempt at intimidation, but Ken's not buying. He pisses Woody off by insisting on a receipt for the $50 rent he hands the jerk.

Ken visits Jerry's room and tries to strike up a friendship based on their mutual hatred of Woody. We learn that Jerry earns his living as an indexer for a publisher. The guys decide to grab a bite to eat together.

Woody, Jerry explains, is the guy who collects the rent from all the tenants, a bit of a tyrant. The only tenant Woody doesn't faze is someone named Ike (Jonathan Ingraffia). That's Ike's dog outside barking its head off. Jerry's a nervous type and dismisses himself quickly after giving Ken a rundown on the other tenants.

In a bizarre scene that takes place in the garden behind the house, we are introduced to Woody and his girlfriend Turquoise (Rachel Winfree). They have a dysfunctional relationship on the verge

> "It was easy for me to get suckered into watching Mongrel because I'm a foaming, rabid lunatic when it comes to killer dog films and the related subgenre of 'killer humans who think they are dogs' movies. Oh shit, did I manage to give away the big twist in the first sentence of the review? That's some tragic irresponsibility on my part. It's true, Mongrel is not about a mongrel at all."
> --*theaterofguts.com*, Goat Scrote, April 25, 2014

Woody plays the *Deep Throat* pinball machine and tells Toad (John Dodson) and the other guys who are hanging out that the new tenant is uppity. Ike comes in still wearing his postal uniform. He has a rare, collectible model of a World War II tank. Woody and Toad take the opportunity to taunt the poor guy. Ken and Jerry return from dinner and now everyone gets to meet face-to-face.

After some juvenile banter, the room clears out, except for Ken and Leon who's been sitting passively on the sofa. Leon makes a half-assed apology for the behavior of the others. Ken's really impressed with the *Deep Throat* pinball machine and can't wait to send some balls between Linda Lovelace's flippers. It turns out the machine belongs to Leon.

Weird video sleeve for **Mongrel**.

The lovely Sharon (Catherine Malloy) returns home and is introduced to Ken. It seems they share a spark of attraction.

During the night, Jerry tosses restlessly in his bed.

Early Saturday morning, the sound of a battle wakes Woody and Ken. It's Ike, playing wargames. Woody tells him to knock it off. Ike uses the opportunity to try to establish a friendship with the new tenant, Ken.

Upstairs, Jerry is doing sit-ups when Sharon knocks on his door. She's returning a book he loaned her and, as a gesture of appreciation, she gives him a couple of small Foo Dog figurines. Jerry thinks the gift is too much and tries to decline, but Sharon insists. The timid Jerry has an obvious crush on Sharon and very much welcomes the peck on the cheek she gives him.

Outside, Ike is feeding his dog. The animal's name is Brute. Jerry is terrified of the creature. When he tries to slip by unnoticed, Ike teases him.

That evening on the front porch, Ken and Sharon have a conversation and get to know each other a little better. Sharon is very protective of Jerry and disdainful of the other "jerks" in the building. She encourages Ken to befriend Jerry to help boost his confidence.

That night, again, Jerry tosses, awakening abruptly from a bad dream.

When Toad taunts Brute with a piece of steak, the dog gets riled and breaks his chain. Soon Toad is on the ground screaming for help as Brute tears into him. All the guys pour out of the boarding house in response and struggle to get the beast off the obnoxious guy. Jerry watches from his bedroom window, transfixed, seemingly hypnotized by the scene unfolding below.

The movie that kicked off Burns' remarkable career, *The Texas Chain Saw Massacre*.

A gunshot brings the uproar to a close. Woody has shot and killed the huge dog. Ike is pissed and shouts at Woody while the others carry the injured and whimpering Toad to a vehicle to get him medical attention.

It's night again at mongrel house. After a few drinks, Ike knocks on Sharon's door. They went out a few times and he took it a lot more seriously than she did. Sharon tells him to take a hike. Ike blames this rejection on the new guy, Ken.

Somewhere in the darkened house, moonlight streams in through the shutters. A hand reaches for a doorknob, then hesitates.

In the morning, Turquoise, the 'Earth-Mother' of the group, is nursing Toad back to health with some super nutritious blue cornmeal mush. Woody intrudes. Luring them down to the basement, he introduces them to his new puppy. Woody shows no real affection for the animal. He only bought the dog because it'll grow up to be a huge animal. He did it to piss off Ike.

When Ike learns about the pup, he goes on a rant, bending Ken's ear.

Sharon warms up to Ken, since he's the closest thing to a likable person living in this little community. She gives him a pendant, just as she'd given Jerry the

Foo Dogs. Jerry raps on Ken's door and is surprised to find Sharon in his room. They encourage him to join them, but he quickly dismisses himself. Ike's drinking again and nursing a grudge against Ken. When he sees Sharon leaving Ken's room, he seethes with anger.

We enter a highly subjective sequence. Once again, the moonlit wall. And again, the hand reaches for the doorknob. This time the door opens. In the hallway is the snarling mongrel. Jerry jerks awake. A dream? His deep-seated anxieties are tormenting him.

Ike can't let go of his animosity toward Ken. He turns to his mortal enemy, Woody, to come up with a plan to bring Ken down a notch.

First, they slip some concert tickets under Sharon's door with a note saying the tickets are from her latest admirer. Later, Woody pretends to be Ken's pal, telling him Sharon is waiting in his bedroom. When Ken goes to check it out, there is indeed someone…or something…in Ken's bed. Assuming it is the lovely young woman Ken slips out of his clothes and moves to join her, but then his nose is assaulted by an awful smell. It's not a beautiful girl in the bed, but the dead body of Ike's dog Brute. By this time, they have locked Ken in the room and are playing loud wargame sound effects.

Ken tries to switch on the old lamp in his room, but there's a puddle of water on the floor. It's been previously established that the lamp has a short in it. Poor Ken is electrocuted. The pranksters hear his screams and are terrified to see the result of their practical joke.

Robert A. Burns and friend.
Photo courtesy of Tim Harden

Leon stumbles onto the aftermath and wants to call the cops immediately, but Ike and Mitch insist on doing some damage control. They want to remove any evidence of their practical joke before the arrival of any authorities.

Sharon realizes she was lured out of the house by someone for some unknown purpose. When she returns, the power is just coming back on in the old house. She finds Ike and Woody trying to cover their tracks. She realizes their trick has resulted in her new friend's death.

Jerry returns home shortly after Sharon and stumbles onto the rotting corpse of Brute, which Ike and Woody have dumped in the back yard. He gags, dashes into the house and soon learns Ken is dead. He freaks out even worse than Sharon. Ken was pretty much his only friend.

Jerry is convinced that Ike and Woody killed Ken intentionally. Sharon believes it was a prank gone bad. They both know they need to get out of this house at the earliest possibility. That night, Jerry has the same dream. He opens the door and the angry mongrel pounces. Waking up, he creeps toward his door, but he's afraid to open it.

Sharon makes arrangements to leave the house the next morning. Jerry's unable to leave because he's broke. Maybe after the publishers pay him for the work he's done. He refuses Sharon's offer of a loan. Her taxi arrives and she has to go, leaving Jerry to fend for himself in his own personal hell.

Woody, Ike and Turquoise are at each other's throats now. Like most conspirators under pressure, they are feeling the pinch and eager to cover their own respective asses.

Jerry cowers in his bedroom. Something, neither mongrel nor human, is growling outside his door.

When Woody goes to feed his puppy, he finds the small dog eviscerated in the basement. Woody blames Ike right away, but Leon thinks he's jumping to conclusions. Jerry tries to tell them that something big and strange was in the house the night before. Woody is convinced of Ike's guilt and, true to his nature, begins plotting revenge. Jerry puts the hard sell on Leon about the unseen intruder, but Leon thinks his fellow tenant has gone 'round the bend.

Robert A. Burns helped create some of the most memorable horror flicks of his generation, like **The Hills Have Eyes.**

Leon warns Ike to avoid Woody while he's in such a volatile state. Leon spends the night out on the town and comes home stumbling-drunk. From the shadows, he hears the same half-belch, half-growl that's been plaguing Jerry. An unseen attacker besets the defenseless Ike. Once he's unconscious the growling apparition drags him into the shadows.

Watering her plants, Turquoise discovers Ike's corpse beneath a hedge. She screams for Woody.

The cops are called and a policeman (Dennis Hill) wants to interview Jerry about the strange sounds he's been hearing.

Finally, we get our second glimpse of the "name" talent. Aldo Ray as Mr. Bouchard shows up while the cops are there and throws a fit. He's understandably annoyed by the dying trend among his renters and wants everyone thrown out. He gives Woody until the end of the month to clear out, along with the rest of the tenants.

Sharon calls and offers Jerry temporary quarters in her new place. He doesn't want to impose, but it certainly sounds better than his present circumstances. After viewing her new digs, Jerry and Sharon return to the old house to find his bedroom in shambles. Sharon gives him a back rub to calm him down. Jerry thinks the phantom mongrel has been in his room, but Sharon is convinced it was Woody. The back rub makes Jerry fall asleep. It is then that Sharon is perplexed to find the necklace she had given Ken in Jerry's bed.

Jerry wakes up alone after the sun has set. He goes to the kitchen for a beverage and hears a voice whispering his name. It seems to come from the basement. Investigating, he stumbles upon the corpse of his old tormentor, Woody.

Jerry wakes up screaming. Was it just a dream?

Leon and Toad listen to Jerry's frantic, half-coherent ravings, then leave Turquoise in charge of their distraught roomie while they investigate the basement. There's no corpse, but they find signs that the door leading to the basement from outside has been jimmied. The cops return but find nothing.

After the police leave, Leon passes out tranquilizers from his own private stash.

As Leon and Toad secure the basement door with hammer and nails, Mr. Bouchard shows up unexpectedly giving them a start. He gives all the tenants an ultimatum; out in the next twelve hours or else he'll return with a shotgun.

When Turquoise awakens from her drug-aided slumber, she hears a growl. There in the disarrayed attic room, she finds Woody with his throat torn out. Perched on top of the corpse is the growling Jerry, teeth drenched with blood.

Leon hears the commotion and runs upstairs. There he finds Jerry cornering the terrified Turquoise. Seizing a nearby tire tool, Leon attacks Jerry. The two men fight their way downstairs and into the kitchen while Turquoise cowers in her closet.

When the noise dies down, Turquoise makes a lengthy, suspenseful trek down to the telephone on the ground floor. She dials for help, but before anyone can answer her call Jerry attacks.

A couple of police officers arrive at the place at Bouchard's behest. They poke around outside, but receive no answer at the door. Inside, the panting Jerry is hunkered down over the body of Turquoise.

Cover art for **Mongrel**.

After the cops leave, Toad returns in his groovy little Metropolitan car. He's been in the process of moving his stuff out. He sees the phone on the floor, but makes no effort to set it right. As he wanders through the house, Sharon tries to call. All she gets is a busy signal.

Toad retrieves a box from the basement and is beset by the snarling, semi-human Jerry. He tries to run, but I think we all know how this encounter will end. After a savage struggle, Toad is impaled on an iron spike protruding from the stone wall.

Sharon comes searching for her friend Jerry. She knocks on his bedroom door. Jerry bursts out and grabs her. But, it's the old Jerry, the timid, fearful Jerry. He's freshened up and brushed all the blood out of his teeth. He drags her in the room and warns her the beast is still somewhere in the house. She comforts him and he finally finds the courage to assert himself romantically. When Sharon rebuffs him, he explodes, accusing her of leading him on.

Looking in Jerry's bathroom, Sharon gets shock. He's redecorated. In red. Screaming, she realizes the truth about her friend. She slams the door in his face and makes a run for it. She races down the stairs, but Jerry takes a short cut by leaping from the floor above. Cut off, she diverts into the basement, throwing an old washing machine in front of the door. She sees Toad standing there and thinks she's found help, but well, you know …

Sharon cannot escape. The door's been nailed shut. Screaming, cowering in a corner, Sharon prepares to meet her doom. Jerry advances. A roaring boom echoes through the basement. It's Bouchard who has returned, as promised, with his shotgun. The human/mongrel is down for the count. "You okay, lady?" he asks the whimpering Sharon. The bewildered Bouchard says, "God damnedest thing I ever saw."

Fade to black. Roll credits.

When I returned to Fort Worth, Texas from Santa Barbara, after studying film production at Brooks Institute, I worked for a time as a printer. While I cast about

One of Robert A. Burns' art direction achievements, *Re-Animator.*

looking for some sort of way to make a living in film or video production I kept my fascination with cinematic schlock alive by interviewing people for a book I hoped to publish someday. (Someday was a long time coming.)

Gradually, I developed contacts with some of the guys at Allied Film Lab. These were folks who'd been around since the 1960s. Since the Dallas film community was not an especially large pond, everyone knew everyone else. Through the film lab connections, I was able to get names and phone numbers of people I wanted to interview. Naturally, I set my sights on talking with Tobe Hooper, but that never came to be. I was, however, referred to Mary Church. She was gracious enough to grant me a phone interview (sometime around 1982) and offered her reminiscences. It was Mary who put me onto Robert A. Burns. She knew him from *Texas Chain Saw Massacre* and later worked on a film he directed called *Mongrel*. I certainly knew his work as an art director/production designer and after talking with Ms. Church, I felt like he was someone I should interview. I cast my inquiries out there, but came up empty-handed. Time passed and before long I was making my own movies, spending much less time gathering data on the films of others.

Robert A. Burns passed away in 2004. I never met him or spoke to him over the phone. In late 2016, when this book project began to coalesce, I recalled Mr.

Burns and tried to seek him out. I was saddened by the knowledge of his death and surprised that he'd gone without my realizing it. Michael H. Price, film historian and multi-talented savant, suggested I contact Robert's brother, C. Ross Burns, via Facebook. I did and found him to be a gracious and cooperative contact. Ross made me aware of the fact that his brother's website: *Robert-A-Burns.com* was archived on the *Wayback Machine*. I spent a few very pleasant hours exploring the entries there. Afterwards, I almost felt like I knew the man. Certainly, I recognized him as a kindred spirit. What I had never known was that he was the foremost authority on Rondo Hatton of the *Creeper* films. Wow!

Robert A. Burns with Tobe Hooper and others.
Photo courtesy of Tim Harden

Truly ground-breaking, iconic indie horror films don't come along that often. Rarely do directors have more than one in their oeuvre. In the arena of design, make-up, effects – all the stuff that makes these little films stand out – Burns' credits read like a who's who of notable horror. Titles include: *Texas Chain Saw Massacre* (1974), *The Hills Have Eyes* (1977), *Re-Animator* (1985), *The Howling* (1981) and *Tourist Trap* (1979)!

I've prepared sections from Robert A. Burns' website for inclusion here. Since everything he posted has a very laid-back, conversational tone, it reads almost like an interview. It's only fitting that his contribution to Texas indie cinema be preserved.

*On Directing*

RB: I'm very proud of the fact that all my projects have come in on time and under budget because of careful planning. They have met with varying degrees of success or failure, hence the term, "That's showbiz."

*Mongrel* received limited release on home video because of a variety of marketing choices and unfortunate timing. It is notable as the feature debut of Mitch Pileggi, "Skinner" on *X-Files*.

*The Man Who Loved Inflatable Women* was a parody pilot for the Playboy Channel. Unfortunately, they ceased all original programming of this sort just as we finished.

*Scream Test* was an experimental black comedy similar to *The Blair Witch Project* in format. A combination of factors led to the film not being what I wanted it to be and it never found a market.

*Out of your Tree!* was described by the NY Times News Service as, "One of the most universally appealing productions ever to grace the original-for-video market." It has sold very well for years, both domestically and in some international markets.

*Mausoleum* poster art.

*Signs of Life* is an entertaining guide to archaeological conservation, funded by the National Park Service. It still sells today.

(Author's note: Prior to his death, Robert had been working very hard for several months on a thriller he called *The Legend of 80-foot John*. In one of his website entries he commented, "I hope to shoot it this winter in Central Texas." Unfortunately, that was not to be.)

*On Mongrel*

RB: I got the idea while working on *Hills* which, like *Chain Saw*, is set in a remote place where isolation can cause madness. I wanted to show the same isolation and madness could occur in town. A young man living in a communal house, psychologically becomes that which he fears most – a killer dog. This is the actual psychosis of lycanthropy, the basis for the werewolf tales.

John Jenkins, a rare book dealer and gambler, raised the $300,000 budget to shoot on 35mm. The entire shoot took place in one house with a very good cast and crew. It was smoothly shot from specific storyboards and the final product looked very good with some genuine fright moments.

By the time we finished editing, however, Jenkins had lost interest in all his businesses. We had an interested theatrical distributor, but instead of putting up a small amount to pay for posters, John chose to make a deal straight to home video. The video market at that time was small, so even with a very good deal, the budget was not fully recovered. A short while later the home market skyrocketed and the film was repackaged and re-released, but we saw no more money.

Mitch Pileggi went on to star in *Shocker* (1989) before finding fame in *X-Files*. Even though he was playing such a jerk, he is such a nice guy that I had to explain to him the art of sarcasm which was totally foreign to him.

*On Scream Test*

RB: This was supposed to represent an unedited home videotape that turns out to be an audition, effects test, and shooting of a sci-fi film made by two young aspiring brothers. As it plays (turned on and off by them or others in it) we see that they are inadvertently killing off the participants. Eventually, we discover that all the offices, labs and sets are merely homemade walls set up in their attic where their mother keeps them protected from the world.

Since there was no editing within the scenes (except for a few hidden edits) we could shoot the whole film in 12 days, again carefully storyboarded. The concept of having the camera an active part of the script worked well. At times, it was picked up and carried around, knocked over, dropped, etc. All the while it was still running. Some of the effects were quite funny.

One problem arose with my strict adherence to the concept. The sets were supposed to look homemade, but until the gimmick was revealed they were just cheap-looking and by the time of the revelation it didn't matter. Also, the lead actor (who had played the lead in *Mongrel* so well) resisted all direction, making for an uneven performance. It turned out he had a mistaken idea about his deal, but never revealed this until the next to last day of shooting.

Another Burns oddity, **Tourist Trap**.

This was aimed at the made-for-home-video market which was red hot when we began. By the time we finished, though, that market had vanished and the final result was too disappointing to market otherwise. Chris Bonno who played one of the brothers moved to L.A. and has appeared in film and TV in comedy roles.

*On The Hills Have Eyes*

RB: Two years after *Chain Saw* I got a call from Peter Locke. He had gone to extraordinary lengths to track me down in Austin since I wasn't working in film. Also, *Chain Saw* was in the midst of lawsuits out the wazzoo (including one I had filed) and nobody was talking to anyone else. Anyhow, Peter was insistent on my being art director of a film he was producing with Wes Craven.

The design was to be a major part of the original story, but by the time we started filming, the scope had been narrowed considerably. The role of the art direction had diminished drastically. I was pleased to have been included in consultations of how to heighten the fright while shooting was in progress.

When we scouted the desert outside Victorville, California, we found perfect locations that were so desolate and dried up that even the thought of anyone living there was frightening. Of course, as always happens in film planning, by the time we shot, record rains had come through and everything was green and inviting.

Although it was a lot of work in a demanding location for not a lot of money, it was a pleasant situation and renewed my interest in working on film. Of all the films I have worked on, I consider *Hills* the best all round in terms of not only fright, but character and drama.

Wes Craven, of course, went on to become WES CRAVEN! Peter Locke is one of the most consistent producers of film and television (Kushner/Locke). Dee Wallace has proven equally resilient with credits including *Cujo* (1983), *ET* (1982) and *The Howling* (1981) which I did as well.

*On Film Designs*

RB: Designing for films was simply an extension of commercial art, at which I had been self-employed in Austin for years. *Chain Saw* made me quite well-known, but it was not a pleasant experience, so I didn't do another film until *Hills* a couple of years later.

On location with the final scenes of **The Texas Chain Saw Massacre**. Photo courtesy of Tim Harden

*Hills* was a lot more pleasant, so I ended up going to L.A. for 2 ½ years where I did several films. A few, while far from classics, have endured through the years, including *Tourist Trap* (1979), *Microwave Massacre* (1983) and Rudy Ray Moore's *Disco Godfather* (1979). Immediately after *The Howling* I moved back to Austin, but worked back and forth on several films, including *Re-Animator* (1985).

While designing *Confessions of a Serial*

*Killer* (1985), the producer and director decided I was the psycho to play the lead role, not having any idea I had ever acted before or that my college degree was in acting. While much preferring to produce projects of my own, I still do design and effects work when it arises.

On December 7, 2016 I interviewed Robert's brother, C. Ross Burns. The interview is presented here in its entirety.

*CRB*: I have a couple of fun stories about "Grannie."[i]

*TS*: Great, I'd love to hear them.

*CRB*: At the time Bob made *Chain Saw* he had his own commercial art shop. It was called the RH Factor. For Rondo Hatton, not the blood type. He took the bone floor lamp and put that in the corner of his office, like in a waiting area. He had Grannie sitting there for several years. Anybody who came into the shop and was looking for a place to sit had to encounter that.[ii]

*TS*: Where was RH Factor located?

*CRB*: The original one was on 12th Street just down from the old Austin High School. There was a little strip mall that had a hangout called the Maroon Mill in it. When he moved into the place he discovered a bunch of duck decoys in the back. He built a barrier out of studs and chicken wire with a row of these ducks across the top. There was a big sign that said, "Office Protected by Rabid Ducks." (laughs) Later he moved onto 7th or 8th Street for a while.

About a year after Bob's death I got a call from the Bob Bullock Museum of Texas History. Big important stuff. The young man said, "Mr. Burns, we are about to exhibit what we believe is the most significant article of Texas History we have ever displayed at the Bob Bullock Museum." I think, *Holy crap, why are you talking to me?* It was "Grannie." (laughs) They were putting together a display on Texas in the movies. (laughs) This is a place that has displayed the Travis letter from the Alamo. The fact that they were so proud of "Grannie" made me worry a little bit about the folks who take care of our cultural heritage!

*TS*: He may have been yanking your chain. I'm sure even those people have a sense of humor.

*CRB*: I thought that was great.

*TS*: It is great. How old was Bob when he began demonstrating creativity in the weird direction?

*CRB*: About one. (laughs) He was always creative. He was the artistic mem-

---

[i] "Grannie" is the affectionate nickname given to the skeletal female remains Robert Burns created for the original Texas Chain Saw Massacre.

[ii] At the time of this writing, "Grannie" was in the possession of Tom Rainone, art dealer and filmmaker from Arlington, Texas. When I produced my first feature I rented camera equipment from Mr. Rainone. I intended to interview him for this chapter, but as I was writing it I learned that he had died unexpectedly on December 7, 2016.

ber of the family. As children, we'd put on plays out of storybooks and what have you. He was always very meticulous.

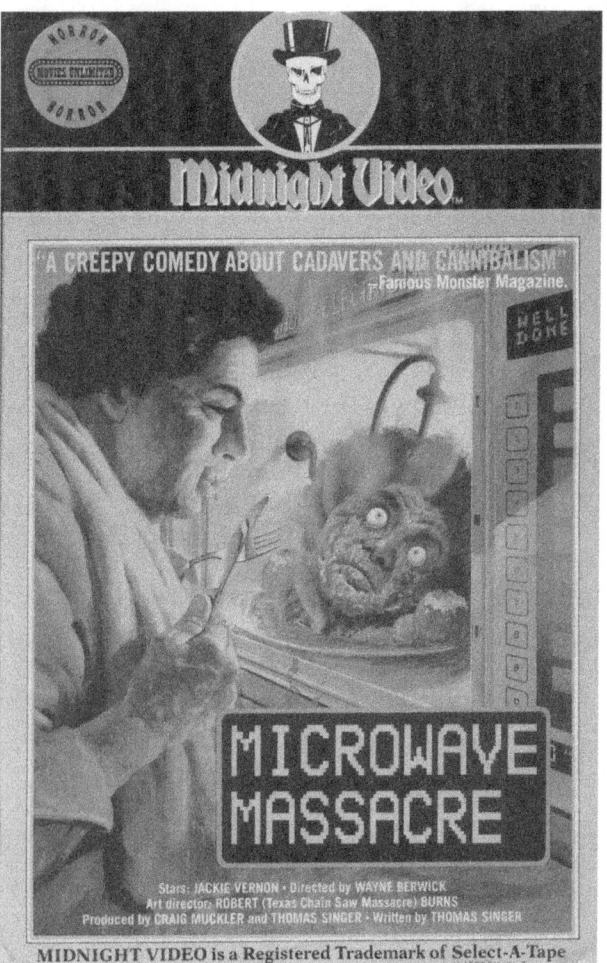

Original art for **Microwave Massacre**.

One time we were visiting friends who lived near a wheat field. He went into the field and gathered a handful of wheat. He brought that wheat home and made his own little loaf of bread about a half inch long. (laughs)

His degree from UT was in acting. He did the commercial art to make a living initially.

There were four of us growing up. I'm the youngest and Bob was second youngest, but he was six years older than I was. The other three were grouped closer together. I was kind of the afterthought.

Three of us attended Austin High and we were all members of the Thespian group there called the Red Dragons. Bob was going to appear in a "mellerdrammer" they were putting on for the Fall Festival. He played a Southern officer and he made a very elaborate set of red mutton chop whiskers. He meticulously applied one hair at a time. If he decided to do something, he was very seriously into it.

His movie work all came up after *Chain Saw*. He really didn't want to get back into the movies. Because he had such a bad experience. *Chain Saw* took longer than they had planned. He was making his living with the commercial art and because of the delays he missed the back-to-school sales. He had a very lean winter. After back-to-school, the local commercial artists didn't really get any more work until Christmas. The commercial art he was doing was for the big department stores around town.

He was always doing unusual things. For a while he was a clown for childrens' parties. At UT they did a James Thurber play called *Thirteen Clocks*, a children's play. He created, out of balsa wood and what-have-you, thirteen clocks to hang out in the lobby. Crazy looking clocks. They were all set to five minutes before midnight because that was in the story.

If the clock struck midnight the Baddie would vanish. He just did these very detailed, creative kinds of things.

*TS*: What do you think of his performance in *Confessions of a Serial Killer*?

Promo art from the theatrical release of **Re-animator**.

*CRB*: (groans) It was creepy! He was a wonderful actor. At UT he was in a Chekov play called *The Cherry Orchard*, about the modernization of old-style Russia. In a summer house, the upper crust are all being waited on by this ancient servant named Firs. Bob played Firs. He created a makeup process for himself that took four hours. He created a head piece with long stringy hair, a beard, a neck piece. You know a wobbly-looking neck piece. Fred, our slightly older brother took a series of photos showing all the steps in the process. At the end of the play Firs is left in the house in the cherry orchard and dies on stage. One of our cousins said, "Oh, he died so wonderfully!" (laughs)

He was a terrific actor. He was already on-board to do Art Direction for *Confessions of a Serial Killer*. The director was asking around, "Who's crazy enough to do this part?" They decided on Bob.

He didn't feel that his co-star was up to the challenge of being a good foil for him. Just this offhand performance. Bob had a very good review in the New York Times for that film. Shortly after that he got tired of hauling couches up and down stairs, so he decided to work on his acting. It just didn't quite take off. Part of it was an ego thing. Craven had looked Bob up. Joe Dante came looking for Bob. Stuart Gordon was told Bob is the go-to guy. Because these guys came looking for him, as Art Director he was an integral part of the movie. As an actor, he's going to cattle calls for bit parts.

Irma P. Hall, Bill Atherton and Bob were all inducted into the Southeast Texas Film Makers Hall of Fame. It was after Bob's death and I went to represent the family. I talked with Irma Hall. She'd started out as a teacher and then went on to little roles in industrial films. She built her career from the ground up. Since Bob had started out at the top, it was hard for him to come back down. If you understand what I'm trying to say.

He was supposed to be in a scene with Clint Eastwood in the film *A Perfect World* (1993). They shot some nice coverage of him, but it ended up not making the final cut. Bob's response was, "It's a very imperfect world!"

*TS*: Anything you'd like to say about *Mongrel*?

*CRB*: I get a kick out of *Mongrel* because almost all the props in it are his, things he had in the house. The vehicles are his. That film was covered pretty well in the Austin paper at the time. They interviewed Aldo Ray. He said he'd be happy to work with Bob any time. It always tickled me to see his stuff in the film – the infamous *Deep Throat* pinball machine – and other things. Things that were in Bob's house all the time. So much of it was just his stuff.

I think that's the film. Bob said the house they used was about to be renovated and the owner told them they could do whatever they wanted as long as they didn't weaken any load-bearing walls. So, they had carte blanche.

I went to school with the Winfree girl. She was in the Red Dragons with me. The blonde in that film. I'm not sure, I never asked her, but I think she might've been the State Librarian's daughter. That was all local people. My understanding is that John H. Jenkins III was the moneybags for that production. He was an author, publisher and rare book dealer. He and Bob were good friends. They shared a love of murder mysteries. One of their favorite games was to speculate on how you could commit suicide and make it look like a murder committed by persons unknown. Considering the circumstances of Jenkins' death, Bob thought he pulled it off.

Jenkins was the leading rare book and document person selling to libraries, museums and collectors in Texas. Another collector died and the widow gave Jenkins a couple of boxes of documents which Jenkins accepted at face value. It turned out they were forgeries and he'd sold them to some places. His documents business took a nosedive and he was about to go bankrupt. His death preceded the bankruptcy filing by a couple of days. Because he was dead the bankruptcy couldn't proceed and his family got to inherit.

The executive producer of *Mongrel* called me a couple years after Bob's death. She was not happy to learn that the film had already been put out on DVD. Some Mom and Pop shop evidently did it. She'd been approached with a legitimate deal for a DVD release, but these bootleggers had already done it.

Sometimes he did just too good a job.

*TS*: How's that?

*CRB*: For instance, on *Re-Animator*. That was Stuart Gordon's very first film. Everyone told Gordon to go to Bob. Bob told him, "Yeah, I'll take care of it." Most people will give you some sketches or some idea of what they plan to do. This worried Stuart a little bit. For that film, they used one of the oldest soundstages in Hollywood. It was the old Essanay stage, going back to the silent days, that's Buster Keaton era stuff. He built a four room, four-wall set. It was over 1600 square feet. The camera never had to be taken off the dolly. The camera could go anywhere it was needed. Gordon was amazed that it included a working elevator. That just tickled him to no end. There were parts of that set you could've just put your hand through. But Gordon said the parts where bodies were going to be flying up against the wall, they were sturdy and they withstood it. He and Bob had looked at morgues in Philadelphia and L.A. As I said this was a huge set and very well done. Bob had colleagues in Hollywood who'd ask, "What hospital let you use their basement?" He did such a good job that even professionals were convinced it wasn't just a set.

That was what Bob wanted. He needed things to be as realistic as possible. He used to say when they did *Chain Saw* he didn't want folks to ask, "Where did they get actors to play these parts?" He wanted them to think, "Where did they get these people!" He wanted it to be grounded in such a realistic world that the surreal horror would stand out.

*TS*: How did Bob initially hook up with Tobe Hooper?

*CRB*: Tobe had a student film called *Eggshells* (1969). Bob helped him with the art for the advertising campaign. Bob was doing a lot of work with student publications on the UT campus. They had a magazine called the Texas Ranger. It was a humorous magazine from the 1880s until 1972. They decided it needed to be serious, they couldn't have a humor magazine. They changed it to a literary magazine that had one issue, then disappeared. So, Bob was known on campus. He did a lot of silk screen posters for musical groups like Double Trouble. You can see some of those on his website. So, Tobe used him for that, then came back when he wanted to do a feature film.

Gunnar Hansen did a neat book called *Chain Saw Confidential* (Chronicle Books 2013). He puts together everybody's stories. It's the ultimate *Chain Saw* book.

# GLEN COBURN

## BLOODSUCKERS FROM OUTER SPACE (1984)

A farmer (Dan Gallion) is up early caring for his livestock. An enigmatic wind assaults the man. Moments later, overcome by nausea, the farmer vomits out all his blood. This annoys his horse and the animal decides to return to the barn. After a brief period of unconsciousness, the farmer revives, full of vim and vigor. He has become our first *Bloodsucker from Outer Space*.

Local Reporter Jeff Rhodes (Thom Meyers) shows up to cover a double homicide. Two bluish corpses in a pasture are attended by law enforcement personnel. Rhodes begins snapping pics, but is pre-empted by his friend, a police officer named Sam (Christopher Heldman.) The young reporter is grossed out by the brutal scene. An older policeman (Charles Coburn, the director's dad) unperturbed by the murders, gnaws on a barbecued rib and opines that this is nothing compared to the axe murders of 1962.

The owner of the property where the bodies were discovered is a yahoo named Buford. It's his conjecture that a couple of "devil-worshipping homos from Hatchet Creek" committed the crime.

> "One of the critical things to realize while watching *Bloodsuckers from Outer Space* is that it's a comedy. It isn't the type of bad movie that *Troll 2* is, in which the cast and crew intended to make a sincere horror movie. There is an obvious parody of horror, but at the same time it has such an awkward sense of humor that it overflows with the charm of a bad movie. Which is an interesting distinction, because horror spoofs, especially these days, are often so over-the-top and obnoxious that they lose any sort of charm. But in the case of *Bloodsuckers from Outer Space*, most of the humor is so awkward, and falls so flat, that it has the appeal of cult classic bad movies. So, for anyone who knows how to enjoy a good bad movie, this is absolutely one you'll want to see. And since Halloween is now right around the corner, I'll point out that this would make a damn good party movie."
>
> --*thebloodsuckinggeek.wordpress.com*, Jonny Dead, September 1, 2013

After sending Buford on his way, Sam confides to Jeff that the victims were "sucked." No, it's not a kinky sex thing. They were sucked dry of blood. Sam's good at math and he calculates there's at least six quarts of blood missing from the crime scene. He wants Jeff to keep this thing under wraps until the police department has more info.

> "*Bloodsuckers from Outer Space* is a parody and homage to many great classics of the sci-fi and horror genres. *Psycho, Body Snatchers, Night of the Living Dead* and even *Dr. Strangelove* all get a poke throughout the flick. The movie even breaks the fourth wall plenty of times to remind us that it knows what it is, and it doesn't give a damn because they're trying to entertain."
> --*dreadcentral.com*, Kryten Syxx, May 24, 2008

> "Completely comprised of static shots, *Bloodsuckers from Outer Space* was written in three days, and subsequently shot over a series of weekends in and around Dallas, Texas. Intended as a spoof of the conventional sci-fi films that were the bread and butter of drive-ins across the country. Glen Coburn, the film's writer/director, describes the movie best in an interview for the reunion documentary found on this release: 'The movie is in color, in focus and you can hear it.' Well said."
> --*dvddrive-in.com*, Jason McElreath

The cops may be clueless, but scientists Ralph Rhodes (Glen Coburn,) B.J. Barton (Wayne Green) and Jeri Jett (Kris Nicolau-Sharpley) at the high-tech facility, Research City, have one of the bloodsuckers in custody and they're working feverishly to unlock the secret of this bizarre interstellar ailment. It seems one of the scientists of Research City, Dr. Pace (John Webb), has himself succumbed to bloodsuckeritis.

Jeff Rhodes takes time out of his busy schedule to visit his Aunt Kate (Billie Keller) and Uncle Joe (Robert Bradeen.) These two are concerned about Jeff's future and disdainful of the wasteful use of government money they attribute to his brother Ralph, over at Research City. If Jeff doesn't agree to become a farmer like his uncle, he's going to lose his inheritance. They give the young fellow until dinner time to make a decision.

Driving away from the farmhouse, Jeff Rhodes is at an all-time emotional low. Then he has a blow-out. Could things get worse?

Yeah, there's no spare.

There is a tire tool, however, and Jeff vents his frustration by smashing all the glass on the old Dodge he's driving. Not a productive choice, but he seems to find it satisfying.

A cute girl in a nice car catches him savaging the Dodge and offers him a ride. Things could be looking up. The girl is Julie (Laura Ellis), a fugitive from her pampered life in Dallas, Texas. Yeah, things are looking up. Julie's got a tank of Nitrous Oxide in the back seat and she doesn't mind sharing.

On location with **Bloodsuckers**.

A hard-core badass named General Sanders (Dennis Letts) barges into Research City. He's not interested in the scientific approach suggested by Rhodes, Jett and Barton. He wants to use weapons. The sooner the better. Offended, the three scientists leave the General to stew in his own juices.

Jeff and Julie make it to Jeff's place and he invites her to take a look at his stamp collection. She consents. Inside they get to know each other a bit better. Julie teaches him the universal answer to every question . . . and it's got nothing to do with stamp collecting.

Jeri and B.J. decide to get boozed up, but Ralph Rhodes is fixated on the bloodsucker enigma. Checking in on Dr. Pace, he finds the captive bloodsucker unresponsive and seemingly dead. Time for a little spontaneous dissection. But, the joke's on Rhodes. Pace was playing possum and soon he's redecorating the lab with Rhodes' blood.

Julie drives Jeff to the planned dinner at Uncle Joe and Aunt Kate's place. Joe is distracted and behaving peculiarly when they arrive. Lying on his back beneath an archaic piece of farm machinery, he is fascinated with its design. Jeff thinks he's snapped and may have murdered Kate. His worst fears may be true. The living room is drenched in blood. But, then, his aunt calls cheerfully from the kitchen. Jeff and Julie discover that she, too, has succumbed to the bloodsucker infection. They do not linger for her explanation of why the house is such a mess.

In the yard, the young couple are cut off by an aggressive Uncle Joe, intent on forcing them to join the bloodsucker club. He just wants his nephew to know the thrill, the ecstasy of sucking. Jeff becomes assertive and engages Joe in a bit of Kung Fu fighting. He doesn't play fair, however. Spotting a machete nearby, Jeff uses it to remove one of Joe's appendages, leading to the most highly touted line of dialog in the movie, "You cut off my fuckin' arm!"

Jeff and Julie have lost their appetites; this dinner thing is not the pleasant event they'd hoped for. They dive into Julie's car, leaving a waving Aunt Kate and a befuddled Uncle Joe standing in their driveway. That settles it. Now Jeff knows for sure farming is not for him.

The two young fugitives stop at a random farmhouse. While Jeff goes inside to make a phone call and pilfer cookies, Julie checks the property out. Seems this is the home of the original bloodsucker, the guy who puked his guts out before the opening credits. Until now, there have been no humans to prey upon, so farmer guy has been ripping the throats out of his sheep. Sheep are fine, but to this ghoul Julie looks a bit yummier. He moves in for the kill.

When Jeff exits the house, he hears a familiar sound – moans and cries from Julie – is she getting it on with some other guy already? No, she's fending off the bloodsucker. Jeff grabs the farmer's chainsaw and decapitates the guy.

The enterprising couple hit the road again. Where can they go? These things are everywhere! Their only hope is Research City.

Three drunk scientists are enjoying themselves. That is, until they discover the gruesome corpse of Ralph Rhodes. Dr. Pace gets the drop on them and insists on a friendly discussion.

The only person in this film who really knows the score is Norman the janitor at Research City. Unfortunately, Jeff and Julie do not heed his warnings, preferring instead to delve further into this weirdness.

Following mysterious noises, the young couple discover Dr. Pace giving a talk in the lecture hall. He's making some nice points, but his words are falling on deaf ears as the audience is composed entirely of dead scientists. The Doc puts the hard sell on Jeff. They want him to play quarterback on the bloodsucker team. Jeff's got a problem with authority. He refuses the offer and drags Julie away from the bloodsucker pep rally.

On an isolated country highway, Julie's car runs out of gas. They hoof it cross country in search of fuel. They find an abandoned gas station. While Julie fills a can with gasoline, Jeff calls his friend and confidante, Officer Sam.

We're an hour into the movie and I was wondering what happened to the gratuitous boobs. They show up just in the nick o' time thanks to Sam's girlfriend, Pam (Samantha Walker.) Jeff's call interrupts a serious game of twister. When Sam learns Jeff is on his way over, he brings the call to a close and moves the sexy game to the shower.

A bloodsucker throws a vanishing dummy at Jeff and Julie, so they steal a car parked at the station and head for Sam's place. A whole flock of bloodsuckers tries to stop them, but Jeff puts the pedal to the metal and disperses them.

Meanwhile, the all too familiar bloodsucker breeze descends on Sam's house, interrupting sexy time in the shower and converting Sam and Pam into you-know-what.

Some expendable army troops explore the bloodsucker-laden community. Skillfully maneuvering past the gas station, they find the dummy is still missing from the sidewalk. Soon bloodsuckers are emerging from every nook and cranny. Lured into the street by a fairly seductive female bloodsucker, three soldiers are swarmed by the entire bloodsucking population.

On the way to Sam's, Jeff swings by Julie's car to grab the Nitrous.

Sam and Pam corner the couple in the house. They go to great lengths to explain the benefits of bloodsucking, but Jeff is immature and stubborn. Julie interrupts another incipient Kung Fu sequence, cold cocks Pam and leads the retreat from the house.

Our president (Pat Paulsen) is hard at work in the oval office when he receives an urgent phone call from General Sanders. Sanders begs, pleads, bullies and badgers until the prez agrees to let him use the nukes. Consent is given and the president returns his attention to more important matters.

Despondent, hopeless and clueless in terms of where to go, Jeff and Julie turn to their only real friend—the Nitrous canister. At that very instant the bloodsucker wind engulfs their car. Desperately, they roll up the windows. The Nitrous Oxide neutralizes the alien lifeforce.

Mankind is saved!

Unaware that an alternate solution has been found, General Sanders enters the nuclear missile launch codes.

Jeff and Julie love one another passionately on the lonely Texas prairie. Their love lights up this brave new world . . .*or is it the thermonuclear explosion?*

As General Sanders rehearses his future conversation with the president, Major Hood informs him the nuke exploded sixty miles from the nearest bloodsucker activity. It's not a total loss, however, as they did eliminate a Methodist Church camp.

So, life gets back to normal. Old bloodsuckers exchange morning greetings. Kid bloodsuckers toss the football around. Redneck bloodsuckers in pickup trucks cruise small town avenues in search of bloodsucker poon. As they say in schlockville, all's well that ends in hell.

One chilly mid-winter morning at Productions West Communications, I was alone in the building, sipping coffee and pecking away at the keys of my electric typewriter, when I heard someone come in. Turns out it was Mike Minton.

Mike and Jess Sherman shared an office at the front of the building, so it was infrequent that he and I just hung out and shot the bull. This morning was different, since we were the only ones there. He joined me in my office, asking what was going on. I filled him in on whatever project I was working on and asked what he'd been up to.

He told me he'd been on an audition and was hopeful he'd land a part. It was some (typical for the time) story of some young people camping out near a river who run afoul of sinister forces. Mike was upbeat as he spoke, enthusiastic about the film. As the conversation continued, he mentioned in passing this film was a cut above some other thing he'd been asked to audition for, a super cheapie called *Bloodsuckers from Outer Space*…

Shriek Show DVD cover for *Bloodsuckers from Outer Space*.

Now, I was interested! This was right up my alley! Why was I only now hearing about it? With a laugh, Mike shook his head, "Yeah, I should've mentioned it. I forget that's sort of your thing."

Italy embraces **Bloodsuckers**.

I pestered Mike several times until he supplied me with contact info for the folks doing the movie with the delightfully cheesy title. I made a few calls and eventually connected with a young guy named Glen Coburn. No, he wasn't related to James Coburn, Charles Coburn or even the Coburn family with the cafeteria on the north side of Fort Worth. But he was friendly and willing to talk.

Not long afterwards, I met with Glen at a restaurant on Lower Greenville. It was early spring, but weather was pleasant enough that we could sit outside on the patio. Our conversation touched upon many of the same topics you'll find elsewhere in this chapter; Universal's horror films, Hammer, Corman and, of course, the overwhelming drive to make movies. I recorded the conversation and later transcribed it, but the record of that first meeting has long since been lost to the sands of time.

Glen and I became casual friends. We didn't spend a great deal of time together, but I always got a kick out of his "out there" sense of humor and I believed he was a very talented guy who'd one day be a famous, successful film director. After he worked with me on *Tabloid!* (1985) we lost touch. He and his lovely partner, Kay Bay, moved to Los Angeles for a time.

Later, through a mutual friend, Tom Alexander, I heard that Glen and Kay had produced a film called *Among the Dead* (1995). It was many years before I had the opportunity to see this intriguing little film noir.

As with lots of other folks, the advent of Facebook put me back in touch with a lot of long-lost friends. Glen and I reconnected and have been in fairly frequent contact ever since. He's a good friend, a great writer, an extremely accomplished photographer and a world-class wit.

*Interview with Glen Coburn 11/21/2016*

TS: Let's start out with a little background; your childhood, any influences that got you started with horror to begin with.

GC: I grew up in Mesquite. Graduated from Mesquite High School. And, as you know, I grew up in, I guess we'll say a haunted house. There was a lot of paranormal activity. It was pretty crazy. It wasn't like, "Oh, a week ago we saw a shadow moving in the kitchen..." There was a lot of stuff happening ALL the time. From the time we moved into the house, when I was seven until I went off to college. Finally, I left after I was out of college and this continued after I was gone. I think that was part of what got me interested in scary, creepy stuff.

I will say by the time I was three years old, we were living in another house in Oak Cliff, I remember getting up and watching the package of films that had been syndicated to television. The one that contained the Universal Horror Films. I think it was called Shock Theater.

TS: Yep, Shock Theater. Locally it was on Channel 11.

GC: Right. Channel 11 was running it. This would've been 64ish when I first started watching these films. I want to say it was Sunday mornings, but it could've been Saturday mornings. Maybe that's why I didn't watch cartoons, because I was watching these movies. I remember my parents were still asleep so I had to get in there quietly to watch all these films. I must've watched the entire Universal Horror cycle by the time I was four or five years old. Frankenstein, the Wolfman, Dracula, all that stuff. I was really fascinated with those traditional monsters.

TS: At that young age, which of the monsters was most appealing?

GC: The least respected of the Universal classics were the ones that had multiple monsters, like *House of Frankenstein* (1944), *House of Dracula* (1945) and *Frankenstein Meets the Wolfman* (1943). I liked when the monsters were teamed up and battling each other. The original *Dracula* (1931) and *Frankenstein* (1931) were a little too clunky. I liked it better when the films became a little slicker, more contemporary. A lot of kids were scared of that stuff, but for me it was fun. I was fascinated, hooked.

When I was older I'd go to the movies on the weekends with my friend, Sam, my best buddy from first grade to junior high. That's when I saw *The Abominable Dr. Phibes* (1971), *Children Shouldn't Play with Dead Things* (1972) and a whole slew of weirdness from the early 1970s.

TS: Those 1970s movies you saw in the theater as opposed to TV, which ones were your favorites?

GC: *Count Yorga, Vampire* (1970), *Dr. Phibes*, those have a very striking memory for me. *Theater of Blood* (1973), *The House that Screamed* (1970) ... some of the titles were more exciting than the movies actually were.

A movie I still think about, from Italy, *The Last Man on Earth* (1964) starring Vincent Price. It was based on the Richard Matheson novel, *I Am Legend*. Later it was remade a couple of times with Charlton Heston and then with Will Smith.

Another thing I realized recently was that *Killers from Space* (1954) and a film called *Invisible Invaders* (1959) with John Agar probably had an influence on me as a child which manifested later as *Bloodsuckers from Outer Space*.

I went to college, East Texas State University. I was a journalism major in radio/TV/film with a group of friends and we began doing stuff on video. We did some fun things, not just the news stuff we had to do for the college TV station, but putting together narrative stories. Most of what I did was funny action and dialog bits. This continued with my friends even after college. This was the group that ended up doing *Bloodsuckers from Outer Space (BFOS)*.

I graduated college in December of 1982. Sometime in early 1983 I wrote the script for *BFOS*. The title came to me before I ever had an idea for the story. It just sounded like it could be the title for a real horror sci-fi film. It had a funny, satirical ring to it. You know, the idea of doing a parody of something that sounded like a real movie I might've grown up with, and a funny edge to it. I wrote the thing on Big Chief tablets. I'm sure you remember those.

We were still in the college frat-boy mode. We drank a lot of beer. Just got crazy and fun as people of that college-age do. Someone threw it out there, "Can you write this thing in three days?" I don't remember if it was a challenge or a bet. The fact that I was twenty-three and doing it for fun precluded any thoughts of spending time on it, fine-tuning it. It would've been better. At the time it didn't matter, because I had no long-term plan of where I was going with this. I was just thinking about Roger Corman and the fast turn-around legends around his early movies.

TS: If someone offered you a challenge today, to write a screenplay in a week or less, would you take it?

GC: For money?

TS: How much money would someone have to pay you?

GC: I would've done it in my twenties and thirties...after that I got a little burned out with the whole film making process. You never totally outgrow it, once you've had the bug to make movies. Once you have a kid and you're trying to pay the bills, you get a bit more serious. There's the part of you that thinks, "Why not do it just for fun?" If someone offered me $500 to write a script in a week, that part of me that just wants to have fun

Uncle Joe glares at Glen Coburn.

would say, "All right man! I'm on it!" So, I'm not saying it would take $20,000 to get me interested. (laughs) If you said, I've got $300 cash right here, write me script in five days . . . I'd probably do it. That's the film enthusiast in me saying that.

*TS*: Interesting! I hope this ends up in the final interview! How big a role did alcohol play in your approach to *BFOS*?

*GC*: There was a lot of beer, a lot of tequila and I smoked a lot of pot. I think that created a frame of mind that colored the whole process for me and probably for anyone else who was involved in the project. That combined with our naivete. "Let's just make a movie, let's do it!"

I'd never really given it any thought, but about five years ago, when *BFOS* was getting some exposure at fan conventions, I started hearing, "This is a stoner movie." It never occurred to me at the time or in the ensuing years, but I realize now that's why young people like it. They have dorm parties to watch it. That cycle's repeating itself with the millennials now. I hear about it from Facebook friends. Lionsgate started a subscription website for Comicon. A lot of my friends on FB are fans. For me it's like, I did this thing a long time ago. Young people since then have found out about it and get a kick out of it. I'm pleased that people continue to have fun with it. For me, that's what's made it all worthwhile.

Even my daughter Claire, her boyfriend and his buddies like to have bad movie night. She's always apprehensive, because she never liked *BFOS*, it was a source of embarrassment for her growing up. So, she's out of college now and her boyfriend and his buds are in their late twenties. While she's at his house, watching this embarrassing film with a group of her peers, I suddenly start getting all these texts, like, "People love this! They're crazy about it! You're famous!" Which, of course, I think is kind of funny. She was able to see the film as something other than an embarrassing thing her father did a long time ago, she sort of saw it through her friends' eyes and she's like, "Now I know why people like this!" Those sorts of validations trickle in and I don't take them too seriously, but I enjoy them in the moment.

Going back to the drinking and smoking pot thing. Yes, it was a pretty consistent everyday thing. That really comes across on the screen I think and colored the whole experience of making the movie.

TS: Aren't you involved in the distribution and marketing of films in the same genre?

GC: I have been. I kind of put the brakes on that about a year ago. I have a distribution label called Whacked Movies and it's still sort of on-going because I haven't taken all the necessary steps to

France goes crazy for
**Bloodsuckers from Outer Space**.

shut it down. I didn't make an announcement, "Whacked Movies is closing down, it's out of business!" So, it still exists. I released only a half-dozen movies. The thirtieth anniversary edition of *BFOS* I put out on the Whacked Movies label. That's the title I continue to make money on over the years. Time passes with nothing happening, then all of a sudden, I'll make what seems a significant amount of money for something I did so long ago.

I released the movie, *Repligator* (1996), which seems to be still making money every month in digital sales. There are some cool movies in that group, *Legend of the Hillbilly Butcher* (2014), for instance. That movie was shot on an iPhone, but it's got this great atmosphere to it. Joaquin Montalvan, is not like a kid making movies. He's probably in his forties. He's like an artist making movies, who does mostly documentary stuff. *Legend of the*

*Hillbilly Butcher* is a film I can always watch and enjoy. I'm glad I released it on my label. The other titles, like *Atom, the Amazing Zombie Killer* (2012), the last movie I released, did okay, got a little attention. Whacked was really not a money maker. The way distribution has always worked is that you try to put out volume, because you know there are going to be duds, then you'll have one that actually makes money.

My friend, Rob Hauschild, who has Wild Eye Releasing by now has put out something like 150 movies. Finally, for him, because of the sheer volume of titles, he's in the black. For him this has been like a six-year process. For every title you put out there's the expense of authoring, artwork and promo items, manufacturing, marketing expenses…it adds up. Sales have to recoup your initial outlay. After that the filmmaker starts getting some money. If the movie only sells a couple hundred units and doesn't get a good digital deal, the distributor eats those costs. For me, with Whacked Movies, it was just a lot of work for no money. I was going in the hole. I wasn't interested in dumping a lot of money into Whacked Movies in hopes that it would eventually make money. So, I entered into a deal with Wild Eye, so that they release any titles that come to me, so I don't have any expense up front. If the films make money, then I make money and pass royalties on to the film maker.

Rob Hauschild and I co-sponsored a film festival called the Polygrind Film Festival in Las Vegas a couple of years ago. We got to be pretty good friends. We talk a couple times a week. He sends me screeners to watch, to give him a yay or nay before he'll even watch them.

*TS*: What I'm hearing here is that there's still a strong movie fan living somewhere inside of your head.

*GC*: Yeah. There is.

*TS*: Distributors have a sketchy reputation among filmmakers. How has your perspective on that changed, now that you've walked in those shoes for a while?

*GC*: Well, that reputation has been confirmed. But with Rob and me there is a, not just a very serious effort, but a commitment to be ethical. To not cook the books and to not write off unrelated expenses so that they get charged to some poor film maker. The film makers legitimately get what they are contractually supposed to get. I know that happens with us, because that is exactly what was impressed upon me by Rob. That's the way he does business.

That said, I do know of a number of situations involving other film makers, other distributors who use a number of tactics to keep movies in the red, so film makers never make any money. Some labels are very congenial and accessible to get a film in the door, but as soon as that contract is signed the poor filmmaker endures months or years of not having calls or emails even answered. That sort of thing happens a lot. That's what's been going on since the beginning of indie films. That is still very much a part of the business.

*TS*: How did *BFOS* do in its initial home video release back in the 80s?

*GC*: Karl Lorimar Home Video and Warner Home Video sold 60,000 units of *Bloodsuckers from Outer Space* on VHS and a little Beta.

This success was largely a result of the desperate need for content in the early home video era. However, *BFOS* was in higher demand because it met the specs of a high-quality product. Despite the issues that reveal the film to be a cheap piece of schlock to modern audiences, it was of relatively high technical quality. It looked and sounded enough like what people were watching on television, that the entertainment value was not muted by the unwatchability factor that dogged much of the cheaply available content of the era.

The cameo appearance of Pat Paulsen as the President added production value. A large segment of the audience for the rental market remembered Paulsen's appearances on *The Smothers Brothers Comedy Hour* and his satiric campaigns for the U.S. Presidency (1968, 1972, 1980, 1988, 1992, and 1996)

I was told (by either distributor, Tom Moore or producer, Gary DePew) that the reason *BFOS* was so popular in foreign territories is that the film showcases rural Texas exteriors, which at the time fascinated foreign audiences. I think the wide-open spaces in Hamilton County exemplify people's perceptions of what Texas is like. Also, lots of interesting exterior locations add production value to any film.

The initial and continuing interest in *BFOS* comes from the movie's quirky, oddball perspective. Upon its release, there really wasn't anything comparable on home video. Of course, there were lots of silly, cheesy movies but not exactly like *BFOS*. In 2008, Art Ettinger, editor of *Ultra Violent* magazine told me that when he was a kid he rented the movie at the video store. When he watched it, he was perplexed. He couldn't figure out what he was watching. It was this weird mix of gore and cerebral humor. Maybe a lot of young people had that reaction and they told their friends and the word got out that they had to watch it because it was sort of off the wall.

*TS*: Tell us a bit about the other key players in *BFOS*.

*GC*: Garl Latham was a good buddy of mine in college and we continued that friendship after college. His dad had an oil and gas appraisal company. He was connected in the Texas political arena going all the way back to Johnson. The point is there was money there. This guy was very successful. We borrowed a little bit of money from Garl's dad and bought some equipment and started a business doing training videos. We actually did one for his dad's company. Our business was really not much more than a break-even proposition, but it legitimized us. That was the business we were in, making videos for these companies.

I'd always wanted to make a movie and I talked about that a lot and Garl got interested because of that. We scraped together whatever money we could from the video business and bought an Eclair NPR motion picture film camera. It was largely my enthusiasm that propelled our move toward doing a feature, but Garl contributed jokes and ideas for the screenplay.

Another of my good friends from college, Chad Smith, who is now a professor in the college of fine arts at Texas A&M Commerce. He'd done some work at a couple TV stations in Odessa by the time I met him. He had that experience with video and he understood how to put together news footage and narrative stuff. He had an understanding of composition, exposure and lighting. He was part of our circle, so we didn't even consider interviewing a bunch of cinematographers. He was just part of the deal.

Chad introduced the idea of composing each scene like a still image and have all the action happen in an artfully composed framework. That's a bit of an oddball thing that happened and determined what the movie is visually.

Thom Meyers, who was cast to play the lead, the character Jeff Rhodes...I'm still in touch with him. He's a great guy and a very good actor. His dream was to be a successful actor, but there are so many great actors out there. If you go to New York or Los Angeles, you just get sort of swallowed up. When we found him, he was studying at Adam Roarke's Film Actors' Lab in Las Colinas. In the early to mid-1980s the Dallas Communications Complex in Las Colinas was going to be a new hub for television and film. Of course, it didn't really go, but it was a big deal at that time.

Glen Coburn and Kay Bay in *Tabloid!*.

Lorimar release of **BFOS** minus Uncle Joe's severed arm.

Adam Roarke was an actor who'd made a splash in the biker films of Richard Rush back in the 1960s. He'd been under contract briefly for Universal at the end of the old contract system. He was in some good early television series like *Twilight Zone* and some western shows. After the studio contract thing, he got into the low-budget indie exploitation titles like *Frogs* with Ray Milland. He had personal issues that derailed his career, as many others did with drinking and stuff. But, he was a very cool guy and the thing he did to earn a living after his film career faded was this Film Actors' Lab. Adam was an excellent actor in technical terms. He knew how to add that little something extra.

Lou Diamond Phillips came out of the Film Actors' Lab. Thom was friends with Lou back in those days. When Thom came into the audition he was very funny. He did his Jack Nicholson impression and we knew he was the guy we wanted.

Another guy who was really good was Dennis Letts who played General Sanders. He did a sort of George C. Scott character from *Dr. Strangelove* (1964). He played it in that vein. Dennis had a great comedic talent, but he was great at any character role. *Bloodsuckers* was his first movie, then he did like forty movies and TV shows and ended up on Broadway in *August Osage County*, which won a Tony for best play. Great play, written by his son, Tracy Letts. He got a Pulitzer for that play. Dennis was just a great guy, a college literature professor and a very funny man.

Dennis's wife, Billie Letts, wrote *Where the Heart Is*, a very successful novel that was made into a well-known film. It's about a poor pregnant woman who is abandoned by her boyfriend at a Wal-Mart in Sequoyah, Oklahoma. She went on to write other novels. A lot of talent in the Letts family.

*TS*: Because of his work in *BFOS*, Dennis was cast in the "BBQ of the Dead" episode of *Tabloid!* Any ideas on *Tabloid!* you'd like to share?

*GC*: *On Tabloid!:* That movie was really fun. Kay and I got to work together for the first time. We played those terrific, comic white trash characters somewhat earnestly. They were ridiculous and I'm not an actor. Kay was good. Janice was priceless as Mama. It was fun working with Thom Meyers again. I knew about his comedic talent but he didn't get to show it off in *Bloodsuckers*. "Baby Born with Full Beard" was the perfect vehicle and I think he went all out. He's really funny in the part of Lester. And, Bret, you were very good as Hipster. I know that you're about as much an actor as me but you were right on the money with your performance. You were really funny. I don't mean you were funny in a bad acting way. You were knowingly funny.

We had to have a baby with a beard so Matt recruited one in his characteristic fashion. He was very pushy and ingratiating, making it sound like a big opportunity. Somewhere in Athens Texas, like downtown or at a shopping center he spotted a young couple with a baby. He got them out to that horrible, abandoned trailer house out in the country. They had no idea what was going on. They got spooked and thought we were going to do something perverted with their baby. Matt somehow convinced them to stay. They very reluctantly let us take their baby into the trailer house. Somebody put the beard on with corn syrup I think. We hurriedly got one take of the wide shot where Debbie and Mama come out of the bedroom, Kay cradling the baby in her arms. Then we got the close up of the baby with the beard. In retrospect, we could've used a doll in the wide shot and picked up that close up of the baby anywhere. We could've even shot a friend or family member's baby in Dallas at any time. I directed that segment so I must've been pretty clueless about that at the time.

I got a kick out of shooting that dull car chase, and the shootout at the trailer house. We used real ammo on the cutaways! The exploding pickup truck was a blast, literally. The top of the truck peeled back like a tin can and the entire vehicle was engulfed in flames. I remember that after it cooled down, you switched on the ignition and the engine started right up. We used multiple cameras to shoot the explosion. The camera operators started the film rolling and then they ran off. They each had to signal when they reached a safe distance so the blast could be set off. There were a few funny things that happened by accident. I remember that during the shootout I was supposed to be sneaking out the front door of the trailer in route to making the Molotov cocktail. None of us had actually come out that door and onto the porch. We didn't do a run through. Film was rolling when I stepped out of the door and onto the wooden porch. The wood was rotten and I fell through the porch. I wasn't expecting it but I just kept going. We didn't shoot another take because that was such a happy accident and because it would've been dangerous to even step onto that porch again.

We all had so much fun on "Baby Born with Full Beard." I wish we could've made it a full-length feature. I'm probably just being nostalgic. That story might not have held up for longer than twenty minutes. I didn't work on any of the rest of *Tabloid!* I wasn't even on the set for one minute. When the movie was finally completed and I saw "Baby Born with Full Beard" cut together, I was totally pleased. It was as good as or better than I hoped for. It's slow going by today's standards but it has its moments.

A DVD release of *Tabloid!* isn't a bad idea. I could get distribution or put it out myself. It's worthy as a little-known oddity from the early home video era. But it's no great loss if it never sees the light of day. *Tabloid!* is not a must see. There are a significant number of movie fans who want a copy of every retro movie that gets released. There are enough of them to make the release at least break even. But *Tabloid!* is not entertaining enough or significant in any way that would excite even the most avid DVD completest. With the exception of new, big budget Hollywood movies on Blu Ray, physical distribution is dead. And I don't think there will ever be a digital market for the film, so *Tabloid!* is basically dead. If we could have put it out on DVD six or eight years ago, it would've had a life.

On the other hand, *The Abomination* (1986) and *Ozone: Attack of the Redneck Mutants* (1986) could still get a collectors' DVD release. Those are actual cult films and as a distributor and a horror film enthusiast, I can tell you with great certainty that a lot of people would really like to see a legitimate DVD release of those films. I could release them myself and I know other niche market, boutique labels that want to put them out. A couple of them have pressed me to try and make it happen. They're offering MGs (minimum guarantee). That's money in the bank right now even if the deal turns out to be a flop. Unfortunately, the time is almost passed for those releases to be viable. I think it's a shame that those will essentially become lost films especially since digital masters with no restoration required are ready to go. There is a little potential for streaming/video on demand. The highest resolution masters that exist don't quite meet the specs for the major aggregators but I see decent numbers coming from Amazon

Thom Meyers and Glen Coburn ogle Baby Born with Full Beard.

Prime and they seem to be more receptive to content of marginal technical quality.

*TS*: The fans always seem to be interested in budgets. Want to talk about that?

*GC*: It was through Garl's dad that we were able to get some money, a little bit at a time to pay the lab bill and rent lighting equipment. I'd say the entire budget was in the neighborhood of fifty thousand dollars. For these young film makers who can take some digital equipment out in the field and start making a movie, that sounds like a lot of money. Basically, they can go out and shoot as many takes as they want for nothing. Film was an entirely different story. It was expensive and you couldn't shoot a lot of takes. It has to be lit and exposed properly and you have to be very careful about the number of takes. With film as opposed to video you can't end up with a bunch of stuff you can't use. It's just not viable financially. That fifty thousand dollars went quick! That's what it took to make the movie.

*TS*: Are there any obscure, indie films made in Texas that you are personally fond of?

*GC*: *Texas Chain Saw Massacre* (1974) is not obscure, but I really like that film. As far as really obscure stuff, Larry Buchanan made a number of films. *Mars Needs Women* (1967) is one that I think is watchable. Brownie Brownrigg's *Don't Look in the Basement* (1973). Most of the Texas indie films are not very striking. Many are technically not good and the scripts aren't great. They're not charming. Some micro-budget indies are fun to watch because they're charming. In other words, you get hooked in because there's some little spark of something from the film maker. Or there's something engaging about the film.

I will have to say the two films produced by Gordon McLendon, *Killer Shrews* (1959) and *Giant Gila Monster* (1959), both are pretty cool. Those are Dallas-based movies from the late 50s. Those two sort of stand out, but they're not truly obscure. A lot of people, especially film buffs, have heard of those.

*TS*: Tell us a little bit about *Among the Dead*.

*GC*: After *BFOS* I wanted to do some other films. I had a couple of projects; *Rescue Girls* and *Dracula's Granddaughter*. I

Japan extends warm welcome to **Bloodsuckers from Outer Space**.

still like *Dracula's Granddaughter*, I think it would be pretty cool to do even now. In those years at the end of the 1980s and into the early 1990s I had no idea what people were thinking about BFOS. The internet was not what it is now and we had access to much less information. I wanted to do something to sort of redeem myself, something that was more serious or artful. It turned out to be a drama called *Among the Dead*. It's the story of a would-be film maker, living in an apartment building with some other eccentric characters. He's on his final drinking bender and he's so enamored of these actors from an earlier era of Hollywood, that they start to integrate themselves into his life. Is it psychological, delusional? Or is it something for real in a paranormal sense?

I shot it in black and white. Kind of film noir. I remember in 1989 when I was still in L.A., writing the script. I had a little money in savings. That movie ended up costing exactly $50,000. That included everything from pre-production to conforming the negative and having a projectable print. It had some festival screenings. There was a guy named John Pierson who was the independent film guru at that time. He helped launch Spike Lee's career and some others. I sent him a rough cut. He said, "This is a great movie. I love it. You're going to get some festivals and an art house theatrical release. Finish the movie, get back in touch with me and I'll help you out."

We shot the film in 1992, but it took me almost three years to finish it. I'd run out of money and needed fifteen grand to finish it. I know that doesn't sound like a lot. By the time I finished the movie and got back to John Pierson everything had changed. He had a two movie per year development deal with Touchstone. He said, "I'm sorry, but I can't help you." I was like, "What do I do now?" In 1995 *Pulp Fiction* had become the new model for indie films as opposed to say, *She's Gotta Have It* (1986). The little indie stuff that had been getting theatrical, that was over. If I'd finished it a couple years earlier, it might've gone somewhere. It might not. It exists. It's a movie.

We had a lot of fun making it. The story takes place in L.A. But we shot it here in Dallas. We found some great locations locally that looked like Los Angeles. Kay and I and the main actor and the Director of Photography went to California and shot some second unit stuff on a Bolex. The movie was very carefully planned. I had every scene planned out, so I knew exactly what I needed to sell the idea that it had been shot in L.A. And it worked. A guy at Miramax in acquisitions, who was very interested in the movie was absolutely convinced it was shot there and was blown away when we told him it was shot in Dallas. So, I think we really sold it as an L.A. Movie.

It's a tragedy. The main character is sort of deplorable and meets with a tragic fate at the end of the film. That's one of the things about it; he had no redemption and there's no happy ending. That turned a lot of people off. The main actor, Craig DuPree, did a great job. Later he ended up having some major problems with depression. He was a professor at a university in Florida. They shut down his department and he couldn't find another job. One of the scenes has this old Hollywood director hanging himself from a curtain rod in the main character's apartment. Then in 2008 or 2009, Craig ends up hanging himself from a tree in his 80-year-old mother's yard. It's a very depressing story both on and off screen.

Despite all that, I really enjoyed making it. I was able to put together a great crew of Dallas people. I'm still connected socially to all the people who worked on the movie. At parties, they'll still talk about how much they enjoyed making the film. These were people working in the industry, then basically working for free on the weekends to do this project. At the end they were still like, "When are we going to do another one?" The experience of making that was much more fun than making *Bloodsuckers*. The camaraderie we established in 1992 is still going strong in 2016.

A couple of years ago I had an Emmy Award Winning editor, Phil Allen, re-cut the film. It was 110 minutes long as *Among the Dead*. We got it down to 90 minutes and retitled it *Hollywood Deadbeat* (2005). I tried to get some action on that, but once again, it didn't go anywhere. I spent a lot of time on that movie and nothing ever really happened from it.

*TS*: I can imagine some of the readers wanting to watch *Hollywood Deadbeat*. Is it available for potential viewers?

*GC*: I thought about putting it out on the Whacked Movies label, but it doesn't really fall into that genre. It's more of a vanity project for me. I'm pretty sure I'll end up putting it out there as a video download on Vimeo or sites like that. I think it would be cool for people to be able to see it.

Author's note: Glen Coburn contributed some very funny film commentary for the Bret McCormick chapter of this book. He was instrumental in putting together the limited edition releases of *Bio-tech Warrior* (1995) and *Time Trap* (1995).

# TERRY LOFTON

## NAIL GUN MASSACRE (1985)

No time wasted here. After a really fast fade in, we see a young woman named Linda (Michelle Meyer) being dragged by a group of men. It's clear they've got rape in mind.

In a scene that has its roots in the biker flicks released by A.I.P. and Crown International, these rowdy yahoos hold the woman down and have their way with her, ignoring her screams and pleas. The main instigator of the crime is a moron with a light green cap with white polka dots. That brought back memories, because my buddy Terry Himes wore a hat just like that back in the early 1970s.

Elsewhere, in a misty, backwoods environ, a big ol' country gal, Mary Sue, is hanging laundry, her tow-headed offspring at her feet. The woman's old man comes out of the shitter and flies into a tirade on account of she ain't got him a clean shirt to wear. We've all been there. Maybe a good ass-whuppin's in order?

Beyond the clothesline, a character in a camo jumpsuit, wearing a black helmet with some black gaff tape on it, steps into frame and gives us a lesson on the proper loading of a nail gun. This fellow has ninja powers and uses them to walk right past Mary Sue, unnoticed.

The nail-gunner goes inside, where the man of the house is still spouting a lecture

> "When the Nailer is finally unmasked, I was more than a little pissed off. The killer did wear a motorcycle helmet and camouflage the whole time, but the person inside the costume was obviously female. They were shorter than Bubba, had hips like a woman, and even ran like a woman (you know - arms straight down at the sides, swinging back and forth) - but Bubba was the killer. Reading the ending credits, I realized that the person(s) playing the Nailer throughout the film had indeed been a woman. I bet that the writer/director thought it was a neat twist to have the brother be the nail gun psycho. Yeah, you sure fooled us. We thought the Nailer was a woman the whole time ... That's because it was a woman, you freaking jerk!"
> 
> --*badmovies.org*, Andrew Borntreger, March 2, 2008

to the oblivious Mary Sue. This bastion of redneck manhood sizes up the intruder and imagines he can kick the stranger's ass, but he gets a tad nervous when the nail-gunner staples his hand to his forehead. It was a neat shot, I'll admit. The sort of thing that scores high points at any nail-gunning competition.

The killer has a weakness for one-liners and rehearses new material on his victim, but Mary Sue's ol' man is having trouble paying attention, because of all the nails in his body.

When Mary Sue finishes hanging clothes, she scoops up her young 'un and her cardboard laundry box and heads to the house. She's only in there a moment before she runs back out screaming and gagging. Not sure if it was her bloody ol' man or the smelly laundry stacked everywhere that made her carry on so.

A young couple are frolicking in the sack. This ain't no skin-flick, but it sure seems like one for a second there. The dialog's porn-worthy and the music sounds like it was lifted straight out of one of those early 1970s "adult" movie classics. She's feeling frisky, but he's got to abandon his morning wood and go cut some firewood.

The guy, whose name happens to be Mark, gets dressed and she checks her hair in the mirror. The cameraman's not interested in her hairdo, he zeroes in on her awesomely augmented bazoongas.

Later, Mark and his buddy arrive in the woods. His pal's a bit nervous. He heard

> "*Nail Gun Massacre* takes place in a nameless small town in the rural south. They probably mention the name of the town once or twice in the movie, but there's no establishing shot of a sign with the town's name and population on it. Without that I have no concrete sense of location, so let's just make up a name. *Nail Gun Massacre* is set in New Shittington, South Carolina. It's a town in the throes of economic decline, with jobless families lining up to take cabins in the middle of nowhere as soon as the previous inhabitants are murdered. Despite the recession wracking New Shittington, construction seems to be the biggest source of employment."
> --*somethingawful.com*, Zach "Geist Editor" Parsons, July 13, 2006

> "What do you get when you cross *The Texas Chainsaw Massacre* (use of a power tool), *I Spit on Your Grave* (someone seeking revenge for someone being raped), and *A Nightmare on Elm Street* (the killer spouting off corny one-liners before, during, and after killing someone)? You get the wonderful, fun cheesefest that is *Nail Gun Massacre*."
> --*horrornews.net*, Todd Martin, March, 14, 2012

about the nail gun murder that happened not far from there. As they're selecting a tree to cut down, a hearse pulls in behind their truck on the nearby road. When the buddy goes to take a leak, he thinks Mark is trying to spook him by sneaking

Terry Lofton tries a nail sans gun at Cinema Wasteland.

up from behind. In retribution, he wheels around and sprays the unknown creeper with urine. Nope, it's not Mark. And the nail-gunner takes offense at having his boots peed on. Pretty soon, the guy's lying on the ground in agony with three nails in him. One right in the Johnson.

Mark starts up a chainsaw and gets busy on a fallen tree. The nail-gunner fills him full of rust-resistant fasteners. When he slumps over the tree, the chainsaw falls from his grasp and takes one of his hands along for the ride.

Okay, here's the key to *Nail Gun Massacre*'s staying power; we're twelve minutes into the movie and we've already witnessed a rape, three brutal murders and some bodacious tatas.

The Sheriff (Ron Queen) happens onto the woodsmen's abandoned pickup. He radios in for info on the vehicle.

Later, Doc (Rocky Patterson) shows up to examine the bodies the Sheriff has found. This doctor likes to dress like a folksinger, blue denim all the way. They examine the bodies and are perturbed by the outbreak of gruesome killings in their previously peaceful community.

The hearse cruises along an isolated country road, encountering a hitchhiker (Thom Meyers) who flips the driver off when it looks like he's not getting a ride. Bad idea. The hearse comes to a stop. When the hitcher starts talking through the window the driver aims the nail gun at him. One of the great mysteries in this movie is why didn't the hitchhiker simply step out of the line of fire, instead of pleading for mercy at the window. He gets what's coming to him.

On a rainy afternoon, Doc and the Sheriff are called to the local auto parts store where a bearded old geezer has found a female victim behind his dumpster. Before they can even finish examining the body, they get another call. Some trucker has discovered the lifeless, nail-ridden body of the hitch hiker.

Like the immortal Alfred Hitchcock, Terry Lofton puts in a cameo appearance as the truck driver.

Some wholesome young folks have moved into the place where Mary Sue's hubby got nailed. They're trying to enjoy a decent dinner of spaghetti-os when they hear some banging out on the porch. It's probably a raccoon, but one of the young fellows goes out to see for sure. He doesn't find anything, but we know the nail-gunner was out there.

These kids have agreed to fix the place up for the landlady in exchange for free rent. The guys go to the lumber yard next day to buy some supplies. They have a strange encounter with the female clerk who blows a fuse because they almost went off without their receipt. Why's she so uptight? She's the rape victim from the opening scene.

A couple of construction workers and their girlfriends show up looking for work. Bubba, (Beau Leland) the guy at the lumberyard - who happens to be our rape victim's brother - sends them out to the old Bailey place. When they show up at the farmhouse, no one's home, so they settle in for a picnic lunch on a blanket.[i]

While the Sheriff checks out the hearse at the side of County Line Road, the picnickers get restless. A couple of them slip off into the woods for some tree sex, while the other two torch a reefer.

The tree-sex couple are just about to experience a happy ending, when things take a turn for the worse. The nail-gunner shoots the guy in the back of the head. This causes him to stop pleasuring his girlfriend and that starts her to complaining. The boyfriend falls on the ground and the killer nails the girl's hand to her face and puts a couple of nails in her chest. As her naked body falls on top of his, I am reminded of a couple of facts. First, there was a time when full frontal nudity was not uncommon in films like this. Second, there was also a time when American women didn't all shave their pubic hair.

**Nail Gun Massacre** promo art.

A third thing, that came to me later, was that when a couple of horny kids get killed in the woods in one of these pictures, somebody always comes looking for them. That person usually ends up

---

[i] I'm guessing Terry Lofton did his casting at Adam Roarke's Film Actors Lab, because one of the girlfriends is Connie Speer, who was married to Rocky Patterson. Both were active at the Film Actors Lab at the time this film was made.

dead, too. The other guy comes looking. Ends up he's a tree hugger who becomes especially attached to a particular tree, if you get my meaning.

The tree-hugger's girlfriend (Connie Speer) has a prolonged scene in which she starts to freak, crying, talking to herself and expecting the worst. When she's got herself plumb worked up, one of the clean-cut young fellows living in the old Bailey place makes the mistake of touching her shoulder. She loses it and it takes him a good while to calm her down.

The Sheriff and Doc are called out to look at this new batch of cadavers. This murder business was a little exciting at first, but the new has worn off and the thrill is gone. They just want the killing to stop. They're sick of driving out to the Bailey property, which is where these corpses mostly end up.

At a nearby construction site, a couple of half-wits are engaged in a nail gun war, just for kicks. Not only are they idiots, they're rapists as well. They were in on the gang rape at the beginning of the movie and they're still gloating. The nail-gunner surprises the two guys when they're inside finishing out the walls. They're fresh out of drywall, so the killer tacks these guys to the studs instead. The way the killer is talking leads us to believe that behind the gaff tape, under the helmet, it's the rape victim shooting all those nails at folks. And I suppose she'd be within her rights.

A guy we've never seen before, but who seems to share some biographical and professional similarities with the film's director, Terry Lofton, takes a young lady to get a nice meal at the local DQ. Their waitress is upset about something. Maybe she thinks the young guy in the beat-up convertible stole Doc's wardrobe. In any case, she takes her frustration out on his car's radio antenna.

After enjoying their meal, the two young folks head to an isolated road to get frisky. In one of the hottest (and yet tender) scenes ever committed to film, the lovers practice their contortions in the small car for a few minutes, warming up for the real action which takes place on the hood of the vehicle.

Terry Lofton has no intention of allowing any of his actors to achieve an orgasm. Nail-gunner shows up and does what he (or she) does best.

As a construction foreman and his daughter are preparing to enjoy some grilled steaks, the killer pulls a commando move, bursting from the waters of the swimming pool and firing a volley of nails. The guy not only gets nailed, he falls onto the grill and gets cooked. When his daughter finds him, instead of pulling him off the fire, she applies pressure to his back. Is she making sure he's well-done?

Doc's frazzled. He's searching for answers. Why has someone gone on a killing spree? When will these senseless murders stop? And who stole his denim jacket? After viewing some crime scene photos, he calls a dude named Howard to request a psychological profile on power tool killers. Then, he receives a call informing him that he's needed at the latest murder scene.

As Doc and the Sheriff talk about the killings, it becomes clear they know about the rape. We're left with the impression that no charges were filed, even though the victim identified her attackers.

A couple of young women wander through the woods. They must not have heard about all the murders. They seem very friendly with one another and the 1970s porn-style music on the soundtrack inspires hope that we're about to witness some girl-on-girl action. No such luck.

They wander onto the killer's property. The hearse is in the driveway. The nail-gunner surprises them near an old barn and soon there are two more victims on the tally sheet.

Doc shows up at Linda's trailer. He warns her that the Sheriff is about to arrest her. She claims she didn't commit the murders. Doc drags her off to search for her brother who is out joyriding in the hearse somewhere. Ah, the days before cell phones. The shiny surface of Doc's black Camaro gives us an impressionistic view of the camera crew as they speed away.

Not far down the road, the Camaro crosses paths with the hearse. Doc hangs a U-turn and pursues. The chase scene that ensues, with its blaring synth track, brings back fond memories of Crown International's drive-in classics, *The Teacher* (1974) and *Trip with the Teacher* (1975). The hearse races up a mountain of gravel at a concrete plant and plummets off the edge. The camoed killer tumbles out of the disabled vehicle and scrambles away with Doc close on his heels. The killer and Doc scale the metal structures on the property, evoking comparison to the final scenes of *The Hideous Sun Demon* (1958).

Bubba falls to his death. As Linda grieves over his body, the Sheriff arrives. Doc says the killing's over. The Sheriff is not so sure. The audience is pretty sure there will be more killings since Linda is still living. She cradles the black helmet in her arms while Doc leads her away. Yes, there is a sunset. And, yes, Doc and Linda walk into it.

I met Terry Lofton only once, to the best of my recollection, and may have had a phone conversation or two with the guy. I spent an evening at Terry's house in the late 1980s, eating pizza, drinking Coronas and strategizing marketing ploys for low-budget producers like us. I don't recall us solving the world's problems (or any problem, for that matter), but, I found him to be a likable, down-to-earth guy with a practical approach to indie film production. His film, despised by some,

Lofton hawks **Nail Gun Massacre** at Cinema Wasteland 3.

adored by others, definitely punched the right buttons for a large enough number of viewers to ensure its place in the annals of B-movie classics.

Glen Coburn, of *Bloodsuckers from Outer Space* fame, told me Loyd Cryer, creator of the Southwest's premier horror convention, Texas Frightmare Weekend, knew Terry and might have some memories to share. I approached Loyd and he graciously consented to take time from his busy schedule to answer a few questions.

*TS:* How did you first become aware of Terry and *Nail Gun Massacre*?

*LC:* I think I've been aware of it since seeing it in video stores in the 1980's. However, I never actually saw it until I met Terry.

I used to run an online movie store. We specialized in the harder to find horror DVD's. I bought a couple of copies of *Nail Gun Massacre* on VHS from a distributor and put them on the website. A few weeks later I received a phone call. When I picked up a gentleman was asking me why I was bootlegging his movie. I was a little thrown off of course. But, he proceeded to tell me that he was the director of *Nail Gun Massacre*. I told him that I was a big horror fan and had no idea that I was "bootlegging" anything. We talked for quite a bit and quickly became friends. Terry was a big-hearted guy and he was easy to get along with. We met up about a week later so he could see the tapes. He realized that they were actually original VHS copies of the film that were produced by Magnum back in 1986. The guy I bought them from later told me that he purchased a big box of them somewhere.

Terry had health problems for a long time. I had helped him out over the years when he needed it. Due to his diabetes, his vision was failing. I bought some new glasses for him. I loaned him money when he needed it. At one point, he was living in his car. I offered for him to stay with us but he wouldn't accept that. He eventually moved in to the back storage of that country store that is seen in the movie.

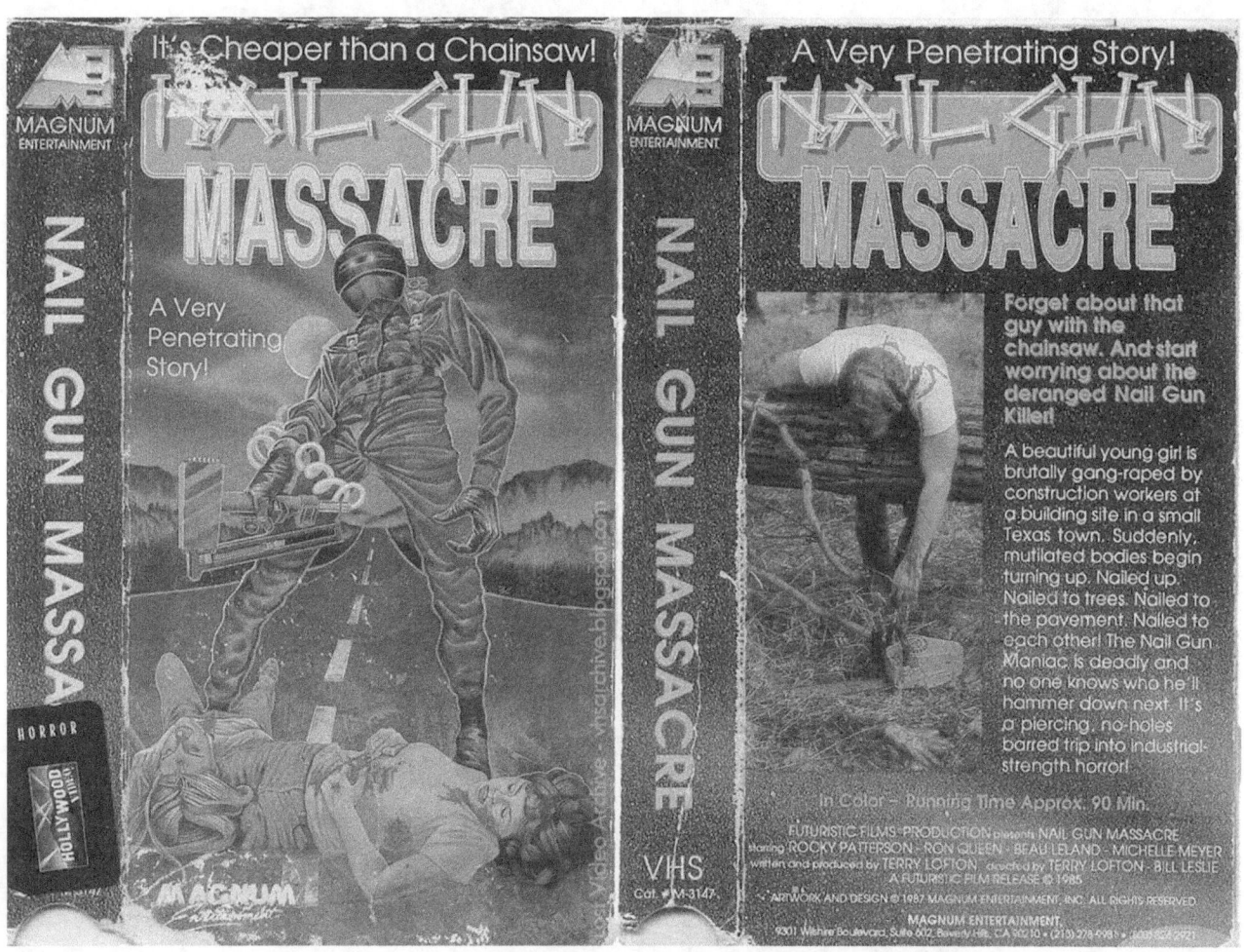

Original VHS sleeve for Magnum's release of **Nail Gun Massacre**.

Terry Lofton with Art Ettinger, editor of ***Ultra Violent Magazine***.

The point is, we'd gotten really close over the years. He called me one day and told me that he didn't have much longer to live and asked if I'd be interested in taking over *Nail Gun Massacre*. He set a price. I talked to my wife and got the ok. Then I called him back and accepted the offer. Since then I've been trying to keep the movie alive for Terry. We've released it in the US and the UK on Blu-ray. We're currently planning a remake as well.

It actually has a pretty big worldwide following. I've met a few super fans. Mostly in the US. But, I do know of at least one in Australia. We screened it at the Alamo Drafthouse a few years ago and packed the house. People came up to us after the screening and told us that they have been big fans. A couple even gave us fan art for the film that they had drawn!

*TS*: How long have you been a fan of schlock cinema?

*LC*: I grew up on these films. My Mom took me to see everything at the drive-in in Ennis. Of course, I had a steady diet of movies from the video store as well. I've always been particularly interested in movies that were filmed around the Dallas/Ft. Worth area. I started Texas Frightmare Weekend in 2005 because there just wasn't anywhere that fans of horror could get together in Texas.

Loyd Cryer has certainly done a bang-up job of providing a venue for fans of the genre. I visited Texas Frightmare Weekend 12 and was amazed at the number of people in attendance. Practically the first person I saw when I entered the DFW Airport Sheraton was Udo Kier. Yeah! The guy who recommended having sex with a dead gall bladder if one really wishes to understand life, in *Andy Warhol's Frankenstein in 3-D*! A couple minutes later I exchanged a greeting with Michael Berryman of *The Hills Have Eyes*. In no time at all I was having lunch with Frank Henenlotter, director of *Basket Case* and *Frankenhooker*. There's never before been a venue like Texas Frightmare Weekend in the Lone Star State.

Another fan of Terry Lofton is a guy named Art Ettinger. Art is the editor of *Ultra Violent Magazine*. I spoke to Art by phone in August 2017.

*AE:* Terry was a great guy. I always really liked regional horror movies. Movies that were made in places you don't usually see movies from. I would say, unquestionably, *The Nail Gun Massacre* is the greatest movie ever made in Seagoville, Texas, right? It's an interesting setting and an odd-ball movie. It has its own sensibilities. It's got a cool look. It's shot on film in a time when some people were starting to shoot on video. It's an unusual movie.

I liked Terry. When I interviewed him, he'd just started talking to people. He'd never been contacted really about the movie, by journalists or from a fan point of view until he put up that website and started re-releasing the movie on DVD. He had a good sense of his place in the big picture. He didn't take himself too seriously. But, he also understood that there were people who really liked his movie.

A few other things, too. Like he'd re-edited this movie called *My Friends Need Killing* (1976), an amazing Vietnam era exploitation movie that I was obsessed with for a while. I had no idea Terry Lofton was involved with trying to re-release it.

His health was really deteriorating when I met him. It was sad to see him go from his state the first time I met him to just a couple of years later, when I hung out with him again. He was starting to go blind and really having a hard time from complications of diabetes. Unfortunately, he passed away shortly after that second time. I didn't get to know him as well as I would've liked. We used to talk on the phone, we used to email back and forth. He had a great sense of humor. But, I only hung out with him in person those two times when he came up to Cinema Wasteland.[ii]

I took his film very seriously, rewatched it and got him to comment on some very specific things that happened on the set. It's not a bad little interview. It's fun. When you're a kid, watching something like *Nail Gun Massacre*, you never ever expect that you'll be talking to the guy that made it, you know? It was pretty cool.

Art Ettinger granted us permission to print some excerpts from his piece which originally appeared in *Ultra Violent; A Very Penetrating Interview with Terry Lofton, Director of Nail Gun Massacre.*

*TL:* When I made *Nail Gun Massacre*, I actually didn't have a background as far as making movies. I previously, before that, worked for Warner Brothers for the television show *The Dukes of Hazard* (TV series 1979-1985). I worked in the promotion department, and went around doing fairs and car shows, showing one of the General Lees. They had special cars built for doing car shows. There were about fifteen of those General Lees, and I actually owned one of them. That's what got me interest-

---

[ii]Cinema Wasteland is a movie and memorabilia expo held in April and October in Strongsville, Ohio.

ed in shooting television or movies, was watching them shoot the show. I had also been a stuntman for a couple of years doing racecar tracks and state fairs, doing car stunts and motorcycle stunts, so I had a collaborative interest in the actual shooting of movies from the angle of stunt work.

I was talking to some people about shooting a horror movie, and everyone told me it was expensive to do what I wanted. I knew I probably couldn't scare people, but I might be able to come up with a good blood and guts one. So, I was developing ideas, and one day I went to visit a friend of mine at his business, and he worked for a pallet shop where they made pallets to move stuff, and they built them with nail guns. When I drove up there, I heard nail guns going off, and he was hiding behind the corner of the building, and they were shooting at each other, literally with a nail gun. I got out, and they stopped and were laughing. I said, "What are y'all doing?" They told me they were having a nail gun fight. I talked to them about it, and I thought about it, and I realized they've used just about everything to kill people with, but I hadn't seen a nail gun yet, and I thought that would be great. Seeing that nail gun fight is where I got the idea.

It was shot on 16mm, in and around Seagoville, Texas, all within a five-mile radius. Seagoville is a rural, country town. It's not real big, although it's growing. In the country parts, we were way off the road, in the woods, by a gravel pit. Seagoville is about fifteen minutes from Dallas. It was shot in 1985 for about $60,000, financed mainly through family and a few investors.

We always see women naked in movies, and I thought maybe I could give the women a shot of a guy for a little bit, with some muscle action. It was shot from behind, five feet away, with both of them in the shot, and I shot it from two different angles for the close-ups. I knew Blockbuster and the major video chains wouldn't take it because of that scene. I didn't think the nudity was any big deal. It came out unrated, even with the cuts. We call it the tree sex scene in the DVD. The wife of the actor in that scene didn't like it when she saw it, and they got a divorce over it.

Most of the movie was kind of ad-libbed because as we were going along, we literally didn't know what direction we were going in. We were just trying to wing it, and do the best we could. I did all of the special effects myself. I made a point of using a lot of blood.

I took such a beating on the distribution from *Nail Gun Massacre*, and got screwed out of a lot of money. I got totally disgusted with the movie business, threw up my hands, and walked away from it.

I kept getting calls from people telling me that the film gets talked about over the internet, so I typed in *Nail Gun Massacre*, and all these reviews and sites popped up. I dug further and asked questions, and found out others were selling copies of it. I realized that I could maybe get some of my money back and could release it on DVD. I scraped some money together, transferred it over, and authored it a little bit. I couldn't do it like a Warner Brothers DVD, but I did the best I could. I put up the website and did some press releases. I've been winging it, like in the olden days when independents sold their own films to theaters.

In June 2017, Daniel Redd of RDM Productions in Plano, Texas offered to comment on *Nail Gun Massacre* and his relationship with Terry Lofton.

*TS*: How did you come in contact with Terry Loftin?

*DR*: I first met Terry in 1984. We were introduced by Bill Leslie. Bill used to do some work with us and he was the one who shot *Nail Gun*.

Terry was a good person. He really wanted to make movies, but like a lot of folks in the same boat, he had no money. He borrowed money from his folks to make *Nail Gun*.

*TS*: Did you know Loyd Cryer is planning a remake of *Nail Gun Massacre*?

*DR*: I wasn't aware that there was a remake of *Nail Gun* in the works.

*TS*: Did you see *Nail Gun*? What did you think about it?

*DR*: It was a cheaper production for sure, but it stacks up pretty well against other films in the same genre. It's about the same quality as a Roger Corman or Larry Buchanan movie. Over the years my father's lab provided processing for a number of low budget movies, but mostly we did corporate films.

*TS*: So, your father was involved peripherally with a lot of low-budget movies?

Art Ettinger and Terry Lofton display **Nail Gun Massacre** art.

*DR*: My dad, Bob Redd, was a Vice President at Jamieson Film Company back in the 1950s. He's the one who hired Brownie Brownrigg to work there. They became best friends. When Dad started Producers Services Incorporated, Brownie came to work for PSI. Brownie shot and produced projects for PSI, mostly for their client Tracey Locke, an ad agency. Larry Buchanan's *Zontar* was shot at my house and on the PSI stage.

*TS*: PSI was involved with all of Brownrigg's movies?

*DR*: PSI processed all the 16mm film for all four of Brownie's movies. They were blown up to 35mm somewhere else. Dad didn't get into 35mm until the late 1970s.

Bob Redd started a number of film production-related businesses in Dallas; Producer Services Inc., WBS, Universal Cine Photo. He was a partner with Brownrigg in Century Studios.

*TS*: In 2015, you and Dave Rennke produced the sequel to Brownrigg's drive-in classic, *Don't Look in the Basement*.

*DR*: I consider my decision to get involved in producing *Don't Look in the Basement 2* a dumb-ass mistake. Even so, I'm considering producing Justin Powers' next feature, *Rotten Riders*.[iii]

As I was completing this chapter, Glen Coburn unexpectedly agreed to add some thoughts of his own.

*GC*: In 2007, when I was mulling over the possibility of self-releasing *Bloodsuckers from Outer Space* on DVD, Terry encouraged me to go for it. He had recently done his own release of *Nail Gun Massacre* just prior to the Synapse release. I made my movie in 1984 and he made *Nail Gun* in 1985 so they were relatively of the same ilk. They came out at the time when the home video market was hungry for content. A couple of decades later they both had the allure of "cheap retro horror" that fans were hooked on. There's the nostalgia component that finds appreciation among a devoted fan base that loves the gritty, anything-goes quality of those movies.

Terry was not only encouraging but he jumped right in to help me make it happen. He set up the authoring and manufacturing. He understood the process and knew where to get the best deals. He was involved from the start through completion. His support was critical in stoking the fire under my ass to keep me moving. And that self-release stirred up the interest that led to the Shriek Show deal, which gave the fans an awesome official release with superb image quality, special features, and really cool art for the sleeve.

During that time, he was working diligently to raise the money to make a sequel to *Nail Gun Massacre*. That's all he talked about. He was going through some rough times. His health was failing. He was going to dialysis a few days a week. His eyesight was failing. I think the *Nail Gun* sequel was something he could focus on that made him hopeful. He didn't talk a lot about his health problems. He didn't dwell on it, so none of us really knew that he was at the end. At some point, he disappeared. We were all calling each other trying to find out where he was. Then we found out that he had passed away. It was very sad and I know that some people who were really close to him wished they had been there for him in his last days, but I think he didn't want to make a big deal of it.

---

[iii] Justin Powers is the Dallas-based filmmaker responsible for *Pot Zombies*. *Rotten Riders* is a proposed production dealing with zombie bikers.

# BRET McCORMICK

## I, Schlockmeister

Author's Note: I made the mistake of asking my former friend[i], Glen Coburn, to write reviews/synopses for the films in this chapter. Oh well, I asked for it. In reality, I chose to have Mr. Coburn write the reviews of my films for two reasons. First, I didn't want to describe my own work. Second, his reviews of cheesy flicks are always hilarious! Check out his book, *Whacked!; Skewed Views of Horror Movies that Simply Refuse to Die.*

### THE ABOMINATION (1986)

This movie does have a cult following and I can see why. There is plenty of nasty garbage on screen throughout. There's so much stabbing, slicing, gut-munching horribleness in this movie that most mentally unstable male youngsters will wallow in it. When I was a kid, we were fascinated at the sight of African women with exposed udders that looked like zucchi-

"Taking the good with the bad, is *The Abomination* worth tracking down in the end? It's quite a memorable little oddity, with its bible-infused weirdness, rivers of blood and odd sound effects. Only low budget filmmaking can play with the sort of stuff we see, so we have to be prepared to live with the inevitable shortcomings of such a fringe production. At the very least, it's a memorable, distinctive effort so I'd say give it a look if you can. Probably after twenty-two years you won't be knocked over by the splatter, but that allows the other oddball qualities that McCormick has created to come through."

--*girlsgunsandghouls.com*, Boris Lugosi, May 12, 2008

"There are many VHS I get excited about. Hell, there's even many VHS that cause me to start jumping up and down like a teen girl at a Green Day concert. But very few VHS make me stage pictures of myself cuddling and sleeping with them on my pillow. I don't think a single one has, actually, until now."

--*vhshitfest.tumblr.com,* Dan Kinem, November 24, 2011

[i] That's a joke, I say, that's a joke, son.

nis as long as a yardstick. Nowadays the boys would laugh at that sight but in my generation the elongated mammary tubes stirred unspeakable desires.

Bret McCormick.

Scooter (Scott) Davis is the star of the movie. He played a whiney ass little baby in *Ozone Attack of the Redneck Mutants* but, in *The Abomination*, he was lucky enough to be a devil-possessed murderer. His acts of brutality are caused by Cronenbergian Sliver worms. Scooter's mama, who is bugged out on Lithium, spits up a chicken liver after watching Brother Fogg on television. Fogg is a bogus but hilarious preacher. If his show was real, I would watch it every day. Mama gets hypnotized by this man of the cloth. Her devotion to him brings about a healing that is otherwise known only to Medjugorje visitors.

The worms turn into giant balloons of hemorrhoidal tissue. Before you know it, the bilious, slimy gourds grow teeth and take over mama's filthy shithouse. Scooter spends the rest of the movie gathering plant food. This results in lots of images resembling the inside of a pig rendering plant. This is the kind of ugly carnage

> "Now, was all of this Greek drama and pop cultural meta-referencing intentionally put into the film? Probably not, but that means a lot of it was done subconsciously, which means Bret McCormick, as writer and director, had some serious demons to exorcise in 1986. Without a doubt, it can be said his existential struggle is to the viewer's benefit."
> 
> --*horrorpedia.com*, Ben Spurling, January 20, 2017

that made gory Drivers-Ed films obsolete. When I was a young person, girls were allowed to leave the room so as to avoid seeing people turned into dog meat during the commission of auto accidents. I remember one scene with a couple of African-American re-enactors jabbering like retards while barreling down the highway in an antique Pontiac. Then, they fall asleep from inhaling carbon monoxide. The next thing you know, the film cuts to real footage of a meat wagon driver holding a black man by his one attached arm and dragging him off the highway with his brains falling out. I think my friend; Louis Justin is releasing that film on Massacre Video next spring. That horribleness passes for entertainment in our current condition of collapsed family values.

Promotional flyer for **The Abomination**.

Scooters girlfriend is played by Blue Thompson, which is obviously a made-up name. It sounds like a porn name. She probably combined the name of her first pet with the name of the street she grew up on. Blue is pretty good in this movie considering all the shit she has to deal with.

The movie takes place in Texas. Naturally, the moviemaker chose the most putrid, backwoods, Crapsville of inbred morons for the location. It's impossible to pinpoint the exact location because this describes about ninety percent of the state. So, the victims are all rednecks, drunks, meth-heads, and religious fanatics, which leads me to believe that the story is based on actual events.

The one thing I can say about *The Abomination* is that it's not boring. There's not much time between grotesque plot points. Many depraved individuals will consider this the highest form of entertainment and they are welcome to it. I warn all viewers to turn the sound down as soon as you hear something resembling narration because it is truly terrible. Crank up some Black Sabbath or other devil music. Then turn up the sound on the movie when the preacher talks.

## OZONE! ATTACK OF THE REDNECK MUTANTS (1986)

The first time I saw this movie, I was stoned. It must've been twenty-five years ago. I was stupefied by the profundity of the subject matter and its relentless depiction on my television screen. Upon later reflection, I remembered nothing. And when I say nothing, I mean literally nothing. This movie was only one of the many

"What *Ozone! Attack of the Redneck Mutants* lacks in quality, it more than makes up for in heart and determination."
    --*horrornews.net*, Sean Leonard, October 19, 2014

"Since we don't ever give zero stars (boy, how I wish *Ozone! Attack of the Redneck Mutants* could be the only exception!), it'll leave me no other choice than giving this movie half a star."
    --*slashingthrough.com*, Kries Tyfus, May 5, 2012

"Most of its faults are because of things that are actually in the movie. This movie does take full advantage of the fact that it was filmed in such a precious format as Super 8. It even has fun with itself, as all the sound is dubbed in post-production. But more than anything there is an underlying beauty in the filmed events portrayed here."
    --*criticsroundup.com*, Jaime Grijalba, August 15, 2015

"This film is a masterpiece."
    --*badmovies.org*, MBrown06, April 23, 2012

things included in that black hole of nothingness. A cataclysmic tectonic shift in my brain meat was precipitated by a neurologic electrical storm that caused the two hemispheres to be fundamentally at odds. This movie is the fraternal twin of *The Abomination*. They are similar in some ways because they emerged from the same womb of adversity. Bret McCormick is responsible for *The Abomination*. *Ozone* is superior visually but it took over twice as long to shoot.

The first rule of Super 8 movie making is that social commentary is anathema to the medium. Shit in. Shit out. A polished turd is still a turd only smoother. They both stink up the place. As far as I can tell, there is a message in this movie. It is a cautionary tale about what happens when a smoke bomb is released into the atmosphere. Hillbillies turn into crispy-faced cannibals. The first casualty is a man who drives an air-conditioned tractor. He gets sick from drinking trash can punch the night before so he vomits on the driver-side window of his tractor. After exiting the farm utensil, he wanders off until he falls down, turns red and develops wings on either side of his forehead. Every other mutant in the movie is black. The preponderance of Negro mutants creates a vehicle of expression for the moviemaker's liberal political agenda. Paralleling the terrifying Watts Riots of 1965, *Ozone* relates the sentiment that the only way for black people to get attention is to act up.

*Ozone* is a road movie. The main part of the movie is all about two people driving in various automobiles through mutant infested territory. The driver of the car is Arlene (Blue Thompson), a biology student from the local community college. She wears a summer hat while taking a stool sample from a pastoral lagoon full

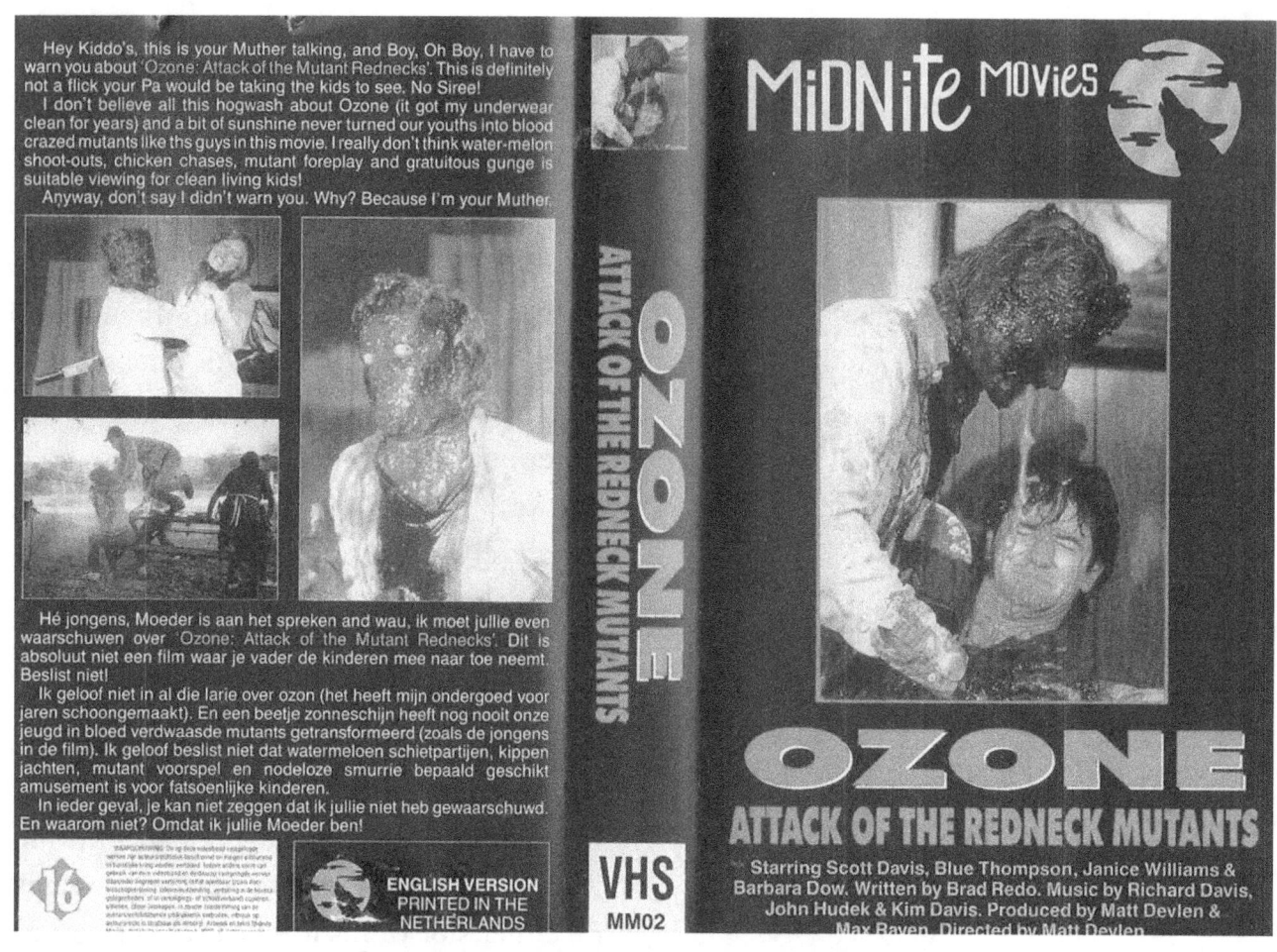

*Ozone Attack of the Redneck Mutants* VHS sleeve.

of raw sewage. When she returns to her Rambler, she finds a whiney boy named Kevin (Scott Davis) sleeping in the trunk. She gives him a ride and for the rest of the movie she relentlessly bitches at him while he cries like a baby.

There are subplots. The movie also includes a cooking show. Grandma is featured preparing a chicken dinner in real time. There is a watermelon-shooting contest. The most heart-warming part of the movie is a documentary about a country-fried talent show. In this isolated, wooded garbage dump, a profound incidence of genetic drift has occurred. All the white people have turned into toothless, bloated water-heads. The talent contest is hugely entertaining and all the entrants do a fine job considering their highly developed mental retardation. The Master of Ceremonies is the token normal person. He is the only humanoid being at the talent show who possesses an I.Q. above sixty. He chooses to stay drunk all the time due to a horrible, chronic bout of acid reflux disease which he attributes to his proximity to so many inbred, pig-faced, Pentecostals.

Kevin, the whiny boy, turns out to be a stooge and this angers Arlene to such an extent that she harangues him even more than usual. Her behavior sets a new elevation for bitchiness that is seldom seen except in real life. Other people get mad at him too. They throw fried chicken at him. This reminds me of the time I was walking down the sidewalk on Sunset near the intersection of Western. A passerby flung a half-eaten fried chicken leg out the window of a ghetto Impala and hit me hard on the side of the head. I was dizzy but not angry. I had no business walking in such a crime-infested neighborhood.

Much driving and watermelon activity continues throughout the movie. The mutants do attack and they are scary. In one horrifying scene, Kim Davis takes a bath while a mutant pokes a hole in the door. The hole gets bigger and bigger until the African American gentleman bursts in and does mean things to Miss Davis. There are scenes of blood drinking and organ harvesting that should not be viewed by persons implanted with pacemakers. Pregnant mothers should also avoid this movie as viewing it could cause miscarriage. At some point, Matt Devlen acquired a hearse. The two leads ride around in that death wagon for a while.

If you enjoy watching the Food Network and *American Idol*, you will find something to like in *Ozone! Attack of the Redneck Mutants*.

## BIO-TECH WARRIOR (1996)

I used to have a shrink who was a hypnotherapy hobbyist. I once asked him if he could use hypnotherapy to cure my addiction to baked goods. He told me he couldn't. I asked why and he informed me that I couldn't be hypnotized. I continued to press him on the subject. He said that some people can't be hypnotized and that I was a member of that group of sad-sack rejects of humanity. I finally proved him wrong. *Bio-Tech Warrior* led me down the path of the most worrisome and demoralizing hypnosis experience imaginable. It reminded me of when my parents would give me a tablespoon of Paregoric to shut me up for twelve hours. Most movies have a beginning, middle, and end. This one seemed like a week of an interminable middle. I blocked most of the unnerving viewing experience so I had to endure it a second time just so I could write something about it.

After six hours of rocket launch footage, moon landing stills, and clips from a Lithuanian space opera, the story begins. A couple of Hell's Angels abandon their

**Author's Note:** At the time of this writing, there were no reviews of *Bio-tech Warrior* from which to pull quotes. Perhaps that will change now that the film is available as a limited-edition DVD.

Appalachian girlfriends at a junkyard RV. The bikers' extreme body odor attracts the attention of a cyborg that turns out to be the title character. For all the movie's flaws, at least the *Bio-Tech Warrior* is pretty realistic and scary. So, in order to shut down this assault to its senses, the cyborg turns his arm into a laser gun that burns up the bikers in blaze of amateurish CGI. This is the only time in the movie when he uses the laser arm. After that he shoots a killer beam from his right ear.

The star of the movie is a semi-professional actor (Chris Heldman) who does his best ham salad impression, which is eclipsed only by his mom jeans. He meets up with a blond scientist who specializes in uncovering alien and government co-conspiracies. Ham Salad looks her up and down and stares at her ass in an act of blatant misogyny that would make Bill O'Reilly jealous. Blondie (T.J. Myers) accepts this heinous behavior with light-hearted aplomb. We know at this juncture that the two cross-eyed lovers will soon be banging away.

The plot thickens like a lard roux in a cast iron skillet. I won't reveal all the details because I can't remember most of them. Part of the story is set in Arizona. There are many beautiful desert scenes including some dizzying aerial footage. The main characters take a helicopter ride for no apparent reason except that it gives the viewer a break from the rest of the movie. Much of the story is set in Dallas. We know this because a caption at the bottom of the screen always reminds us. It's especially enchanting to see the cyborg walking around in the Trinity River bottoms with the Dallas skyline looming large and shiny.

There's a man in a black suit that looks just like Don Draper without the muscle tone. He kills a few people and then we find that he's a clone and there are many Don Drapers. These clones can morph into anybody, so if Abe Lincoln turns up, he's probably just another Don Draper clone. And he's likely to have a loaded musket under his sports coat. In this scenario, every character could be killed at any time by either the cyborg or by Don Draper disguised as a friendly human. One of the clones gets turned into mashed potatoes. That also happens to one of the humans. But I can't remember which one.

Scenes of Ham Salad and the Blondie are interspersed throughout the action. They're always trying to crack the case because they don't have much else to do after the helicopter ride. I almost forgot. Ham Salad has some pretty good Kung Fu scenes. He's as good as Chuck Norris and Ham Salad can go all out because he doesn't have to worry about his wig flying off. Sometime in the movie, some men are sitting around a folding card table in a school cafeteria. They talk about the military, the cyborg, aliens, gambling, and the

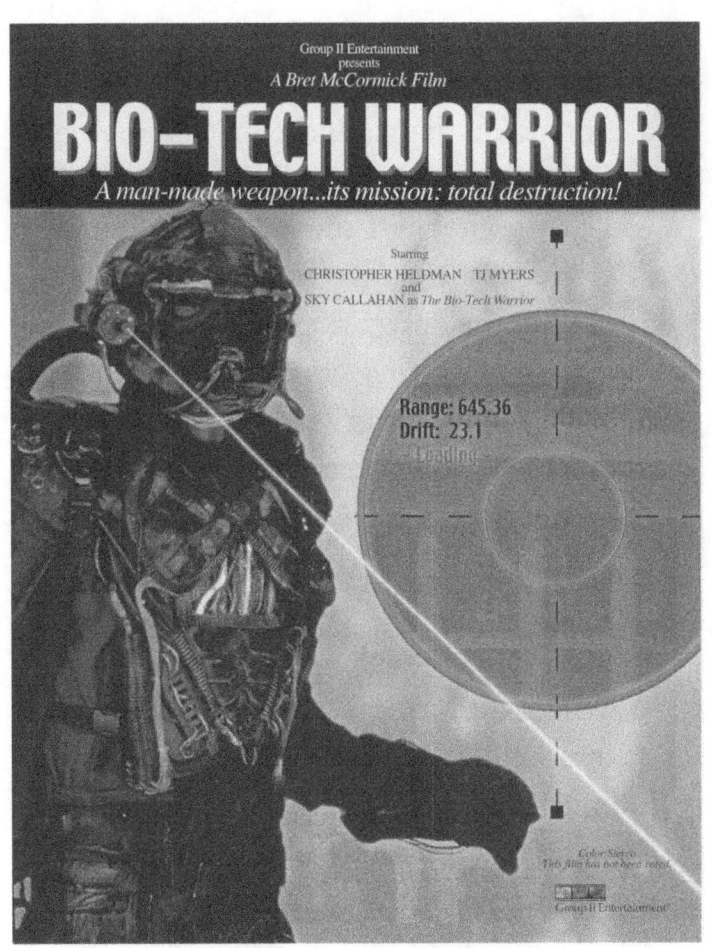

Original promo art for **Bio-tech Warrior**.

the factory and the creepy cyborg turned to the dark side. The sweaty man teaches Blondie how to use a typewriter to stop the madness. She types away for a long time but it takes her awhile to figure the sequence of keys it takes to turn off the cyborg.

*Bio-Tech Warrior* ends up standing at attention in a practically empty warehouse. The only things in there are boxes for the good guys to hide behind when they finally show up. A menacing, curly-haired guy comes by to serve up some toxic sewage to the cyborg. This guy appeared in the movie a couple of times before. Eventually, Ham Salad assaults Jerry Garcia and squeezes his arm really hard until Jerry coughs up the awful truth. They head over to the warehouse. When they arrive, Jerry takes a look around and discovers three pickle jars containing miniature Don Drapers in their underwear. Jerry sets up a plastic explosive device.

Just in the nick of time, Blondie figures out which typewriter keys to hit and the cyborg shuts down during a martial arts scene. For some reason, little Jerry Garcia floats around like a helium-filled, birthday balloon. He shoots a death ray out of his mouth and saves the day. The closing credits feature movie clips of every actor while their name is displayed on the screen. This goes on and on. First, we see every actor who has a speaking part. Then we get acquainted with every featured ex-

lunch menu. Thursday, it's Sloppy Joes. After a while they stop talking.

Jerry Garcia plays a fat hippie who's also trying to crack the case. He's the only sympathetic character who knows the whole truth. The purpose of his character is that if all else fails, he'll be there to turn the tables. A sweaty scientist does a Skype call with Blondie. He talks for a long time about Roswell and earthlings and extraterrestrials secretly working together. It turns out that *Bio-Tech Warrior* was made by humans using alien technology. There was some kind of mix up at tra and background player. This goes on until we see actors who aren't even in the movie. Then I took some Dramamine and Advil and went to bed.

## TIME TRACERS (AKA TIME TRAP) (1997)

There's a lot of sand in this movie. The characters spend a good portion of time in the prehistoric age. This was an age when sand was plentiful. It's no surprise that I was visited by the Sandman as I watched this one. The script reminded me of a decent but dull science fiction screenplay from the 1950s. The movie would've had a couple of familiar faces and running-time a half hour shorter than *Time Tracers*.

This one starts out with a kidnapping followed by a low-speed motor vehicle chase. That story line evaporates into a scene with the two leads getting liquored up poolside at a crappy tract house in the worst suburb of the worst city on earth. When I got a load of our leading man named Van in his swim trunks, my first thought was that gym memberships were plentiful in 1997. So why didn't he have one? Or if he did, why didn't he make use of it? The sight of him shirtless wasn't ironic or whacky like Will Farrell or Seth Rogan with their shirts off. Instead, it was an assault on human decency. Van steps on his watch. This event puts the wheels in motion. The broken watch establishes a plot point that launches a fascinating trajectory that takes us all the way to the end of the movie. I think there's a scene after that where a lady in a hat walks around in the desert and finds a fossilized monster hand. There's no archaeological dig. The hand is on the ground right out in the open. I don't remember if it's wearing a watch.

Author's Note: Ditto. No reviews were available at the time of this writing.

When the critical character development is behind us, *Time Tracers* turns into a time machine movie. A bunch of people show up at a top-secret time travel facility. Confusion ensues. The lab is state of the art. There's a beautiful cardboard panel with geometric cutouts. Each one is covered in colorful Saran Wrap. This panel could've once been used to teach a monkey how to match pegs of various shapes into the appropriate holes. The control panel appears to be a remnant of a rejected set piece from an early pilot episode of *Lost in Space*. The television pilot is lost but this discarded hunk of junk lives on. Jeffrey (*Re-Animator*) Combs is tethered to this thing. He says some heady scientific mumbo jumbo and a couple of times he does a countdown. The first one is from ten to zero. The second starts at five because we've already seen him start at ten.

When you hear the word zero, an item placed on a lightbox dematerializes. One of these items is the film's featured prop, the broken watch. Another is a faded diploma from the University of Phoenix.

The group of random people who showed up at the lab get dressed in *Power Rangers* outfits. One guy goes to a Civil War re-enactment. He shows up with a large camcorder hidden in his underwear. No videotaping is allowed at this event. The time-travelling journalist finds a man sitting under a bed sheet. This guy gives by far the worst performance in the entire movie. He has absolutely no charisma. But the time traveler pulls the camera out of his underwear and interviews the guy anyway. Fortunately, this horrible performance is cut short when he gets shot by a rubber bullet and dies of a heart attack. The time traveler finds the bad actor's widow riding on a train and shows her a clip of the video interview. It's her dream come true. Finally rid of her abusive husband, she's free to marry an attractive man with money.

The real excitement begins when all the super heroes go back in time to shortly after the creation of earth, six thousand years ago. The bald-headed villain plots against everyone, concealing the fact that he's carrying a quartz crystal that he stole during a dramatic train ride. Instead of using the crystal for meditation purposes, he cooks up a nefarious scheme. This part of the

Original **Time Tracers** promo art.

movie features lots of authentic dinosaur footage. There's a subplot where a muscle man takes his shirt off and forgets to put it back on. The costumed crew-members run around from rock to rock to evade the attention of the dinosaurs. Several of the heroes get eaten by the frightening beasts. The bald man gets gored by a Triceratops. A dino-man shows up and makes trouble for the remaining heroes. For some reason, the creature faints and they carry him around in a prehistoric stretcher.

The super heroes are desperate to get back to the future. They're having a hell of a time because they accidently changed the fossil record and altered the fabric of time. When the money runs out, the filmmakers decide it's time to shut this one down. The group gets beamed back to modern times and forget their names and drivers' license numbers. They get a laugh out of making fun of each other's outfits. Jeffrey Combs shows up as a hillbilly driving a pick-up truck. The time travelers pile into the bed of the truck and ride off down an abandoned country road. The watch makes a final appearance and credits roll.

## REPLIGATOR (1996)

I've watched *Repligator* four times. Each time, was more perilous than the time before. Upon the first viewing, thirty minutes in, I broke out into a cold sweat, which then turned into a warm sweat. This was followed by a hot sweat. At this juncture, I fell into a state of semi-consciousness and the remainder of the movie was a blur of vibrant colors and a headache-inducing, over modulated soundtrack. By the next morning, I had entirely forgotten about the movie. All that remained of the experience was the worst hangover of my life. Glutton for punishment that I am, I endeavored to sit through it three more times. These viewings can only be described as a variation of the seven Stations of the Cross, except truncated into three stages. Each viewing took me deeper into the fiery, cavernous recesses of the pit of hell.

> "The kind of film Edward D. Wood Jr would be making if he was around today."
> --*horrornews.net*, Daniel King, July 5, 2015

> "As for the main body of *Repligator*, the best thing I can say in its favor is that everyone involved in making it looks to have had a ball."
> --*1000misspenthours.com*, Scott Ashlin

> "Oh, where to even start on this film ... Actually, I found this more enjoyable than most of the output of anything associated with Seth Rogan, the Wilson brothers (Owen and Luke), or especially Adam Sandler."
> --*indiehorrorfilms.blogspot.com*, Richard Gary, February 25, 2013

Despite my painful journey, I decided that telling the truth as I remember it might shed some light on the artistic merits of what has been regarded by many as a cinematic masterpiece. *Repligator* was directed by journeyman auteur, Bret McCormick, who is well-known for turning out work that's not only in color but also in focus. From my perspective, I'm not certain he was aware he was making this movie. This style of rudderless filmmaking can be entertaining. Does it work well for this movie? I'll let you decide. There's obviously entertainment value in this piece of work. Unlike many movies of this ilk, it didn't disappear into the abyss of unwatchable, worn-out VHS tapes featuring rolling video and bad tracking. Thanks to a happy intervention by the hands of Fortuna in one of her more fanciful moments, this motion picture is surprisingly well-preserved. It's technically superb in almost every imaginable way. *Repligator* is available on DVD and has found a growing audience on streaming platforms.

Original promo art for **Repligator**.

This one loosely falls into the T & A genre. If you're not familiar with that acronym, the letters stand for Tits and Ass. The movie actually represents the niche subgenre known simply as T. There are plenty of tits but no ass. Whether this was an act of incompetence or a lack of appropriate lighting instruments may never be known. Regardless of the lack of ass, the tits are exceptional and each pair is attached to a lovely vixen with no tattoos or piercings. The lack of skin art and puncture wounds is probably a result of the bygone era of the production. For my money, I'd rather look at a Playboy Bunny than a biker's moll.

In the opening scene, a chubby, seemingly heterosexual Gomer Pyle puts an electrified colander on his head. This futuristic piece of kitchenware enables the military moron to see Brinke Stevens topless. More boobs ensue. This titillating adventure is followed by opening credits, which feature animation created by a pizza delivery boy after huffing paint for three hours. An army colonel whose name you can guess shows up at a business park to find out about a classified government project. Gunnar "Leatherface" Hansen makes an appearance to offer the Colonel a peek through some glasses that enable him to see fully clothed women turn topless. The viewer is introduced to Gunnar as he talks with his back to the camera. He turns around so that we recognize him to be Gunnar Hansen. This bit of inspired direction adds surprise production-value due to the star power of Mr. Hansen. He proceeds to explain the plot of the movie we're about to watch.

The real story plays out on a set that hearkens back to Ed Wood's *Bride of the Monster*. Eddie's sets are significantly better because black and white film disguises their horribleness. *Repligator*'s living color presentation renders them in eye-popping, full-color detail. Fortunately, the producer's nephew worked at a party supply store. His adolescent, hormone-induced fervor was ample motivation for him to abscond with a fog machine for the weekend. The smoky, billowing fog is by far the most compelling special effect in the movie. Two Styrofoam pillars serve as a teleporter and the control panel is a window air conditioning unit with a VCR on top.

Now, the actual movie begins. An expendable army guy is teleported somewhere. It could be into oblivion. The result of the experiment is better than anyone could hope for. A pair of beautifully crafted, cardboard space-ship doors open to reveal an eerie, back-lit fogbank from which a beautiful girl emerges. It turns out that the unappealing white-trash, army reject has transformed into a lovely babe. Thus, a secret weapon is discovered. A brigade of hot chicks will distract the enemy into submission. Of course, the scientist/military contingents aren't inclined to leave well enough alone. They proceed to pad the running time.

The converted girls get put back through the teleporter in hopes of turning them back into men. This stupid idea produces abject failure. The upside is the girls are reconstituted into nymphomaniacs.

The plot thickens as the film cuts away to another location. We're whisked away into an insurance company office. Cubicles ratchet up the suspense. Nymphos dry-hump men and morph into human dinosaurs. Action abounds for the remainder of the movie. People wearing rubber dino masks run amuck. Scientists wielding ray guns fire away, dispatching dino-people into little green and black electronic blobs that fill the screen. At some point we're subjected to a genuinely pathetic attempt at sophomoric humor. For no apparent reason, a couple of poorly, made-up, nelly zombie men desperately seek the affection of any man they can corner. The melee is squelched when all the dinosaur masks are removed.

The singular asset of *Repligator* is its deluge of breasts and nippled, flesh-covered water balloons. If you pop a handful of Phenobarbital tablets followed by a lighter fluid chaser, you'll either enjoy this movie or you'll die. If you've never watched a movie in your entire life and by some twist a fate, you watch this one; you'll be delighted by the vivid colors and well-timed sound effects.

Okay, for twelve years of my adult life I was a schlockmeister. Anyone who truly understands what the word means as I am applying it in this context, anyone who's worked in the slimy lower echelons of feature films understands it's a bit like saying, 'I was a prostitute' or 'I was a drug addict.' I willingly went where few go without the influence of some serious coercion. I have been accused of trafficking in gratuitous violence, promoting the random admiration of the naked female form, following in the footsteps of Larry Buchanan and Ed Wood Jr and engaging in outright stupidity. I plead guilty to all of the above.

I gave all that up more than twenty years ago. To my way of thinking, that places my entire cinematic oeuvre in the category of 'youthful indiscretions.'

Not that I regret a single ill-conceived creation, mind you. I look back on those times with a great deal of fondness.

This book would not exist were it not for the influence of my sometime collaborator E.R. Bills. He overheard Glen Coburn and me reminiscing one night and exclaimed, "This needs to be a book!" His gentle prodding is what brought this thing about. When E.R. suggested the project, I'm sure he had a beast of a different genus in mind. He is a serious nonfiction writer and surely would have preferred I pen the sort academic treatise I would be researching for the next five years. Sorry, E.R., not my style.

Others would've pushed this book in the direction of relentless, comedic mockery. Again, not my thing. Still others would have me to do a gentle, middle-of-the-road volume that approached the subject with whimsy, taking care to offend no one. Meh …

I became a filmmaker because I admired the work of Buchannan, Brownrigg, Ulmer and others. Often, the things critics pointed out as their shortcomings were what I liked most about them. I am fortunate to have met many of the filmmakers in this book and to have become a friend to some.

Texas Schlock is what this book is about. For better or for worse, I'm a part of the story. So, I have to tell it my way. If I come across as a bit narcissistic, please forgive me.

Intuition is a wonderful thing. In an age when we are constantly warned against trusting our own impressions and encouraged to rely on 'the experts,' intuition is largely disrespected, dismissed and downplayed. As a filmmaker, the times I accepted expert opinions and followed a course of action counter to my own internal leanings, I always regretted it.

Following my own gut-feelings led to the creation of *The Abomination* and later, *Repligator*. Out of the twenty or so features I was involved with, these are the only two that still have legs. They are absurd, crude, offensive, inane and some would say sense-

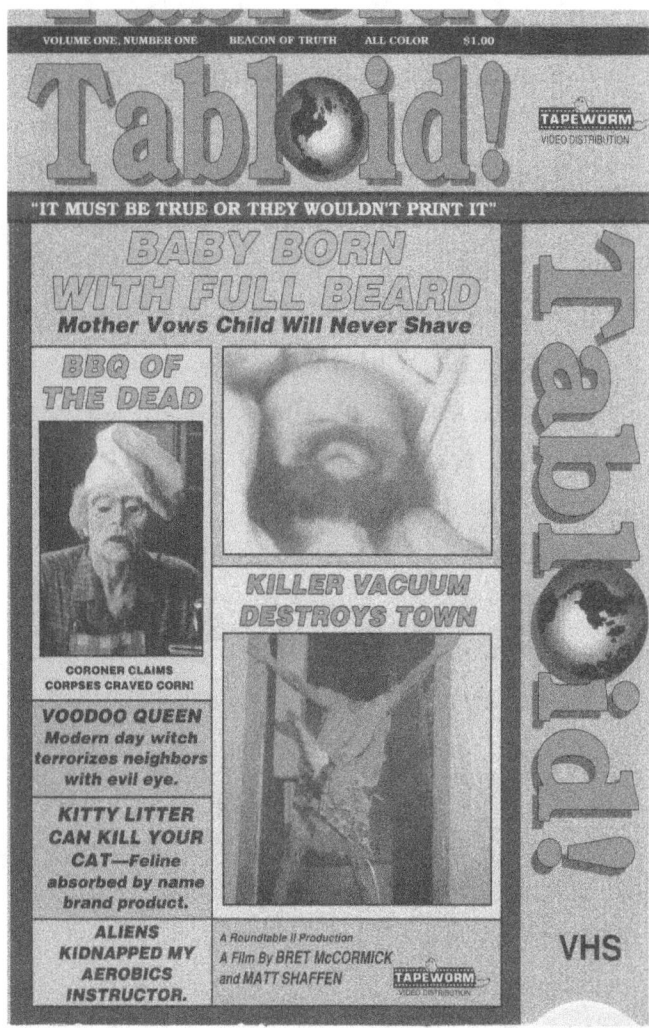

VHS sleeve for *Tabloid!*

less. But a certain sector of the general public still enjoys watching them. What does this prove? Not much. Still I am convinced that artists should follow their intuitive urgings. Following expert advice is not art, but business. It's a shoddy business that is not worth the compromise.

When I entered feature film production in earnest, I wanted nothing more than to make horror films. Had I listened to my internal guidance system, that is exactly what I would've done. Instead of giving in to my feelings of insecurity, I would not have taken on a partner and spent $112,000 on my first feature. I would have shot a horror flick for about $25,000 with a skeleton crew, friends and family. That had been my plan all along and deviating from that plan created a whole slew of problems with far-reaching effects.

My first movie was *Tabloid!* It was an anthology film inspired by the national fascination with tabloid newspapers like *National Enquirer* and *Weekly World News*. It was not a horror film, though my segment *Barbecue of the Dead* mixed horror tropes with existentialist fare like *My Dinner with Andre* (1981). Cinematographer Roger Pistole and Gaffer David Blood gave the segment a nice look. Glen Coburn directed a segment called *Baby Born with Full Beard*. It was funny and Texan-to-the-bone. My partner, Matt Shaffen, directed a whimsical story called *Killer Vacuum Destroys Town*. It had the makings of a pretty good piece, but was stretched beyond its ability to entertain in an attempt to hit our desired running time.

Filmmakers not only make movies. They also make mistakes. Especially beginning filmmakers. *Tabloid!* was a mistake on many levels. It's first failing being we spent too much money creating this clunker. Our second error in judgment was creating a thing that was neither fish nor fowl. *Tabloid!* has its moments, but the viewer has to sift through a lot of yawn-worthy material to get there.

C'est la vie!

Lesson learned. Moving right along.

A few of the distributors we'd contacted while trying to sell *Tabloid!*, said they were selling the hell out of schlocky, gory stuff from the 1960s and 1970s – the sort of stuff Herschel Gordon Lewis pioneered. Based on this information, we began building a couple of projects that could make the most of our limited resources.

We didn't have money to pay actors. We'd be using friends and family. These facts precluded the idea of attempting anything "serious." No real drama, no forays into legitimate suspense. These two movies were designed to be over-the-top gorefests. It was understood from the get-go they'd be as funny as they were repulsive.

I wrote a 20-page treatment with some dialog that I called *The Abomination*. My partner insisted on writing a full-blown script for the project he was calling *Ozone*.[ii] I used the few tricks I'd learned reading Dick Smith's make-up books to create monster prosthetics and facial appliances. Everybody got in on the act. Even my brother, Brad the car salesman, spent his spare time constructing a little mechanical puppet that we'd use in the finale, when it popped out of Cody's torso.

My step dad had a close friend named Curtis Moore who owned a lot of real estate out west of Fort Worth in a community called Poolville. Curtis was a great old guy who willingly gave us carte blanche to destroy an empty old house on one of his ranch properties. If I recall correctly, he even said something like, "Could you just burn the damn thing down? I'd like to be rid of it."

The Bio-Tech Warrior.

We didn't burn it down, but it was a nasty mess by the time we were finished.

As the shoot progressed, we drenched lots of folks in fake gore made from corn syrup and food coloring. It turned humans into an icky, sticky, gooey mess. Bear in

---

[ii] Later, when marketing reality set in, the title was changed to *Ozone: Attack of the Redneck Mutants*.

mind it was a long drive back to civilization. The only plumbing on the property was in the mobile home where the ranch foreman lived. We talked the poor guy into letting us use his shower for the actors. That man was so incredibly glad to see us go when we finally wrapped shooting after about six weeks.

The plan was to shoot each film in ten days. A ten-day shooting schedule? Hell yeah! That's what Roger Corman had on some of our favorite films he made in the 1950s. Why not. My partner was supposed to go first, but he begged off, saying he needed more time to finish his screenplay. This was the same strategy he'd used when we shot *Tabloid!* What it meant in practice was that his portion of the production would be open-ended regarding scheduling and whatever money was left in the budget.

I shot *The Abomination* in ten days. We embarked on *Ozone* and finally stopped shooting after 23 days. Matt, even then, was full of angst and excuses about why he needed just another day or two.

When you're shooting messy movies, using friends and family, there comes a point when people just say, "Hell no. I'm done." That's sort of what happened. Our double-bill was finally in the can. We had neither the manpower nor the resources to continue.

Young and inexperienced, we sought out experts to guide us through the process on *Tabloid!* We'd followed the advice of the guys who were supposed to know. We'd conformed our negative and generated a low-con print which we transferred to a 1" video master. The conforming was just in case there was ever a chance at theatrical exhibition. The result of following expert advice was that we spent $112,000 making a movie we could've created for about $50,000. I may have been slow to come around, but I was waking up to the realization that the "experts" are generally guys who have a vested interest in getting you to spend money. And that's not just true in film production. It's the same in every commercial endeavor, no matter what the field.

By the time we were in postproduction on *Abomination* and *Ozone*, we'd figured out there was no point in spending money on anything that wasn't certain to add money to the back end. Based on this understanding, we transferred our original Super 8mm film to ¾" video and edited on a cheap off-line system we found at a home-video transfer house called MCM Productions on the southside of Fort Worth. The place mainly transferred 8mm home movies to VHS, but they had a decent little editing room.

We had met the gauntlet of production. A new challenge was just beginning. The editing process went on forever! My family members kept asking me when we'd be finished. Finally, when we had an edit

The Melting Man from *Bio-Tech Warrior*.

master for both films, we screened them for the people who'd been involved in the two productions. The consensus was pretty much, "You spent all that time and effort on this? Uh...why?"

Not exactly an auspicious beginning.

In retrospect, (hindsight, as they say, is 20/20) we should've transferred the original film on these two titles to 1" video. It would've been more expensive and the edit would've cost more, too. Still, our chances of making money would've been far greater.

At the American Film Market in Santa Monica, we got representatives from the JVC company in Japan interested in releasing all three of our movies. They gave us $10,000 advances on *Tabloid!*, *Abomination* and *Ozone*. We delivered *Tabloid!* and it appeared in their release catalog right next to a big-budget *Star Trek* movie! Yay! Score one point for the schlockmeisters from Texas. Months later, though, when we delivered the horror movie masters to JVC, they rejected them because they'd been posted on ¾" video. Bummer.

Still living, still learning.

Things dragged on. Even though we were generating very little money, I still had a wife and kids I was trying to sup-

Promo for **Macon County War** starring Dan Haggerty.

port. Things were bleak. I decided to dissolve the partnership and try to keep making movies alone, on my own terms.

Since my pre-teen years, I had always been a horror and sci-fi fanatic. I watched these genres relentlessly. I wanted more than anything to produce and direct these types of film, but because I was intent on maximizing my potential for profit, I entered into a number of deals in which distributors decided for me the genre I'd be working in.

Early on I approached Fred Olen Ray, thinking, "Here's a schlockmeister who's worked in horror. Maybe he'll give me financing for a horror picture." At first, I thought my gambit might pay off. Fred had a short film clip of John Carradine reading from a spooky old book. He wanted an entire feature built around this brief scene. *Crazy to build a whole movie around an old bit of footage less than a minute long.* Still I thought it would be cool to direct what could become the final film of John Carradine! (See how this weird-ass world of schlock works? Crazy, man, crazy!)

My movie featuring Carradine was not to be. Fred called me up one day and said, "I want to focus on your strengths." I anticipated he meant gore. "You're good at rural stuff. Your locations and characters are sort of hillbilly." Long story short, he wanted to send Dan Haggerty, of *Grizzly Adams* (TV series 1977-1980) fame, to Texas for three days and have me write, produce and direct a picture he wanted to call *Macon County War*. Not my first choice, but it was work and I couldn't afford to turn it down, or so I thought at the time.

It would be a few years before I was able to get back to the horror and sci-fi flicks I so wanted to do.

A group of young people calling themselves Open Door Productions, worked with me on an action picture titled *Striking Point* (1995). Initially, they were a bit condescending about working on an exploitation picture. They were serious artists and imagined themselves making the next critically acclaimed indie smash. By the time the production was winding down, they'd decided they wanted to try their hand at an exploitation flick of their own.

They asked if I could help them secure distribution. I did what I could to help them and that's how I became the Producer on a film called *Cyberstalker*[iii] (1996 aka *The Digital Prophet*.) The talent at the core of Open Door Productions was Anthony Brownrigg, youngest son of S.F. Brownrigg. Tony was good at everything; he could write, act, shoot, edit, create special effects. He was a real renaissance man, in a category all by himself.

Matt Trotter, a Dallas-based indie director who'd made a sci-fi action movie called *Stealth Hunters* (1991), somehow ended up in possession of a huge futuristic set from a failed made-for-TV sci-fi series. I arranged to have portions of this set made available, hoping to increase production value. The Open Door guys cannibalized pieces of this big-budget set and put them to good use in *Cyberstalker*.

Annie Biggs pulls off a fantastic performance as a schizoid comic book nerd who goes postal due to the perceived intervention of a weird higher power. Jeff Combs, of *Re-Animator* fame, plays an intense and frightening fringe character who runs a comic book shop. These two make the movie memorable.

While I was gathering old horror trailers for a documentary series based on John McCarty's book *The Fearmakers*, I became friends with a writer in LA named Ted Newsom. Ted was a schlockmeister at heart and he'd written a time travel sci-fi epic built around stock footage from other films he knew he could legitimately license from the rights holders. I don't remember what it was originally called, but when completed, the movie was known as *Time Tracers* (1997 aka *Time Trap*).

For *Time Tracers*, we used a troupe of eager Dallas actors and brought in Jeff Combs to play a scientist named Dr. Carrington. That shoot was a lot of fun. We shot in and around Dallas and even filmed for a couple of days in the Dinosaur Valley State Park in Glenrose, Texas. My son, Joshua, played a half-human/half-reptile missing link. Jeremiah, my middle son, played an extra-terrestrial who corrects the mistakes of foolish humans, mending the dangerous rift they've caused in the time-space continuum. The youngest boy, Joseph, plays a Civil War-era waif on board an antique train. Considering the budget, I'd say we did a very decent job of delivering a marketable (for the time) product.

*Bio-tech Warrior* (1996) was the next sci-fi movie on the slate. A Dallas-based distributor who was heavily into a 'New Age' spiritual belief system and loved anything related to Sedona, Arizona, told me he wanted a sci-fi thriller. Following the lead

---

[iii] Not to be confused with the film of the same title released in 2012.

set by schlockmeister-par-excellence Sam Katzman decades before, I made use of as much stock footage as I could get my hands on. This was satisfying to me in a way only a true schlockmeister would appreciate.

Local actor, filmmaker and college instructor, Randy Clower made a fantastic cyborg costume for the *Bio-tech Warrior*. The warrior itself was played by tall, lanky Dan 'Sky' Callahan. We made use of several actors who'd worked with us on *Time Tracers*. The shoot went pretty smoothly and I felt like I was on a roll.

The sets from *Time Tracers* were still standing and we had a refrigerator full of 35mm short ends. Always a Roger Corman fan-boy, I'd often dreamed of trying to emulate the ultra-short shooting schedule he had on the original *Little Shop of Horrors* (1960).

The video editor who had cut *Bio-tech Warrior* and *Time Tracers* was an aspiring writer named Keith Kjornes.[iv] I asked him if he could come up with something in a week that we could use to make another movie. My only requirements were, it must contain sci-fi elements, naked women and humor (however lame). Keith didn't let me down. Inspired by a notice he'd read in one of the Hollywood trade publications about a movie called *Replikator* (1994),

he and special effects artist T.G. Weems wrote *Repligator*. In a couple weeks' time, we were in production. Kjornes did a great job as Dr. Hardy. The man had a natural talent for buffoonery.

When *Repligator* was edited together, we only had 75 minutes running time. The project languished for several months until Ted and Wynn Winberg, of Aries Productions in Arlington, Texas, agreed to invest some time and money into completing this cinematic oddity. They paid to bring Brinke Stevens and Gunnar Hansen to town. We shot a couple of days to inject additional scenes written by Wynn to fill out the movie's running time. The final product is a bewildering flick that continues to draw viewers.

In October of 1995, I was desperately casting about, trying to get one more project completed by the end of the year. I'd produced *Takedown*[v] (1995), produced and directed *Time Tracers*, *Biotech Warrior* and *Repligator*. I'd read somewhere that Corman had completed five films in one year. I reasoned that this venerable schlockmeister could be the answer to my dilemma.

I drafted a letter stating that I was trying to match his record of five films in a year. I included my demo reel and a news item from the Dallas paper in which Jane Sumner had referred to me as the "Roger Corman of Dallas." The idea I pitched was

---

[iv] Keith Kjornes spent the last years of his life mostly in Los Angeles, building a screenwriting career. He wrote a fairly big budget sci-fi horror flick called *The Devil's Tomb* (2009) that starred Cuba Gooding, Jr and Ron Perlman. He has 16 screenwriting credits listed on imdb.com. Keith passed away in Fort Worth, Texas in 2013.

[v] Not to be confused with the TWO other movies of the same title.

an updated remake of *The Beast with a Million Eyes* (1955), shot forty years after the original on exactly the same meager budget!<sup>vi</sup> Frankly, I was a little surprised about a week later when one of Corman's people called me.

Corman didn't go for the *Beast with a Million Eyes* thing. He did, however, ask me to shoot a remake of a film called *Streets* (1990) he'd done a few years earlier starring Christina Applegate. So, in December of 1995, I managed to squeeze in one more picture; a movie about a maniac motorcycle cop (Patrick de Fazio) who's pursuing a teenage prostitute (actress and Playboy model, Kimberly Rowe). We called it *Rumble in the Streets*[vii] (1996).

Corman came to town to check out the production. It was probably the best all-around experience of my production career. Since I was twelve I had been telling people some day I was going to make movies with Roger Corman. At age thirty-seven my dream came true.

In the fall of 1996, I did a second film for Corman. *The Protector* (1998) starred Ed Marinaro and Lee Majors. It was an action flick written by Chris Heldman, who had hoped to play the lead. Instead he got to produce. Corman cast Kate Rodger, a Dallas native and former Playboy model, to play the female lead. Cyril O'Reilly of *Porky's* (1981) fame played an underworld bad guy. The film's protagonist is a computer-whiz vigilante. The scenes involving his virtual reality relationship with his dead wife add a sci-fi flavor to the film.

The spring of 1997 brought a slew of disappointments into my life. Not the least of which was Dallas-based distributor, Tom. T. Moore, filing bankruptcy. Moore had been licensing the rights to four of my films in foreign territories. He announced his bankruptcy the month before he was contractually obligated to make specific payments to me and other filmmakers. In the light of this development, I decided to throw in the towel.

It had been a blast, but I knew there had to be an easier way to make a living.

These days I write books and a lot of short horror tales. This satisfies my creative urges without costing me anything. In fact, it sometimes puts money *into* my pocket. What a concept! A few years ago, when Joseph Ziemba interviewed me for his on-line fan magazine, *Bleeding Skull*, he asked if I would ever return to filmmaking; was a belated sequel to *The Abomination* a possibility? I suppose it's possible. After all, anything's possible. Isn't that what the quantum theorists tell us? Some things are just a lot more probable than others. In some divergent dimension, I'm sure that sequel is already resting on the shelves of horror fans.

[vi] *The Beast with a Million Eyes* was made in 1955 for about $33,000.
[vii] It is no coincidence that Jackie Chan's similarly titled movie *Rumble in the Bronx* had recently made a splash at the box office.

# SHERMAN AND MINTON

Author's note: As with the chapters on Larry Buchanan and Jacob Grim and Sal Hernandez, the format applied to most of the book seemed to inhibit best use of the material available. Consequently, this chapter dealing with the work of Jess Sherman and Mike Minton has a slightly different layout.

## CREEP TALES (2004)

Before I got my first film production gig going in Texas, after graduating from Brooks Institute in Santa Barbara, California, I worked for a time as a printer for a little offset franchise called Quik-Print. The location where I worked was located on Rosedale near the intersection of 8th Avenue, in the heart of the Medical District. My boss was a likable guy named Rod Bertram. The Bertram family had three Quik-Print franchise locations in Fort Worth; one in the heart of downtown on Houston Street, a second on 7th Street near the Museum District and the third, as I said before, in the Medical District.

"Here's a horror anthology you may have missed. The title, of course, is clearly meant to allude to another anthology hit directed by some guy you may have heard of named George A. Romero. While all five tales contained within Mr. Romero's *Creepshow* (1982) were lensed specifically for that film, here the director (Mandel) has gathered together six short films from other filmmakers and shot a silly framing device to tie them all together."
--*thebloodypitofhorror.blogspot.com*, September 21, 2011

"*Creep Tales* is a horror-anthology which began filming in 1985, was finished in 1989, but wasn't released until 2004. With a PG-rating, each segment is rather tame but still very entertaining."
--*letterboxd.com*, Hollie Horror

On a typical day at Quik-Print I would stand all day long at one of the AB Dick 360 presses and churn out thousands of 8 ½ x 11 or legal-size sheets of printed material. Rarely did I interact with customers at the front counter. One day, Rod asked me to help a young man who was standing at the counter with a manuscript in his hand. This chance encounter had far-reaching implications in years to come. As it turns out, the young man was Jesse (Jess) Sherman. In his hand was a screenplay Jess was developing with Greg Bransom[i], called *Support Your Local Monsters*. He was there to have additional copies made of the script.

> "So, we begin with two monsters bringing a horror movie to a monster party. This is the wraparound and it's rather meaningless. It's similar to the anthology *Screamtime* where some no-gooders steal some tapes from a video store and each represents a different tale. That one was done much better, but the wraparound is similar. The monsters are rather stupid and just laugh at everything. I think this was the comic relief for the film, but the movie isn't scary. It reminded me of *Monsters*, that old TV show from the 1980s. Okay, I know, I'm comparing this movie to about fifteen other movies and I'm only in the second paragraph. I'll stop. Sorry."
>
> --*scaredstiffreviews.com*, Geno McGahee, December 23, 2015

Monsters? Screenplays? Since my return to Fort Worth I had begun to feel like a fish out of water. I was struggling to make ends meet and I rarely encountered others who shared my interests. I made a couple of copies of the screenplay for Jess and struck up a conversation. "Are you a filmmaker?" I asked.

Jess cleared his throat and said, a little self-consciously, "Tentatively." I laughed then and I laugh to myself now as I recall it.

"Aren't we all?" I replied. Like all film school grads who had no relatives or close friends in "the industry," I was clueless. I knew how to use a light meter, how to focus a camera. I knew the difference between a workprint and a negative or positive original. I had shot and edited student film projects. I knew why A and B rolling was necessary on a 16mm project. Even so, I was virtually unprepared for a career as an independent filmmaker. What film school grads did not know then, and probably still do not know, what even many seasoned schlockmeisters did not and do not know, was the "business" end of the equation. Here were a couple of local guys who appeared to share my aspirations. I wasn't going to miss the opportunity to strike up a friendship.

I told Jess I had watched Greg Bransom's late-night horror show on Channel 5. He lit up and told me he'd been a supporting player on the program. He mentioned another local I'd met at high school, Jody Dean. Dean, a big kid, had portrayed the Frankenstein monster on Bransom's *Museum of Horrors* show. It was a lot like other horror film venues on local TV stations that had come before; things like *Nightmare Theater* with Bill

[i] Greg Bransom was known for playing 'Dr. Cerberus,' the weird host of *Museum of Horrors*, KXAS Channel 5's Saturday night horror movie venue in the Dallas/Fort Worth television market.

Camfield as the Gorgon on Fort Worth's Channel 11 and elsewhere in the country; *Ghoulardi*[ii], *Vampira*[iii] and later, *Elvira, Mistress of the Dark*[iv].

In the ensuing months, Jess and I got to know each other fairly well. I was extremely interested in special effects and had done some stop-motion in film school, including a TV ad with an animated pirate character for a place called Schooner Inn Donuts. There was a disembodied hand in the *Support Your Local Monsters* script and Jess hoped I'd be able to create the effects to bring it to life on screen.

Jess was one of the staunchest fans of the classic Universal Studios horror pictures that I ever met. I thought I was a fan-boy, but he put me to shame. He'd seen pretty much every horror film ever made up to that point. The ones he hadn't seen, he knew about from reading fan publications. He had a nodding acquaintance with Forrest J. Ackerman of *Famous Monsters of Filmland*[v] fame and had crossed paths with most of the Dallas old-timers; people like S.F. "Brownie" Brownrigg. His devotion to the Universal monsters and the actors who portrayed them bordered on being religious. His esteem for the likes of Boris Karloff, Bela Lugosi and Lon Chaney Jr. was unbounded. Jess wanted more than anything to create a character through which he would be remembered. With this in mind, he'd written a hunchbacked assistant into the *Support Your Local Monsters* screenplay. When that project didn't materialize, he came up with a cable TV concept called *Monster Bargains*, in which a hunchbacked bargain-hunter would whiz around the metroplex in a hearse looking for great deals. One way or another he was going to create a persona for himself as a creepy, comical hunchback!

Somewhere along the way, Jess and some cohorts rented the empty half of a building in Deep Ellum. He talked me into becoming a part of this "film co-op" for which privilege I paid something like $65 per month toward the rent. I referred to this venture briefly in the introduction to this book. Others in the co-op actually lived on the premises, so the thing was a lot more like a frat house than a business. I could write an entire book on the colorful episodes that occurred in the mid-1980s at Productions West Communications.

Later, after I'd lost touch with Mike Minton and Jess Sherman, they assembled several short horror films together with the intention of creating an anthology film for the direct-to-video market. Their vision was something like *The House that*

---

[ii] Ghoulardi, played by Ernie Anderson, was the host of WJW-TV's *Shock Theater* in Cleveland, Ohio from 1963 to 1966.

[iii] Maila Nurmi was American TV's first horror movie host, playing the Vampira character on KABC-TV Channel 7 in Los Angeles, California from 1954 to 1955.

[iv] Cassandra Petersen played Elvira, the hostess of *Movie Macabre* on KHJ-TV Los Angeles beginning in 1981. The show was quite popular and was soon syndicated all over the nation.

[v] *Famous Monsters of Filmland* was a print magazine for horror fans, published from 1958 to 1983.

*Dripped Blood* (1971) or *Tales from the Crypt* (1972), movies Amicus Films had produced in the UK. Those films had been moderately successful in US theaters and were fondly remembered by fans like myself. Jess and Mike enlisted the help of Ken Mandel. A Dallas filmmaker with something of a counter-culture reputation, Ken had produced a number of music videos during the early heyday of MTV.[vi] So was born one of the most outrageous cheese fests ever known to horror fans – *Creep Tales!* Jess Sherman's dream of portraying a zany hunchback on screen had finally come true.

Though I hadn't seen Jess and Mike in decades, I reached out to them via Facebook and asked if they'd like to be the subject of a chapter in *Texas Schlock*. They graciously consented. These guys very meticulously answered my questions in great detail, providing a lot of color and interesting flavor to the behind-the-scenes story of how *Creep Tales* came to be.

TS: Why don't we start out with a bit of background? How did you guys develop an interest in making movies?

JS: I grew up in Ft. Worth, Texas. At age 12, I knew what I wanted to be; a monster actor in the tradition of Boris Karloff and

Jesse Sherman, half of the duo responsible for **Creep Tales**.

Lon Chaney. I grew up watching the classic Universal monster movies of the 30's and 40's. Then I began acting in school plays and making home movies.

At 15, I joined the local television show, Museum of Horrors on the NBC affiliate KXAS TV channel 5 in the Dallas/Ft Worth market. I played various characters and the Frankenstein monster was my favorite. *Museum of Horrors* was a horror host show on late night Saturdays. The cast of *Museum of Horrors* also presented live shows and personal appearances at theaters and shopping

---

[vi] This wasn't the first time Mandel had considered putting together an anthology feature. He'd hired me to do a bit of writing on a similar concept in 1984. I took some material he had and expanded it into a screenplay, he paid me and that was the last I heard of the project, because I soon became involved with the production of my own first feature, *Tabloid!*

centers. The show's host once nailed me into a sarcophagus as the Mummy, and on stage they had to use a crow bar to pry me out before I suffocated.

I also starred in my high school's musical, *You're a Good Man, Charlie Brown*. I was a mainstay in the drama department. I continued to act through high school and signed with a talent agent at nineteen. I landed work in a national commercial, a TV movie and performed in other projects. Soon afterwards, I wrote my first screenplay *Mad Lab*[vii], a horror comedy about the classic movie monsters. At twenty-two, I began managing the Texas State Fair Haunted House.[viii]

*MM*: I grew up in Dallas, Texas. At an early age, I was fascinated by my dad's home movies and the 8mm camera. I was always doing magic shows and performing it front of his family and friends. Television and movies of the 1970's had a big impact on me. I spent the summer of '75 with friends in Corpus Christi, Texas. During my stay, we went and saw a movie called *Jaws* (1975) and that changed everything. It was then I knew I wanted to be in the movies. Later, I performed in high school plays and took drama classes and then started attending advanced acting workshops.

At eighteen I signed with my first agent and landed national commercials, TV movies and voice-overs. I worked at a local movie theater and was heavily influenced by the films of Steven Spielberg and James Cameron in particular *Raiders of the Lost Ark* (1981) and *The Terminator* (1984). I picked up a camera and started shooting everything I could, including weddings, sporting events, corporate events. From there, it was a short leap to writing, shooting and editing my own short films.

*TS*: So, how did Productions West Communications come to be?

*JS*: Mike and I met at a local 1980's dance club. I was performing the Elwood half of a lip sync version of the Blues Brothers.

*MM*: I was there shooting some party footage. We hit it off and then joined forces.

*JS*: I had parlayed my State Fair Haunted House money to cover the first and last month's rent on a warehouse in the Deep Ellum district of Dallas[ix]. Later, we brought in other partners, including the author of this book. We turned the group into Productions West, an artist co-op and all-purpose entertainment studio where we created, hung out and some of us even lived there.

*MM*: At Productions West we pro-

---

[vii] Also known as *Support Your Local Monsters*.

[viii] Also known as *Haunted Verdun Manor*. Because of Jess's affiliation with the State Fair's haunted house and the production value it could potentially lend a low-budget horror film, I wrote a spec screenplay called *The Last Attraction*, one of the many attempts we made at breaking into the movie business.

[ix] Jess was something of a visionary in his choice of location. At the time he leased the building on Commerce Street, Deep Ellum was just beginning to undergo its historic make-over. It was not yet the night-life destination it would soon become.

duced a TV Pilot for a children's' program called *Caveman George*. A pilot focusing on indie filmmakers was produced called *Independent Cinema*.

*JS*: We even did an adult gameshow at the popular Monopoly's Park Place night spot. We had a Santa Claus service and staged a Santa graduation ceremony at the Hyatt Regency in Dallas that made national news and got picked up by the AP and UPI.

*MM*: We continued to manage the Haunted House for the State Fair of Texas and provided other creative services such as photography, graphic arts, set construction, acting workshops, musical rehearsal space and variety talent …

*JS*: Including Bob the Gorilla. Anything to make a buck. All the while, keeping our 80-year-old landlord, Murray, at bay.

*MM*: After all we had been through, we finally got focused and decided it was time to make a feature film which was our original intention. We were doing everything under the sun but making films. We brainstormed ideas and decided comedy-horror was the most marketable genre and set out to write the script.

*JS*: We started out thinking big, with an ambitious, high-budget, comedy-horror anthology concept and locked in on the title, *NightCreeps*. The story centered around two guys on a cross country road trip who stumble across a small, creepy town with an old, haunted movie theater that featured a midnight movie on the marquee.

*MM*: The car screeches to a stop. Out of curiosity, they enter the lobby which is covered in cobwebs and dust. They meet the old, creepy projectionist who tells them to "enjoy the show." They get their popcorn and have a seat in the mysteriously empty auditorium.

*JS*: When the clock strikes midnight, the *NightCreeps* appear and attack the two goofy guys. They run out screaming for their lives, hop in the car, burn rubber and screech off. Back in the old theater, the *NightCreeps* laugh, whoop it up, eat their popcorn then watch the first of many horror tales.

*MM*: We were really excited about the *NightCreeps* story and started writing the script. We hammered out the screenplay, then got Kerry Gammill, who penciled for DC and Marvel including *Spider-Man* and *The Death of Superman*, to create the storyboards for us.

*JS*: Kerry later worked as a conceptual artist on big budget Hollywood movies including *Virus* and *Superman Lives*. Once the script and storyboards were complete we worked with a Dallas creature shop to start work on the prototype creature designs.

*MM*: We scouted locations, hired an attorney, raised seed money, formed a limited partnership and created a private offering. We flew to LA and met with the American Film Institute and other film distributors to line up award-winning

Mike Minton, co-creator of **Creep Tales**.

short films.

*JS*: We met with director Frank DePalma who had directed episodes of the TV show, *Tales from the Darkside*, created by George Romero. We scouted locations, started pre-production and did re-writes on the script with Frank DePalma. We also met with art director Robert Burns of *Texas Chainsaw Massacre* fame. We had our above-the-line items covered and a detailed budget of one million dollars.

*MM*: For the old, creepy projectionist we wanted old, classic horror star John Carradine. We later met with Carradine and company while they were shooting a horror film on location in Tulsa, Oklahoma, which co-starred John Wayne's son Patrick.

*JS*: When we got there, it was a second-rate hotel. Poor Mr. Carradine, at his age, had a severe case of arthritis and could barely hold his fork and had a personal assistant. We were getting ready to hire him. However, Mr. Carradine showed such class as we dined and talked classic movies and old Hollywood including, *The Bride of Frankenstein* (1935), *The Grapes of Wrath* (1940) and *The Ten Commandments* (1956). It was a memorable evening and one we'll never forget.

*MM*: Then came the negotiations. We spent all night and part of the next day, with no sleep, negotiating with Mr. Carradine's manager, Byron. He was one of a kind. He had a short temper, a wild limp and a wooden cane. When we had a dispute, he would wildly swing that leg and flail his cane, so we just tried to stay out of the way until he settled down.

*JS*: As part of the agreement, we had to pay for some of their hotel expenses. We finally agreed on everything and signed the contract. We had Mr. Carradine committed for the film and drove back to Texas. We were prepared, committed, had accomplished a lot.

*MM*: Later, we heard on the news that John Carradine had kicked the bucket. He was 82. It all went down-hill from there.

*JS*: Our seed money was running out, our star had just died, and then our funding fell through. That's when we slowly descended into the dark cave of despair.

*MM*: We decided, screw it! We moved to Plan B. We scrapped the *NightCreeps* concept and decided to go guerilla-style. Robert Rodriguez would have been proud. After all the big budget development, we went through on *NightCreeps*, and to limit our risk with the previous investors, we started fresh and re-titled it *Creep Tales*.

*JS*: We then sat our butts down and cranked out the new wrap-around script. Our two protagonists were a hunchback and a mute gravedigger on a Halloween night who journey to locate their favorite movie, *Creep Tales*, which they will take back to their creepy bunch of friends to watch and enjoy.

*MM*: On imdb.com the logline reads, "On Halloween night, two shabby, dimwitted hunchbacks dig up the anthology horror video *Creep Tales*, that was buried with their Uncle Munger and show it to their dimwitted monster friends." It was brilliant.

*JS*: We also cast, ourselves as the endearing numbskull Pizza Guys 1 & 2 and at one point literally scare ourselves at the front door.

*MM*: The antagonist was the imposing Uncle Munger played by Tim Choate. As the Halloween full moon rises, and after an unsuccessful attempt to rent the movie from a cheap video store (managed by long-time Dallas production personality, Bill Peck) they have an epiphany; "UNCLE MUNGER!!" They howl at the full moon.

*JS*: Their ominous shadows are illuminated by an old kerosene lantern as we hear the clanging of their graveyard tools. They enter the graveyard and hear the moans and groans of the unrested as they trek onward. Suddenly they see the grave of Uncle Munger. They feverishly dig and finally hit the coffin. As they slowly open the creaky lid, there lies the dormant Uncle Munger. A rat scurries across his hands and reveals a copy of the movie, *Creep Tales*! they pry loose the movie from Munger's rotted hands. They jump out of the grave and head home as Uncle Munger remains motionless. They run back to the house and display the movie to an assorted group of creeps, ghouls and monsters who howl in excitement. The Creeps party it up as popcorn flies and they settle in for their Halloween night entertainment. They insert the movie, move in close and our first short film begins...

*MM*: We brainstormed the production, scrounged up the money and scouted for the location. The script called for a spooky old house which Jesse finally found, in what some would consider to be the bad part of town. The house was set on a wooded, acre-lot and was planned for demolition soon. It was dangerous, creepy, decrepit and condemned. We had ourselves a "set-piece." It was perfect.

*JS*: Our plan was to shoot the wrap-around to help sell the project and acquire the completion funds. We went ahead and hired music video director/DP, Ken Mandel, and his crew and started prepping the wrap-around shoot.

*MM*: With the help of family and friends we plowed ahead and scheduled the production. We shot it on 16mm with an Éclair NPR camera.

*JS*: Michael had a lot of experience with film and really liked the Éclair's features.

*MM*: On Day One and because of all the action required, plan was to use the standard 10-120mm, shot day-for-night and go handheld. On Day Two, plan was to black out the house windows, lock the camera down and shoot with some primes for the close-ups of the Creeps, rat footage and on the shots where Munger was sitting up in his grave.

*JS*: We had a big casting call for the Creeps. We scrapped all the *NightCreeps* design plans and went with some really cool, prosthetic monster masks that the new make-up guy, Joe Riley, had laying around. He also did all the Munger, Hunchback and Gravedigger makeup and did a great job.

*MM*: We created the shooting schedule and secured the locations. We brought in a generator for the shooting but later tied in to the neighbor's power to save on gasoline. We even had a production trailer.

*JS*: And Michael's family generously provided all the catering. Finally, we hired a couple of shady, local characters as our real grave-digger crew, to dig Uncle Munger's grave on our wooded, one-acre lot. We paid them some cash and kept them in beer and pizza all day until the job was done. By the time the sun had gone down, they were exhausted and it was time to shoot. It took those poor guys all day in the hundred-degree heat to dig a six-foot grave. We were afraid the cops might suspect foul play, but were fortunate they never did.

*MM*: We ended up having a crew of about ten. We also had the editing scheduled with the director as soon as the principal photography was completed. Because the story took place over the course of a Halloween night, we decided to shoot all of the exterior and B-Roll footage on Day One as day-for-night. We were ready to shoot.

*JS*: The first day of shooting, we shot the cryptic duo at a "real" graveyard, climbing over the wall and nearly getting run over by a truck (our grip truck). Later that day we shot the video store scenes with the late, great Bill Peck. For many years, Bill had a production studio and equipment rental facility in Irving, TX. Many local independent filmmakers relied on Bill's generosity and love for the film business.

*MM*: We were shooting in summer time so it was hot and both of us we're sweating like pigs. We had a number of scenes where we were running all over the county it seemed like. We would shoot

Sherman and Minton on location.

scenes, then rest and cool off. Once the sun went down, we brought out the 5K's and shot the Pizza Guys walking up to the house. Jess and I had a lot of fun playing those two guys.

*JS*: They were the only normal guys in the film. We went old school with the Pizza Guy scenes, utilizing the old Laurel and Hardy approach. On the end of day one, we finished with the Munger grave yard scenes.

*MM*: Tim Choate was a real trooper, he let us treat him any way we wanted, including being buried, having rats walk across him and he even let a tarantula crawl across his face. I was the 2nd Unit Director on all these scenes and utilized a number of low, obscure angles, shooting varying focal lengths including a fish eye effect and also shot all the Steadicam footage of Munger.

*JS*: The martini shot of Day One was Munger's slow rise out of his grave. It's Michael's favorite shot in the film. By the end of the day we had shot some fifteen hours and were exhausted. We packed up the equipment and sat out under the stars, drinking beer.

*MM*: Day Two came early. The focus on day 2 was all the interior shots at the house with the two protagonists, Karl and Cleeg, and the Creeps watching TV until Munger's vengeful arrival.

*JS*: The conditions inside the house were

brutal. The house was condemned, it was dirty, hot and cramped. Fortunately, we used the original furniture left behind which included a worn-out old couch, a lazy boy recliner, some chairs and an old TV set.

MM: The story took place at night so we had to black out all the windows. With the lights radiating, windows covered and hot, prosthetic masks on the Creeps faces in August it was hot as hell. We would shoot a scene then quickly bail out to the front yard and cool off. It was a busy day of shooting coverage. We basically shot in sequence. We had a great time shooting all the Creep footage and utilized lots of lenses including the 10mm fish-eye.

JS: The highlight of the day was the Munger sequence. After all the short films finished then Munger kicks down the front door. To accomplish this, we took the hinges off the door and Tim was able to kick it in on the rehearsals. For the final martini sequence, we decided to do it in one take. We knew we only had one shot at tearing the whole set apart.

MM: We went hand-held and called "Action!" Munger kicks the door in. Chaos ensues. Munger proceeds to tear the place apart. He knocks chairs over, overturns the table and chases Creeps. It was so funny watching all those actors blindly scatter and run for their lives as Munger chases them down. They could barely see out of those hot masks. Tim even threw one guy out the window, which we did some extra coverage on.

JS: Karl and Cleeg manage to survive and squirm by Munger, out the door and into the night. Munger then calmly sits down and watches his favorite movie, Creep Tales. Silence fell over the room. The crew broke into applause. "We got

DVD art for *Creep Tales*.

MM: The place was a wreck, we were exhausted and it was almost sundown. We packed the equipment and left the house in shambles for the demolition crew.

JS: We now had the wraparound in the can, had completed an assembly edit and

were ready to start the next step, which was acquiring all the short films to complete the anthology. The short film search was on.

*MM:* We wanted the film at least 90 minutes long but not over 110. Since we'd already completed an off-line edit on the wrap-around, which was approximately fifteen mins long, we needed to fill about 75 minutes. We wanted top quality, award winning, short, horror films that we could get at a reasonable price, paying each film maker an acquisition fee for use of their film in our anthology. We carried on a national short film search for several months.

*JS:* We practically had our own short film festival underway. It was fun going through all those films. We saw some really good films and some really, really, bad ones. In the end, we screened over 200 short films and finally narrowed it down to the list below:

*WARPED,* Directed by Roger Nygard was a really cool film that was well-directed and nicely shot. It was a SAG-deferred production and had great actors. It was over twenty minutes long, had high production value and was creepy, weird and started off with a bang. Roger went on to direct the cult classic films *Trekkies* (1997) and *Trekkies 2* (2004).

*SNATCHER,* Directed by Tim Boxell starred the famed Tom Kenny (the voice of television's *Sponge Bob Squarepants.*) Tom Kenny ended up being the only name actor we had in *Creep Tales,* so we ran with it. Sometimes you get lucky like that. Originally, comic actor Bobcat Goldthwaite was scheduled to play the lead in the film, but something came up and his good friend Tom Kenny took over. It was a really humorous film, shot music-video-style on the streets of San Francisco. Tom was hilarious as the Purse Snatcher and seemed to be having a lot of fun making the film. We really wanted it in *CreepTales* and fortunately were able to secure the rights.

*THE CLOSET,* Directed by Stephen Hegyes/Greg Middleton, this Canadian film is the classic monster-in-the-closet, don't go in there story. It was a very short, fun film that everybody really liked. It had suspense, some humor and seemed like a good fit for us. Stephen Hegyes went on to produce *White Noise* (2005, starring Michael Keaton) and *White Noise 2* (2007).

*GROOVY GHOULIE GARAGE,* Directed by James Salisbury. *Groovy Ghoulie* is a quirky buddy comedy with radioactive undead, stuck in the 1960s. These two guys end up in a small town full of undead hippies and have to run for their lives to escape the radioactive zombies. The film was a little longer, came in the middle and was good follow up to *The Closet.*

*HOWLING NIGHTMARE,* Directed by

Steve Hegyi was another Canadian film. This one had a Werewolf. It paid homage to the classic horror film, *The Howling* (1981). We really liked it. The film had a dark atmosphere, some cool action, a good transformation sequence and a lot of fog.

*SUCKER*, Directed by Rod Slane. This film was one of our favorites. It was originally made as a pilot for a TV show running at just under 22 mins. The film had great production value, was well directed and had some really good effects. It also had a good buildup and a strong finish with the metamorphosis of the wife. It taught a good lesson. We were really glad to include the film in *Creep Tales*.

*MM*: From a production value standpoint, we were very pleased with the short films we had selected. All the films had some humor in them, which integrated well with the wraparound humor. That said, we now had ourselves a horror/comedy, anthology feature-film we had to assemble.

*JS*: Of course, before we could acquire any short film rights we had to secure some finishing funds. We looked under a lot of rocks, made a lot of calls and pitched it around town. Our goal was to utilize the off-line version of the wraparound and videos of each short film to secure the finishing funds. We hammered out a short film acquisition contract, ran it past our lawyer and secured all the films. The contract was exclusive for the first year and non-exclusive thereafter for the life of *Creep Tales*. We had to make sure that we had releases for everything including music, actors and locations. It was certainly a challenge and we had to grind on it for a while, but finally got it all worked out. We took care of all the short filmmakers and paid them an upfront acquisition fee which is a rare thing in projects like this. We had the wraparound completed, the short films secured and were ready for post-production.

*MM*: We already had an off-line edit completed on the wraparound but still needed to complete an online version. All the short films were shot in either 16mm or 35mm. We had already secured the acquisition rights to the short films and the film prints were rolling in. Now we needed to transfer all the short films from their film print masters to video, so that we could insert all the short films into a final *Creep Tales* master.

*JS*: We got a weekend night rate at Video Post & Transfer working from 6PM to 6AM in their top editing suite. We also had their best editor and color corrector who was a friend of Ken Mandel. During the film transfers, Michael mentioned he was going up to Wisconsin. The editor was from Milwaukee and asked Michael to bring back a case of Old Style beer and he'd give us some extra time on the house. Michael was happy to oblige and carted a case of Old Style beer back to Texas. After the last, late night session, we toasted a good night of work with some ice cold Old Style beer on the house.

*MM*: Now that the transfers were completed, it was time to start the online edit. We completed the wraparound footage, did the color correction and added in the sound. We did have to do some Foley work, which is always fun. The credits were a challenge because we had to create the wraparound credits and re-create the short film credits into a final credit master, which ended up making the film look like an epic.

*JS*: On imdb.com, over 200 credits are listed for *Creep Tales*. People kept adding and adding to it. Almost all the people who worked on the wraparound or any of the short films are credited, including "Special Thanks." They rival *Gone with The Wind* (1939).

*MM*: We even produced a cool theme song to run during those epic credits. It was so sweet to finally watch, from start to finish, the anthology feature film *Creep Tales*. It had monsters, humor horror, suspense. The final film was 105 minutes long.

The film was finally completed. After all we'd been through, we decided to have a premiere at the classic Granada movie theatre on Greenville Avenue in Dallas, back when they still ran movies there. It just made sense to have the premiere on Halloween night, so we rolled out the red carpet, sent out a press release, brought in a spotlight and hired a limo. We even had an emcee comic warm-up act. Both Jess and I thanked the cast and crew and everybody that had contributed to the success of the film. For a cold Halloween night, we had a great crowd, the house was packed. We rented the theatre for the one screening, but it went so well the theatre management let *Creep Tales* play the whole weekend and we split the take with the house. We got a check, the money was already rolling in!

*JS*: We were pretty excited by now and our executive producer starting reaching out to distributors right away. Unfortunately, he insisted on selecting the distributor, who turned out to be a dud. The film was under contract and nothing was happening.

*MM*: Nada. Not jack shit. We finally moved on and the film languished for several years. Then, while we were promoting our independent comedy film feature, *Young Producers*, in New York at the Independent Feature Film Market, a distributor passed on our comedy but really wanted horror films and liked *Creep Tales*.

*JS*: After all the negotiations, it ended up on three multi-disc DVD sets at Blockbuster and Hollywood Video nationwide titled, *Afraid of the Dark*, *Night Chills* and *Bite Night*. We also made *Creep Tales* available as a single title DVD on Amazon (which is still available at the printing of this publication.) It was a blast the first time we walked into a video store and saw the film on the shelf. We each bought a copy.

*MM*: As a footnote, in 2016 some bozo from France pirated the film and uploaded it to You Tube. One of the short film directors from *Creep Tales* emailed us. We checked it out and sure enough, it had over 700,000 hits in six months. Not bad. Shortly thereafter it was taken down.

*TS*: So, what have you guys been up to since then?

*JS*: After all the experiences we had with short films on the *Creep Tales* project, ironically, we had never made a short film of our own. We had screened so many short films and had seen the good, the bad and the ugly. We also were selected to screen short films for the USA Film Festival and saw even more short films. That said, we felt like we had a little extra insight into shorts. So, we decided to make a high-budget short film. Both of us are native Texans and Michael is a big Texas historian.

*MM*: So, we wrote a script. In the end, Jess produced and I directed the award winning modern-day, western titled, *Mortal Dilemma* (2012). It's a crime drama with action, suspense and an anti-hero. We shot exteriors in far west Texas and the interiors near Waco. The film screened all over the world, in major markets including Los Angeles, New York, England, Germany, India and took home a number of top honors. We were excited when we heard *Mortal Dilemma* was a qualifying film to compete for the Academy Award in the Short Film category.

*TS*: Any film makers you'd like to mention as major influences?

*JS*: Certainly, there have been Texas Indie filmmakers that have inspired us, including Tobe Hooper, Richard Linklater and Robert Rodriguez. These filmmakers made their marks overcoming odds and breaking down doors, paving the way for guys like us. Films like *Poltergeist* (1982), *Dazed and Confused* (1993) and *El Mariachi* (1992) are among our favorites and films that have taught us much.

*MM*: In the end, *Creep Tales* took on a life of its own. If you Google it today, there's tons of info on it. Our goal was to make a fun, entertaining comedy-horror feature film and that's what we did. Remember, less is more, set goals and finish it. And finally, it's all about the journey, not the destination.

# JUSTIN POWERS

## POT ZOMBIES (2005)

Although Justin Powers and the other talented people involved in the creation of *Pot Zombies* do not condone the use of cannabis (or any illicit substances for that matter), I suspect that this movie has a great deal in common with the classic *Easy Rider* (1969), namely that all involved (especially the on-camera talent) were high as a kite most of the time. This is a random supposition on my part and should not be taken as gospel.

As the movie opens, we find three yahoos traipsing through the East Texas countryside, armed to the teeth and looking for something to kill. They share a little bit of the we're-manly-men-getting-away-from-the-women-folk banter, as hunters are wont to do. And, naturally, they try to out-gross one another. Before long, they're torching a doobie. The leader of the pack warns them to watch out for the creeper tendency of this particular weed. Now, these guys are not the sort of folks I'd ever want to get stoned with (if I was the sort of scoff-law who partook of

"For all its gaping flaws, for its need to entertain and its middling ability to do so successfully, *Pot Zombies* should be celebrated. Go in expecting Mozart and you'll be kicking yourself for days. Drop those designs down a couple hundred notches and you'll be giggling all the way to the nearest Santeria head shop."
   --*popmatters.com*, Bill Gibron, June 27, 2009

"If I say 'independent, low-budget movie' and you think of *Juno*, this is not for you. If on the other hand, you're a Troma fan and you are watching this one knowingly, *Pot Zombies* will provide a fair amount of entertainment. Don't expect anything else from it, and it will deliver. I'm not saying it's great, or even good, but it is watchable, and that's something to be said for such a low-budget, obviously labor of love endeavor."
   --*silveremulsion.com*, WILL, September 5, 2012

"I don't even know what to say about Pot Zombies. You just need to see it. It's something I actually recommend to watch, it's hilarious."
   --*slasherstudios.com*, Tim's Horror Tweet Reviews, November 18, 2012

such things); in fact, they're three of the biggest buzz-killers I could ever imagine.

The pot seems to inspire a primal urge in our Alpha Buzzkill. When he hears a sound, he raises his shotgun and fires. Seems like he hit something!

Oops, it's another human being and they're not in season!

Alpha Buzzkill subsequently freaks out a little and bends down to see if his target is really and truly dead. A park ranger, alerted by the sound of gunfire, simultaneously approaches.

Before we know it, that special creeper weed has turned Alpha Buzzkill into a snarling, hungry zombie with a bad case of the brain munchies. One of his friends is a little put off by this and wants nothing to do with the walking dead. When he turns to leave, he finds the third member of their hunting expedition has likewise reacted to the joint. He's caught between two hungry, green-eyed terrors.

"What the hell?" is the ranger's response. That's pretty much what we'd all say if we happened onto the crimson squirt-fest he finds under the pines. Thank god, he's got his handgun loaded and ready. Lickety-split he puts those pot zombies low. This is a good time to start the opening credits and that's just what Justin Powers did.

Intermingled with the credits we see the bad guys of the movie packaging cannabis in large bags in a grim industrial location where the secret ingredient is added, turning plain old weed into zombie pot.

At Henenlotter High School[i], we see some serious smoke billowing out of a small vehicle as it attempts to park in the lot. Class is underway—a thrilling examination of cost/benefit analysis. The guy and gal who were in that car, and may have accidentally inhaled some of that smoke, stumble into class. The students are uncooperative and resentful. And possibly stoned.

Soon, it's all over the news!

There's some weird virus infecting the weed.

It quickly becomes apparent that the guy and the chick from the smoke-billowing car in the parking lot did inhale some of the ganja gas. As the boy snores, his skin turns green like the Hulk's. We know this is a bad thing on account of what happened earlier with the Buzzkill hunting party. His girlfriend's awake, but not entirely alert and she's pretty certain to make the change, too. Yep, about the time her boyfriend is snatching the heart out of the instructor's chest, she begins vomiting Day-Glo green.

Meanwhile, an unfortunate young man lounges on his back-yard deck. There are cucumbers on his eyes and he holds a reflector around his neck in order to insure an even tan. Somebody probably

---

[i] A nifty reference to B-Movie genius, Frank Henenlotter, creator of the wild exploitation flick *Basket Case* (1982).

Lloyd Kaufman in *Pot Zombies*.

should've told him the only thing worse than that toxic weed is ultra-violet rays.

A couple of stoned zombies wander into his yard. When he flips on his belly to get a little sun on his back, these opportunistic monsters jump on him. He's not really into three-way zombie action, but they've got the upper hand. One of them pokes a large fish hook into his back. These zombies are a little smarter and more creative than some of the others. They suspend the sunbather by multiple fish hooks above the deck and munch on his body parts.

*Singing doobie segue!*

Three mellow musicians watch *Night of the Living Dead* (1968) and try to come up with a name for their band. There's a report on the news about the incident at the high school (those zombies left a mess!). These band members used to attend that school. As the report concludes, they start thinking maybe they should've stayed in school. One of the guys is feeling a little green around the gills.

Turns out they've ordered a pizza. Lloyd Kaufman (co-founder of Troma Entertainment) as the pizza delivery guy is worth the price of admission. While he's waiting to be paid for the pizza, the musicians change their minds. They're not hungry for pizza after all. They want pizza delivery guy instead. As the zombies shamble out of the house into the world we see they are capable of learning. When one falls off a ledge, another decides to make a detour.

Elsewhere in the city, a guy wakes up with his bitchy girlfriend. He tries to mellow her out with a pre-work taste of herb, but she just wants him to call her a cab. At the coffee table, he packs a pipe. The cab shows up and his gal changes her mind about the morning mood enhancer. After one taste, she decides she's taking the grass with her. The cab pulls away and he sets about removing the stems from his stash. The prop greenery used by the film makers is amazingly convincing, though I'm sure it was just parsley or oregano or something.

He rolls a joint and smokes. Pretty soon he finds himself in a psychedelic wonderland. That's some trippy parsley. As the visions recede, we find him green on the sofa. His poor pooch wonders what's going on. He gives the pup an air hit and the little canine soon has glowing green eyes.

A happy toker in a cool looking VW that sounds like it's low on oil, looks in the rearview mirror to see a patrol car with flashing lights. At first, we think it's serious, then we see it's just one of the friendly cops from Wankerville. What's the worst that could happen?

Video cover art for *Pot Zombies*.

The cop pulls an authority trip on the hapless victim and makes him get out of the car. While the driver tries to raise the cop's level of consciousness by sharing some righteous perspectives, the officer sniffs the VW seats and finds a bag o' weed under one. This activates the driver's problem with authority and causes him to glow green.

I think the cop feels guilty for taking the guy's weed. He knows he's crossed a line, so he lets the zombie throw him to the pavement and rip him open. He doesn't fight back much. He knows he deserves it and he takes it like a man. Earlier, the driver voiced a hankering for chicken and now he's plucking M'Nuggets out of the cop's body. A dough nut, too!

*Happy doobie segue!*

The bitchy girlfriend who swiped her boyfriend's pipe is riding in the cab. The cabbie is an expert on tabby cats and ponies and I was fascinated with this sort of "documentary" segment of the movie, but naturally the girl doesn't care for it. Cabbie's a little freaked when he glances in the rearview and sees her frothing at the mouth. This is a kinder, gentler sort of zombie. Instead of tearing the cabbie's head off, she pays him and gets out, saying she doesn't feel well. Cabbie's eyes light up when he sees she's left a bag of weed behind.

Somewhere in Deep Ellum, a punk rock show is getting underway. Backstage bandmembers are getting high.

When I was a kid, my mom bought me a book about all sorts of insects at the Fort Worth Museum of Science and History. A cute blond, who looks like a walking, talking version of my insect book, meets with a friend and shares a bag of pot. The two girls get inspired to explore one another's bodies.

The band's really rocking the house tonight. One of the guitar players is wearing a black mask. Period.

The girls backstage are getting it on. Just when things are really hot and heavy, one of them gets that greenish glow and it interrupts their "sky rockets in flight."

In the front of the house, the band has taken on a zombie vibe. One of them flings his guitar like a weapon and skewers a poor girl in the audience. Then it's every zombie for him (or her) self, chowing down on anything that moves.

*Farting doobie segue!*

Porch party! Everyone's having a great time. Couple of guys show up with the intent of getting everybody high. They're carrying a bag of something they like to call Demonic Chronic. Smokers get all wavy gravy and Lloyd Kaufman puts in another appearance in a flashback about a caring father. Stoney's friend reveals she's got a crush on him. His transformation puts a damper on their first kiss. Soon everyone has the munchies.

In a groovy sort of location heavily decorated with graffiti, the zombies are having a parade. Some of them are a little self-conscious when it comes to eating. They never really thought of humans as finger food, so a bit of social awkwardness ensues.

Zombies are everywhere! Every sort of zombie! There's even a cute little kid zombie and maybe a mangy grackle zombie. Hey, somebody left a perfectly good brain lying there! Can't let that go to waste. The apocalypse has arrived.

Great tail credits with plenty of funky outtakes.

## POT ZOMBIES 2 (2012)

So, a guy who just woke up is taking some extremely healthy hits off a pipe. When he exhales, it's like one of those smoke machines they use at a party or a concert. He blows smoke in his girlfriend's face to wake her up. She's pissed that he's smoking so early in the day.

I'd like to digress a moment. They say all great artists examine the same issue over and over again from slightly varying perspectives. I'm starting to think Justin's artistic focal point is the observation that people don't like their jobs, but they do like sex, just not their bitchy girlfriends; and they use weed to escape from the daily friction of these circumstances. I may be going out on a high-brow limb here, but that's my take on it so far.

This guy may be right when he says, "Nobody ever got their head crushed by smoking a little pot." But, you and I know by now, they damn sure can get their guts ripped out.

No-brainer there. This is a sequel after all.

He's a huffaholic and tokes steadily, even on the toilet. The ol' lady turned him down when he suggested a bit of early morning gratification, so he opens a skin mag and spanks the monkey. While his girl continues to pound on the bathroom door, he pursues his passion. There's your wet shot! And we head into a very groovy opening credit sequence.

Okay, on second thought, make that a disturbingly sick credit sequence. Justin, you may want to consider counseling, dude.

"Oh, god. I thought the title was *Pot Zombies 2: More Pot, More Zombies*. Unfortunately, it's *Pot Zombies 2: More Pot, Less Plot*. I'm just wondering how this is even possible since the first film had virtually no plot already."
--*horrorsociety.com*, MGDSQUAN, August 8, 2012

"Smoking pot and getting the munchies always go hand in hand. But what if instead of craving potato chips and candy bars, you start to crave brains and human flesh? Welcome to Justin Powers' film *Pot Zombies 2: More Pot, Less Plot*."
--*playwithdeath.com*

"Marijuana smokers turn into zombies with the "munchies" for human flesh when a strain of radioactive pot infects the stoners of America. A hilarious warning sign of what may come from the legalization craze sweeping the nation."
--*flixster.com*

A sleazy corporate-type with nice teeth locates a couple of working girls on the east end of town. Soon, he's in a motel room with one of them. As he undresses, his "date" notices there's news footage on the tube showing the John being accused of child pornography violations. The sleaze-ball slips into something more comfortable. While he's acting out his fantasy, a hard-working journalist is snapping photos through the window. Uh-oh! The climax of this scene is just too much for words. (You'll have to watch for yourself.)

The journalist meets his media contact that night. He's annoyed that the guy's smoking a reefer. After the contact sees the photos of the "senator," he starts barfing. Is he just grossed out by the pics? No, it's the zombie pot working on him. Journalist hangs out, waiting for his pay, but all he gets is a fist through his torso.

A couple of partiers stumble by. When they see the mini-van rocking, they peek in hoping to catch some sexy action. They misinterpret the slaughter inside as just a couple of guys getting it on. Later, as they cruise along in their own car, whatever they've seen, begins to work on the libido of one of the guys.

They crash a friend's house. Nobody's home, so they round up the beer and weed and settle in to get even more wasted. After toking, a dude in a white hat decides the time is right to "come out." His friend freaks. Even so, pretty soon they're having some hot zombie sex that concludes with a "head job" you won't soon forget.

Cops working the east side discover the blood-drenched mini-van. They seek out their favorite pusher. Pusher tries to turn zombie on the guys, but they put more bullets in him than there are crabs on a crack ho. They split for a taco.

An aspiring romance novelist gets a visit from one of her four "serious" boyfriends. They make out, but then she succumbs suddenly to a virus she contracted from eating acorns. She bites his lip and chases him into the bathroom. He arms himself with a spike-heeled shoe and sneaks out, finding her at the fridge. When she turns to attack, he vanquishes her with a deft display of shoe-jitsu.

If the eyes are green, the zombie's mean.

In an episode of "My Dumbshit Wife" dad has a confrontation with Junior over his pot usage. When it is revealed that the boy learned to use pot from watching his dad, the family has an epiphany. Later, Junior turns zombie, eviscerates his father and strangles his mother with pop's intestines.

Brownies! Who doesn't like them? They've been bringing people of different persuasions together forever. An underappreciated guy feeds his bitchy mother-in-law a batch of his electric-rapid-onset brownies and the party is on! It's a pre-zombie vomit-fest at the dinner table.

The senator who got mixed up with the zombie ho is big news on the TV.

A foolish teen girl accepts a ride from a stranger. Before you know it, she's drinking beer and smoking weed. The coolest thing about this scene is Powers indulges in a bit of product advertising for his first movie! The badass driver uses force to make the girl help him get off. She has a change of heart and helps him get totally off. Ripped off, as in removed from his body.

In a secret facility, ordinary weed becomes zombie pot.

Mike gets lucky and picks up a good-looking lady at a local bar. She takes him home and soon he gets it on with her and a hot roommate. Mike hasn't got words to express his excitement, so he mostly makes sounds like Chewbacca from *Star Wars*. The next morning, as he's making coffee, one of the girls gives him a glowing green wink. That's when we know some serious shit is about to go down. Gross-out alert on this scene's conclusion!

For the next few minutes, we visit a psychedelic zone where I'm pretty certain David Lynch has just left the building. One of my favorite shots in the whole film is when the dude exits the psychedelic zone via fire escape into a starker, high contrast reality.

Some kids see a trippy dude stumbling down the street and think maybe he needs some help. They reach out and try to get inside his head. The problem is they use a piece of pipe to do it. The kids take this zombie captive and have him chained up in a bedroom when Mom walks in. They want to know if they can keep this stray. Mom sheds a tear, remembering that her deceased hubby became a zombie just before he died.

Feeling sorry for the lonely mom, one of the dudes slips into her bedroom and tries to offer her comfort…and vomit. Soon zombie dude is slipping Mom the green weenie. She's getting close when her daughter barges in and ruins the moment. The girl barfs at the sight of her mom having sex with one of her friends… no, wait, it's because she's going zombie herself. Mom pulls an automatic weapon out from under the pillow and sprays her daughter with bullets. Call it tough love.

When she's taken care of the girl, she sweeps into the bedroom where the zombie's tied up and wastes everything that moves. Turns out Mom is a sort of cougar with a thing for zombies. She saves one to pull out of her closet whenever she's feeling lonely.

A scream queen is plying her trade in front of a green screen. When that's a wrap, the sleazy director invites her back to his office. He insists on a blow job and the poor girl, worried about her career, obliges. He lights up. The girl gets distracted when she hears a sound and goes to make sure nobody's going to walk in on them. While her back is turned, the sleaze auteur turns a bit sleazier. She runs out. On her way out, she notifies the armed security guy there's a zombie killing people. But, foremost in her mind is making her call on the set of a pot zombie movie. It's her close-up she's most concerned about.

The film crew is a task force of efficient professionals. They are standing by, waiting to capture her scene. The director's a little annoyed that she's running late. In the exchange that follows, the director offers up some very sage wisdom regarding cheap-ass-exploitation-genre-pictures, so pay attention. The goal is to offend people. Without that, you haven't got a chance in the competitive market place (Take note, aspiring schlockmeisters!).

What happens next is unavoidable. When you combine an aspiring actress and a pregnant, do-anything ho, ask them to engage in lesbo sex and throw in a dose of zombie-pot for good measure, this sort of thing is going to happen every time. 'Nuff said?

*Masturbating doobie segue!*

Down at the biker bar, a weary-looking dude comes in to have a couple beers. He chases away a talkative newbie waitress. His eye is on the headliner; a sexy chick with an enormous snake. After her show, he arranges a private party in a secluded booth. They partake of that special weed that's been going around. Unlike some others, these two adjust well to zombie-hood and ride off into the sunset together.

All around town the zombies are becoming more prevalent. It's a new world.

Roll credits.

For decades now, unstoppable fringe entrepreneur, Jason Cohen has been at the center of all the cool underground happenings in Dallas. Back in the early 1990s, Jason was the only local business interested in carrying the full line of Bret McCormick videos. At Forbidden Books, his shop just a stone's throw from Fair Park, I was practically a celebrity, with my own shelf and everything. I'd stop by to check in with Jason every now and then. He offered me advice on my first self-published book, *How to Produce Your First Feature Film for $20,000 (or Less)*. He even let us use his business as a shooting location for *Cyberstalker* (aka *The Digital Prophet*) starring Jeffrey Combs.

When I started working in earnest on this book, I contacted Jason at his new store Curiosities to rehash old times and stir up memories. Jason suggested I talk with Justin Powers, the genius behind the *Pot Zombies* movies. I'd heard of the films, but had never watched them and didn't know they were homegrown.

Justin was real accessible and cooperative. I had a blast watching his flicks.

Here are some random thoughts from the *Pot Zombies* creator, himself, Justin Powers:

*JP*: I kind of did things backwards. I started making movies, then I actually got into production and learned how to do stuff. When I did *Pot Zombies* I didn't even know about white-balancing a camera. I didn't know how to use a camera. I knew nothing about lighting. I was pretty clueless. I was just doing it. When I did *Pot Zombies* my plan was just to screen it at a punk show at a punk music venue in Deep Ellum. Then I got Lloyd Kaufman to appear in it. When I gave him his copy, he offered for Troma to release it. That was like a lifetime dream type of thing for me. Basically, I grew up on Troma movies, you know.

When my family got a VHS player and I saw *Toxic Avenger* (1984), that pretty much changed all my ideas about films.

I grew up in Arkansas. I moved to Dallas in 1998. I was promoting punk concerts and tours and stuff. After I moved to Dallas, I met people who were doing movies on their own, which was something I'd always wanted to do. I'd visit their shoots and finally decided I'd try my hand at it. My brother and I bought a Canon GL2 on his credit card. We just started shooting.

Originally, I wanted a real plot and story for the film, but I soon realized I wasn't going to be able to keep the same characters, keep people coming back to participate in the film, because I couldn't pay them anything.[ii] It was going to be impossible for me to shoot it in a couple weeks with all the same actors. So, I just started designing scenes that I thought would be fun to watch. More like a *Kentucky Fried Movie* (1977), crazy skits. I started compiling that stuff, but it took a couple of years.

The exposure Troma gave me was incredible, actually. Troma was such a big influence on my taste in films. After that happened, I thought, "Wow! I don't ever have to make another movie again. This is way farther than I thought I'd ever be!"

I've been slowly putting together a documentary on the history of Dallas punk music for a few years now. I've been shooting interviews and collecting flyers. It's a slow project. It starts out with the 1970s and the Nervebreakers and it'll probably end up with the late 1990s.

I'm still amazed when I get checks for *Pot Zombies*, as bad as that is. It's been a long time.

---

[ii] This was an astute assessment for a first-time film maker. Would that more schlockmeisters were so savvy.

On location weirdness with Justin Powers' ***Pot Zombies***.

Do you know Barak Epstein? He's one of the guys who runs the Texas Theater. I did some film races with their cooperation. We organized a Christmas Horror Film Race and it did really well. People had a great time, they loved it. I think we'll do that again next December. They did the screenings of the work at the Texas Theater.

I was a horror film fan and a big fan of old stoner movies. Cheech and Chong stuff and just random drug movies. We thought it would be fun to have a film race with pot involved. We give them a line of dialog, a prop, a character and they all go out and produce something. We call it the Demonic Horror 48- Hour Stoner Film Race. They have 48 hours to do a 4 to 7-minute film; write it, shoot it and get it turned in. I'm not really sure about the future of that one. I didn't really set out to do a lot of film races. We just did it for fun.

Now, I'm working in film and trying to find time to do my own projects. I can't really spend a lot of time organizing film races. The Christmas Horror one went well, though. December's a slow month anyway for film, so that'd be a fun time to do it again. It's a cool holiday thing for horror fans.

People shoot these things on all sorts of digital cameras. They deliver the finished product on thumb drive. A lot of them are shot on DSLRs. We had a couple that were shot on 4k cameras. That would scare me, just because of the rendering time involved, when you're working with such big files.

The script for *Pot Zombies 2* I thought was really funny. We'd written it a long time ago. I tried to raise the money for it and do it a certain way, but when it came down to it, I had all the days planned, but didn't have the money to do it. So, I ended up making *Pot Zombies 2* for like $3,000. I had to do it all myself and had to write out all the crazy gags and put in cheesy, stupid, additional gags. It worked. It is what it is. My dream for a *Pot Zom-*

bie movie is to do a really cool musical.

I was distributed by Troma on the first movie. On *Pot Zombies 2*, I was talking with this other distributor...do you know Mark Bosco? He did the *Killer Nerd* movies. I got stuck in a contract with him. I just got my rights back at like the end of last month (December 2016). I was in a four-year contract with him. So much time has gone by with nothing happening. I just don't really care anymore.

I shot a low-budget comedy they just put out called *Rocking Reverend* (2013). I shot it just before *Pot Zombies 2*. Another local guy wrote it, starred in it and directed it. It's a funny movie and I think it's the only non-horror film released by Wild Eye. They just released it in December 2016. I may check into Wild Eye for *PZ2*. I don't really want to spend too much time dicking around with an old movie that didn't go anywhere. I just want to make new stuff, show people what I can do, you know?

I grew up around Fort Smith. As a kid, I watched *Texas Chain Saw Massacre* (1974) and *Motel Hell* (1980) on HBO. *The Town that Dreaded Sundown* (1976), all those things that played on HBO back then.

When I was really young, I was scared of everything; clowns, Santa Claus, whatever. After I started watching horror films I think that helped me get over being scared of things. I became obsessed with them.

As a kid, I thought maybe I'd be an actor, but I'm not really very good at it. I'm kind of shy and don't like being in front of cameras. Once I realized the people who really make the movies are the directors, then I wanted to make movies.

I liked *The Town that Dreaded Sundown* because I'm from Arkansas. That's where the killer is. With drug dealers, you get in a gang and then get out before you get caught. Maybe it was the same with the Texarkana Killer.

Before I lived in Dallas, whenever I was in town I'd drop by Forbidden Books and look at all the weird shit Jason Cohen had there. That's where I met Lloyd Kaufman the first time.

When we were finishing *Pot Zombies*, the very first Texas Frightmare Weekend was coming up. They heard about the movie and told me if I finished it in time, they'd give me a premier at the convention. It gave me a deadline to shoot for.

I'm kind of excited. This year Frank Henenlotter's going to be there with the guy who starred in *Brain Damage* (1988). The High School in *Pot Zombies* was Henenlotter High.

# GRIM AND HERNANDEZ

Author's note: The films of Jacob Grim and Sal Hernandez are quite new compared to the other movies discussed in this book. In recognition of this fact, I have foregone detailed synopses. No spoilers here, just enough info to pique the horror film fan's interest.

## DREADTIME STORIES (2014)

I love anthology films, always have. Back in the 1970s, whenever Amicus spit one of these puppies out, I would be first in line to see it. *House that Dripped Blood* (1971), *Tales from the Crypt* (1972) and the like have a very secure soft warm place in my decrepit old heart. I even like the really cheap and cheesy ones. Hell, my very first feature film production, *Tabloid!* was an anthology!

Which brings us to *Dreadtime Stories*, a south Texas flick written by Jacob Grim and Sal Hernandez. Is it cheap? Yeah. But, get this; where most anthology films expect you to be satisfied with three to five stories, this one delivers ten! Ten blood-drenched tales with plots ranging from over-the-top cannibalism to dorky horror fans who get just what they deserve from the working end of a chain saw.

I have just one little problem; the thing's not really schlocky. I mean, it's low-budget for sure, but the performances are competent, the direction (thanks to Jacob Grim)

"All in all, I highly recommend this movie! I would recommend it to anyone who loves horror with a pinch of blood and violence. I do not think you will be disappointed with *Dreadtime Stories*. I certainly was not."
   --*horrornews.net*, Rebecca Brown,
   April 11, 2015

"Overall, *Dreadtime Stories* is a fairly decent anthology. While the segments weren't always cohesive, the filmmaking process that brought this to life is. A lot of the time in horror anthologies, the segments look different from short to short and it's obvious that it's pieces of a puzzle. This had great gore, great actors, great production quality and is a fantastic debut for STX Media."
   --*Horrorsociety.com*, MGDSQUAN,
   February 11, 2015

is professional, cinematography's compelling, editing is top notch and the sound mix is a pleasure to listen to. So, what the hell is *Dreadtime Stories* doing in this book?

> "We've entered a new era of independent filmmaking. The availability of low-cost, high-definition camera and digital editing suites has changed the scope of what can be accomplished with a very small budget. *Dreadtime Stories* is evidence of these changing times. According to director Jacob Grim, this movie only cost around $2,000. It's full color, HD, and not found footage with a cast of three. Rather, it's an ambitious anthology film featuring nine different shorts and a wrap-around with a large cast and a decent amount of visual effects."
>
> --*dreadcentral.com*, Mr. Dark, May 13, 2015

Your guess is as good as mine. Sal and Jacob wanted to be included in this collection of cinematic dregs. I guess the guys grew up watching the same trash I did. Maybe they felt like slumming with some of their unwashed movie brothers.

All I know for sure is, *Dreadtime Stories* deserves a watch. Check it out!

Poster Art for ***Dreadtime Stories***.

had balls…wait, I mean, if he didn't want to have balls? I'm a little confused. Feeling stunned by what I've just watched.

In the time-honored tradition of extreme crime stories, there's an alcoholic ex-cop who earns a meager living as a private investigator. The guy's seen a lot of shit he wishes he could forget. Charlie Reese (Eric Rodrigue) reluctantly takes a job looking for a missing girl. As the PI begins to poke around, someone has him under surveillance.

## DEVIANT BEHAVIOR (2017)

You think Buffalo Bill from *Silence of the Lambs* (1991) was a badass? This disgusting flick features a serial killer who does what Bill would've done if he really

Dr. Walter Firley (Alex Heatherley) is a man with strange appetites. When the working girls see him pull up to the curb, they always smile because he's driving an expensive car. He's a guy with money. It's a good thing. The stuff he wants to do costs extra.

> "I didn't want to shoot myself while watching it, but wasn't exactly thrilled either. It wasn't even the type of film smoking excessive weed could improve (believe me, I tried). This low-budget procedural horror can't blast past the humdrum of familiar tropes and an uninspired storyline. It's most likely to find an audience among gorehounds, fans of torture porn and those obsessed with *The Texas Chain Saw Massacre*."
> --*horrorfreaknews.com*, Joshua Millican, August 10, 2017

> "*Deviant Behavior* has that fun, rough and endearing flair that most Texans possess and it doesn't give you the happy ending you want ... in a good way!"
> --*horrorsociety.com*, MGDSQUAN, February 12, 2017

> "I still struggle with the intention. Not necessarily of these characters, but of the movie as a whole."
> --*horrorpedia.com*, Meredith Brown, March 17, 2017

Okay, maybe I drifted too far away from horror over the years. Maybe I got old and soft. Thirty-four minutes into this thing I am wondering why ... why am I doing this to myself? Planting images in my brain that cannot be erased? I don't have an answer.

Charlie runs across an old friend. Murphy (John Dugan - yeah, the same John Dugan that played Grandpa in *Texas Chain Saw Massacre* (1974) – and he looks a lot younger in this!) is a cop who's been doing his own investigation into the missing girl. It seems somebody at City Hall has been trying to put a lid on this thing.

How many tools can be used to kill a human? The killer seems interested in finding out. But, only those instruments that cause a great deal of bleeding. Red's such a pretty color.

Things get personal when Walter invites Charlie's love interest Roxy (Tania Monroy) to a private party. Charlie's never dreamed of a career in film, but the pair of psychos offer him a starring role.

Since this is a new release, I'll have to zip it on what happens in the rest of the movie. It's tense, it's gross and it may be just the nightmare-inducer you are looking for.

Meet Jacob Grim and Sal Hernandez

*SH*: I grew up in a small town called Odem, TX. In 2003, I made my way to Corpus Christi, where I've been ever since.

I started watching horror pretty young; I'd say about 4 or 5 years old. I can remember being in kindergarten asking another kid during nap time if he had ever seen *Cujo* (1983). My television viewing was loosely monitored and unsupervised as you can see.

Sal Hernandez of STX Media.

I saw most of my first horror films on cable and then eventually I was able to rent them via my parents. I was the youngest of four kids and my parents were indifferent about most things for me. As long as I was passing in school and not causing trouble they never really said anything that I can remember.

I don't really have a favorite horror film director, I'm more a fan of the business of horror, people like Sean Cunningham and Bob Shaye. These are the guys I aspire to be like. Basically, Bob Shaye (of New Line Cinema) began by selling movies out of the trunk of his car. His business became a multi-million-dollar studio.

As far as cinematic influences go, anything Dean Cundey and Daniel Pearl have done. Their knowledge and use of lighting and angles are pure art.

I'm a great admirer of Kim Henkel, I've actually gotten to meet him and pick his brain. He gave me some great advice that served STX Media well.

With regard to the response to our work, they are pretty positive for the most part, but there will always be negative reviews. You just can't help that. However, they serve at least for me, as motivation to do better on the next film. Our current film, *Deviant Behavior* is getting rave reviews so we have definitely learned from past mistakes.

We have a long list of slated films to keep us busy for the next 10 years or so, but we are starting pre-production on our next feature *Dreadtime Stories-Volume 2*. We hope to begin filming in January or February of 2018.

We're not even low-budget film makers yet. We're more like micro-budget or no-budget film makers. We've pulled some things off pretty well for what we had to work with. We're at the point where we want to reach out and pull in some outside support, because we can produce high-quality product for very little money. Our first movie was made for $2000 and our second film cost about $5000.

My personal goal is for STX Media to be a full-fledged studio and be self-sufficient with funding to ensure that we can continue to make movies how and when we want.

What works marketing-wise? Shameless self-promotion. We spend a lot of time designing, tweaking and consistently implementing our marketing strategies.

The future of the horror genre? I think horror fans of the world will be the deciding factor. I think if the large studios put out more remakes and reboots, horror fans will be pushed to spend their attention and dollars on more independent films which is fine by me.

Top five favorite horror writers:
Kim Henkel
H.P. Lovecraft
Edgar Allen Poe
Wes Craven
John Carpenter

*JG*: I grew up in Refugio, Texas until I was about 16 when my family moved to Corpus Christi, Texas and I've been here ever since.

My interest in horror films started when I was in elementary school. I remember in the school library they had a couple of books based on the Universal Studios monster movies. I would always go right to them. I loved looking at make-up for the Wolfman and Frankenstein monster.

I definitely started watching horror films on TV late at night. We didn't really have horror movies around the house when I was a kid, but I was lucky enough to have a TV in my room when I was little. So, a lot of my introductions to horror movies came from watching TNT Monster vision with Joe Bob Briggs every week.

Jacob Grim of STX Media.

I was lucky that my parents were pretty open to the movies they let me watch. One of my favorite movies in rotation at my house as a kid was *Robocop* (1987). As I got older we used to have horror movie marathons on Halloween night.

Some of my favorite directors are David Fincher, Steven Spielberg, Ridley Scott and John Carpenter.

I would have to say one of my biggest inspirations would be the original 1978 *Halloween*. Even though I had always been interested in film and filmmaking, that film was the first one to get me to think it was possible for me to make a movie. I'm a big

Poster Art for **Deviant Behavior**.

fan of documentaries on the making of movies and after watching the making of *Halloween* and seeing how they did it, making a movie seemed like an achievable dream.

As far as favorite film makers from Texas, a big one is Robert Rodriguez; his book *Rebel Without a Crew* was another big inspiration to me. I'm also a big fan of Mike Judge and, of course, Tobe Hooper.

So far, the response to our movies has been really positive, which is great. We've had some not so great reviews as well, but that's to be expected. People really seem to appreciate what we are able to accomplish with limited budgets. Our first movie cost about $2,000 and our second movie was $5,000.

We have a number of projects in various stages of development. At the moment, we are about to start pre-production on our next feature; a sequel to our first movie *Dreadtime Stories*.

My personal long-term goal is to just be able to keep making movies. I love the filmmaking process and collaborating with the crew around me, so to be able to continue to do this by our films finding their audience and being successful, that would be a dream come true.

Our most successful marketing springs from just putting ourselves out there on Facebook and contacting the horror websites. We've gotten great responses from just taking that first step and reaching out.

I believe franchise will continue to be the name of the game. I know it's not a popular thing to say, and people talk about it like it's a new thing that's taken over the major studios, but it's been that way since the Universal Studios monster films. On that note, I also think there will still be room for those great original ideas that break through and become the next big trend in horror cinema.

Top five horror writers:
Stephen King
John Carpenter
Clive Barker
H.P. Lovecraft
Edgar Allen Poe

# AFTERWORD

This book has been a labor of love. In the past year I've spent a lot of time reconnecting with old memories and old friends. I was once an avid schlockmeister, but that all ended in 1996. If you've paid attention, you've probably noticed most (if not all) the filmmakers in this book voiced misgivings about the direction their careers had taken. There are a lot of "what ifs" associated with the world of no-budget indies. It's a great deal of fun for the fans, but often financially brutal for the filmmakers.

I am very happy to see that digital technologies have placed filmmaking within the reach of virtually everyone. Anyone who really wants to, can shoot a movie and get it in front of viewers. The best part is the price. Some very nice pictures are being produced for less than $5,000. Like Jeff Buchanan says elsewhere in this book, that means the public has to wade through a glut of features, many of which are not very good. But, as I've repeatedly pointed out, value is in the eye of the beholder. Some very crude little movies are actually brilliant and irresistible to a schlock-minded individual like me.

Writing *Texas Schlock*, I realized there are many more terrific schlock (or at least low-budget indie) movies from Texas than I'd previously realized. Far too many for a single book. Larry Stouffer's *Horror High* (1973), Gordon McLendon's classic double-bill, *Giant Gila Monster* and *The Killer Shrews* (1959), Harold Hoffman's *The Black Cat* (1966), Paul Maslansky's classic blaxploitation flick, *Sugar Hill* (1974), Matt Trotter's *Stealth Hunters* (1991), Dwight Greene's *Ramming Speed* (1997), Gary Marcum's *Through the Fire* (1988) and the UTA student production, *Interface* (1985) all come to mind. But, there are so many more!

With this wealth of material, perhaps a *Texas Schlock Volume 2* is in order. We'll see. If you have suggestions for titles to include in a subsequent book, feel free to contact me on Facebook or using the email address listed on the copyright page.

*The Texas Chain Saw Massacre* (1974) is the gold standard of indie horror flicks. It spawned many imitators and a rebirth of the genre. The film succeeds on so many levels, something few other indie flicks achieve. Though Tobe Hooper's film is often referenced in *Texas Schlock*, I did not devote a chapter to it because it's not schlock. Low-budget? Yes. But, brilliant! So much has been written about *TCSM* that I did not believe I had anything new to add.

Once again, I want to thank everyone who played a part in making this book a reality. I am sincerely grateful.

*Bret McCormick, Bedford, Texas*
*January 2018*

# INDEX

*3DO*: 35
*8mm*: 26, 71, 212, 222
*16mm*: 12, 18, 27, 71, 83, 109, 120, 194, 219, 226
*20th Century Fox*: 11, 25
*35mm*: 13, 14, 195, 216, 230
*1000misspenthours.com*: 45, 206

*A Boy and His Dog*: 44
*A Bullet for Pretty Boy*: 23, 27
*A Matter of Honor*: 94
*A Perfect World*: 160
*A Stripper is Born*: 17
*Abominable Dr. Phibes*: 169
*Abomination, The*: 6, 178, 196-199, 209, 211-213, 217
*Ackerman, Forrest J.*: 220
*Adelson, Diane*: 72
*ADR (automatic dialog replacement)*: 84
*Afraid of the Dark*: 231
*Agar, John*: 19, 26, 32, 88, 89, 90, 92, 93, 170
*Alamo Draft House*: 191
*Alcott, Robert*: 120
*Alexander, Claude*: 10, 17, 140
*Allen, Phil*: 182
*Allied + WBS Film and Video*: 7, 19, 67, 93, 100, 130, 152
*Allingham, William*: 113
*allmovie.com*: 120
*Amazing Transparent Man, The*: 44-51
*amazon.com*: 178, 231
*American Idol*: 201
*American International Pictures (AIP)*: 18, 19, 20, 21, 22, 26, 31, 36, 40, 51, 101, 104, 108, 110, 131, 183
*American Film Institute*: 223
*American Film Market*: 30, 36, 213
*American Playhouse*: 35
*Amicus Films*: 221, 245
*Among the Dead*: 168, 181, 182
*Anderson, Andy*: 5
*Anderson, Max*: 142
*Andy Warhol's Frankenstein*: 191
*Applegate, Christina*: 217
*Archie Comics*: 60
*Argento, Dario*: 119, 120
*Aries Productions*: 216
*Arkoff, Sam*: 18, 19, 20, 22, 23, 26, 29, 30, 36, 51, 104, 108, 110, 111, 131
*Arlington, Texas*: 157, 216
*Army Signal Corps*: 25
*Ashley, John*: 27
*Ashlin, Scott*: 45, 206

*Athens, Texas*: 177
*Atherton, Bill*: 159
*Atlas Comics*: 60
*Atom, the Amazing Zombie Killer*: 173
*August Osage County*: 176
*Austin High School*: 157
*Avalon, Frankie*: 20
*axs.com*: 125

*badmovies.org*: 73, 144, 183, 199
*Baker Jr., Ralph*: 88
*Barker, Clive*: 250
*Barsamain, Robert*: 109
*Basket Case*: 191, 234
*Batgirl*: 20, 96
*Batman*: 20, 101
*Bava, Mario*: 56, 59, 96, 120
*Bay, Kay*: 168, 175, 177, 181
*Baylor University*: 14, 25
*Bayou*: 115
*Beast of Yucca Flats, The*: 84
*Beast with a Million Eyes*: 217
*Beatles, The*: 94
*beatnik*: 6
*Beatty, Warren*: 70
*Beauty and the Cave*: 142
*Begg, Ken*: 61
*Beldin, Fred*: 120
*Bennett, Jack*: 19, 27, 92
*Bergman, Ingmar*: 23
*Berri, Claude*: 103
*Berry, Dale*: 142
*Berryman, Michael*: 191
*Bertram, Rod*: 218
*Bethard, Robert E.*: 96

*Beverly Hilton*: 36
*Beyond Help*: 108-115
*Beyond the Planet of the Apes*: 42
*Beyond the Time Barrier*: 40, 41, 42, 49-51
*Bills, E.R.*: 209
*Bio-tech Warrior*: 182, 201-204, 215, 216
*Bird with the Crystal Plumage*: 120
*Bite Night*: 231
*Black Cat, The*: 49, 251
*Black Sabbath*: 58, 198
*Black Sunday*: 58, 95, 96
*Blackwood, Christian*: 14
*Blair Witch Project, The*: 153
*Blaisdell, Paul*: 21
*bleedingskull.com*: 217
*Blob, The*: 5
*Blockbuster*: 231
*Blood, David*: 210
*Blood and Black Lace*: 120
*Blood Feast*: 6
*Bloom, John*: 101
*Blues Brothers*: 7
*Bloodsuckers from Outer Space*: 7, 10, 162-167, 170, 174, 176, 177, 180, 182, 189, 195
*Blues Brothers*: 222
*bmoviecentral.com*: 53, 88
*bmovies.org*: 73
*Bob Bullock Museum of Texas History*: 157
*Body Snatchers*: 162
*Bogart, Humphrey*: 69, 70
*Bonnie and Clyde*: 13, 23, 25, 70
*Bonno, Chris*: 155

*Booth, Edwin*: 142
*Booth, General William*: 142
*Booth, John Wilkes*: 142
*Booth, Libby*: 140
*Borntreger, Andrew*: 73, 144, 183
*Bosco, Mark*: 244
*Bowery Boys*: 4
*Boxell, Tim*: 229
*Boxoffice International*: 16
*Boyette, Pat*: 53-60
*Bracken, Eddie*: 120
*Bracken, Susan*: 120
*Bradeen, Robert*: 163
*Brain Damage*: 244
*Bransom, Greg*: 219
*Breakfast at Tiffany's*: 119
*Bride of Frankenstein, The*: 224
*Bride of the Monster*: 208
*Bridge Over the River Kwai*: 31, 34
*Britton, James*: 62, 68
*Brody, Richard*: 45
*Brooks Institute*: 6, 151, 218
*Brown, Meredith*: 247
*Brown, Rebecca*: 245
*Brownrigg, Anthony*: 131, 140, 141, 143, 215
*Brownrigg, Libby*: 131, 140
*Brownrigg, S.F. "Brownie"*: 7, 19, 102, 108-143, 180, 194, 195, 209, 215, 220
*Brownrigg, Stacey*: 143
*Buchanan, Jack*: 11
*Buchanan, Jane*: 14
*Buchanan, Jeff*: 31, 32-39, 251
*Buchanan, Larry*: 7, 10-39, 49, 51, 68, 91, 92, 95, 109, 112, 124, 128, 131, 133, 140, 142, 194, 209
*Buck Rogers*: 44
*Buckner Children's' Home*: 13, 14, 25
*Burn, Witch, Burn*: 95
*Burns, C. Ross*: 153, 157-161
*Burns, Robert A.*: 49, 144-161
*Burroughs, William S.*: 10

*Caddo Lake*: 28
*Cagney, James*: 44
*Cahn, Edward*: 18
*Callahan, Dan "Sky"*: 216
*Cameron, James*: 222
*Camfield, Bill*: 219, 220
*Camp, Bob*: 5
*Camp, Joe*: 107
*Cannes Film Festival*: 29, 34
*Canon Super 8 camera*: 5
*Capri Theater*: 16
*Captain Flame*: 59
*Carey, Timothy*: 115
*Carpenter, John*: 249, 250
*Carr, Camilla*: 111, 116, 117, 118, 124, 137
*Carradine, John*: 214, 224
*Carver Sound Equipment*: 132
*Caveman George*: 223
*Century Studios*: 119, 137, 195
*Chain Saw Confidential*: 161
*Chan, Jackie*: 217
*Chaney, Lon*: 221
*Chaney, Jr., Lon*: 220
*Chapman, Marguerite*: 44
*Charlton Comics*: 59

*Cheech and Chong*: 243
*Chekhov, Anton*: 159
*Cherry Orchard, The*: 159
*Children Shouldn't Play with Dead Things*: 169
*Choate, Tim*: 225
*Chopin, Frederic*: 36
*Church, Mary*: 152
*Church of the SubGenius*: 124
*Cinema Paradiso*: 25
*Cinema Wasteland*: 185, 192
*Cinesound*: 31
*Cineworld Theater*: 5
*Civil War*: 62
*Clarke, Robert*: 40, 49-51
*Cleaver, June*: 9
*Closet, The*: 229
*Clower, Randy*: 216
*Coburn, Charles*: 162
*Coburn, Glen*: 7, 162-182, 189, 195, 196, 209, 210
*Coburn, James*: 168
*Cohen, Jason*: 241, 244
*Cohen, Larry*: 22
*Combs, Jeffrey*: 204, 206, 215, 241
*Common Law Wife*: 17, 142
*Confessions of a Serial Killer*: 156, 157, 159
*Confessions of a Schlockmeister*: 24
*Connelly, Chris*: 105
*Conway, Tom*: 21
*Coppola, Francis Ford*: 102
*Corman, Roger*: 6, 10, 14, 19, 29, 36, 58, 96, 104, 108, 131, 168, 170, 194, 212, 216, 217

*Corpus Christi, Texas*: 222, 247, 249
*Count Yorga, Vampire*: 169
*Cowboy, The*: 15, 25
*Craig, Yvonne*: 20, 21, 96
*Cranshaw, Pat*: 46, 70
*Craven, Wes*: 109, 131, 132, 156, 249
*Creature from the Black Lagoon*: 19, 22
*Creature of Destruction*: 21, 22, 29
*Creep Tales*: 218, 221, 225, 228-231, 232
*Creeper, The*: 153
*Creeping Terror, The*: 84
*Creepshow*: 218
*Creepy*: 60
*criticsroundup.com*: 199
*Crown International*: 108, 183, 188
*Crumb, Robert*: 9
*Cryer, Loyd*: 189, 194
*Crypt of Dark Secrets*: 141
*Cujo*: 156, 248
*Cukor, George*: 15
*Cundey, Dean*: 248
*Cunningham, Sean*: 248
*Cultmovieforums.com*: 116
*Cure, The*: 109
*Curse of the Swamp Creature*: 28, 32, 91
*Cyberstalker*: 215, 241

*Dallas Communications Complex*: 7, 50, 175
*Dallas, Texas*: 7, 12-14, 16, 18, 19, 25, 26, 49, 62, 71, 84, 92, 94, 100, 101, 119, 131, 132, 140, 163, 181, 182, 193, 202, 215, 220, 222, 241, 242, 244
*Dallas/Fort Worth Metroplex*: 7, 31, 219

*Danna, Corey*: 108
*Dante, Joe*: 159
*Dark Crystal, The*: 130
*Dark Mirror*: 129, 130
*Davis, Dorothy*: 88
*Davis, Mary*: 96, 116
*Davis, Scott*: 200
*Day the World Ended, The*: 20
*Dazed and Confused*: 232
*DC Comics*: 60, 223
*Dead Poets Society*: 94
*Dean, Jody*: 219
*Death is a Family Affair*: 115-118
*Death of Superman, The*: 223
*Death Ward 13*: 108-115, 129
*Decker, Nathan*: 45, 61
*Dedd, Jonny*: 162
*Deep Ellum*: 7
*Deep Throat*: 145, 146, 160
*de Fazio, Patrick*: 217
*Delany, Pat*: 22
*Dell, Charlie*: 117
*Demon of Devil's Lake*: 94
*Demonic Horror 48-Hour Stoner Film Race*: 243
*DePalma, Frank*: 224
*DePew, Gary*: 174
*Detour*: 49, 51
*Deviant Behavior*: 246, 248, 250
*Devil's Tomb, The*: 216
*Die Nakte Zauberin*: 29
*Digital Prophet, The*: 215, 241
*Dinosaur Valley State Park*: 215
*Disco Godfather*: 156
*Disney, Walt*: 20, 107

*Dodson, John*: 145
*Don't Hang Up*: 119, 132
*Don't Look in the Basement*: 7, 108-115, 125, 129, 136, 138, 141, 180, 195
*Don't Look in the Basement 2*: 131, 132, 134, 195
*Don't Open the Door*: 116, 118, 119-124, 132
*Double Trouble*: 161
*Down on Us*: 37
*Dr. Strangelove*: 162, 176
*Dracula*: 169
*Dracula Has Risen from the Grave*: 4
*Dracula's Granddaughter*: 180, 181
*Draculina Magazine*: 131
*Draper, Don*: 202
*dreadcentral.com*: 163, 246
*Dreadtime Stories*: 245-250
*Dreadtime Stories Volume 2*: 248
*Dropsen*: 128
*Dugan, John*: 247
*Dukes of Hazard*: 192
*Dungeon of Harrow*: 53-60
*DuPree, Craig*: 182
*dvddrive-in.com*: 96, 163

*Eagle Mountain Lake*: 40
*East Texas State University*: 170
*Eastern Hills High School*: 5
*Eastwood, Clint*: 160
*Easy Rider*: 233
*EDGE, the, (radio station)*: 131
*Eerie*: 60
*Eggshells*: 161
*El Mariachi*: 232

*El Paso Herald-Post*: 72
*El Paso Playhouse*: 84
*El Paso, Texas*: 80, 81, 84
Ellis, Laura: 163
Elston, Robert: 95
*Elvira*: 220
*Elysian Fields*: 39
Emmy Awards: 182
English, Marla: 21
Ennis, Texas: 191
Ensenada, Mexico: 30
*Entertainment Weekly*: 83
Epstein, Barak: 243
*Equinox*: 53
Erickson, Roky: 9
Esquire Theaters: 109
Essanay: 161
*ET*: 156
Ettinger, Art: 174, 191-194
Evans, Terry: 144
*Eye Creatures, The*: 15, 18, 27
*Eye of the Tiger*: 107

Facebook: 81, 250, 251
*Fair Play*: 94
*Fairies, The*: 113
Family Channel Network, The: 106
*Famous Monsters of Filmland*: 220
*Fangoria Magazine*: 137
Farrar, Bob: 121
Feagin, Hugh: 116, 120
*Fearmakers, The*: 215
Federation Against Ridiculous Trademarks (FART): 8
Ferrell, Will: 204

Festival Theater (El Paso, TX): 84
Film Actors Lab: 175, 176, 186
Fincher, David: 249
*Flash Gordon*: 4, 5, 44
flixster.com: 238
Floyd, Charles Arthur "Pretty Boy": 23
Food Network: 201
*For the Love of Benji*: 107
Forbidden Books: 241, 244
*Forgotten, The*: 108-115, 131, 138
Fort Smith, Arkansas: 244
Fort Worth, Texas: 4, 7, 13, 16, 60, 96, 108, 151, 168, 212, 216, 221
Fort Worth Twin Drive-In Theater: 108
Forte, Fabian: 23
Franco, Jesus: 16, 119
*Frankenhooker*: 191
*Frankenstein*: 43, 169, 249
*Frankenstein Meets the Wolfman*: 169
*Freaks*: 140
*Free, White and 21*: 17, 18, 26, 51
Friedman, David: 10,
Friendly, Fred: 25
*Frogs*: 176
Funicello, Annette: 20

Gallion, Dan: 162
Gallman, Brett: 109
Gambin, Lee: 144
Gammill, Kerry: 223
Garcia, Jerry: 203
Gardner, Jack: 98
Gary, Richard: 206
Gateway Theater: 4
*Ghastly Ones, The*: 58

*Ghostbusters*: 9
*Ghostly Tales*: 60
*Ghoulardi*: 220
*Giant Gila Monster*: 180, 251
Gibron, Bill: 233
Gibsland, Louisiana: 25
Gilley, Carol: 90
*Gilligan's Island*: 105
girlsgunsandghouls.com: 196
Glenrose, Texas: 215
*Godfather, The*: 102
*Godzilla*: 4
Goldthwaite, Bobcat: 229
*Gomer Pyle*: 206
*Gone with the Wind*: 231
Gonzaullas, Manuel T. 'Lone Wolf': 105
*Goodbye, Norma Jean*: 35
Gooding, Jr., Cuba: 216
*Goodnight, Sweet Marilyn*: 34, 35
Goodsell, Greg: 22, 84
Gordon, Stuart: 159, 161
Granada Theater: 231
Grand Prairie, Texas: 70
*Grapes of Wrath, The*: 224
Graves, Peter: 115
*Green Acres*: 117
*Green Slime, The*: 4
Green, Wayne: 163
Greene, Dwight: 251
Griffith, James: 44
Grim, Jacob: 218, 245-250
*Grizzly Adams*: 214
*Groovy Ghoulie Garage*: 229
Guerilla Cinema: 24, 25, 100, 101

Haggerty, Dan: 130, 214
Hall, Irma P.: 159
Hall, Libby: 140, 142
Hallmark Releasing: 109, 110, 131
*Halloween*: 249
Hamilton County: 174
Hammer Films: 58, 108, 168
Hansen, Gunnar: 161, 206
*Happy Days*: 137
Harden, Tim: 148, 156
Harlow, Jean: 23
Harrell, James: 121
Harris, Jack H.: 53
Harris, Maurice: 54
Hart, Trella: 96
Harvey Michael: 111
Harvey Russ: 53, 59
Hatton, Rondo: 153
Haunted Verdun Manor: 222
Hauschild, Rob: 173
Hawaii: 6
Hays Code: 16
Hays, Herb: 11, 12
*Headless Horseman of Heth*: 93
Heatherley, Alex: 247
Hegyes, Stephen: 229
Hegyi, Steve: 230
Heldman, Christopher: 162, 202, 217
Henenlotter, Frank: 191, 234, 244
Henkel, Kim: 248, 249
Henson, Jim: 130
*Hercules*: 4
Hernandez, Sal: 218, 245-250
Heston, Charlton: 170
*Hideous Sun Demon, The*: 49, 50, 188

*Highway to Hell*: 6, 14, 81
Hill, Dennis: 150
*Hills Have Eyes, The*: 132, 149, 153-156, 191
Himes, Terry: 183
Hitchcock, Alfred: 101, 134, 185
Hitler, Adolf: 9, 51, 65
Hoffman, Harold: 251
Hogan, Helen: 55
Holiday, Judy: 15
Hollywood, California: 10, 16, 19, 32, 33, 49, 53, 101, 119, 132, 137, 161, 178, 182, 216, 224
*Hollywood Deadbeat*: 182
Holotik, Rosie: 112
Holt, Tim: 62, 64, 67-70
Hooper, Tobe: 28, 71, 152, 161, 232, 250, 251
Horror, Hollie: 218
*Horror High*: 7, 101, 102, 124, 251
*Horror Hotel*: 95
horrorandsons.com: 88
horror-movie-a-day.blogspot.com: 53, 88, 125
horrorfreaknews.com: 108, 247
horrornews.net: 108, 184, 199, 206, 245
horrorpedia.com: 120, 125, 197, 247
horrorsociety.com: 238, 245, 247
*House of Dracula*: 169
*House of Frankenstein*: 169
*House of the (Four) Seasons*: 119, 120, 121, 122
*House that Dripped Blood, The*: 220, 221, 245
*House that Screamed, The*: 170

Houston, Texas: 7
*How to Produce Your First Feature Film for $20,000 (or Less)*: 241
Howard, Ron: 106
Howe, Jimmy: 68
*Howling, The*: 153, 156, 230
*Howling Nightmare*: 229
Hughes, Howard: 23
*Hughes and Harlow*: 30
*Hullaballoo*: 78
Hundahl, Mark: 118
*Hurry Sundown*: 32
Huston, John: 69, 70

*I Hate Your Guts*: 115
*I Spit on Your Grave*: 184
*Ice, Ice, Baby*: 14
imdb.com: 231
*In the Year 2889*: 20
*Independent Cinema*: 223
Independent Feature Film Market: 231
indiehorrorfilms.blogspot.com: 206
Ingraffia, Jonathan: 145
*Interface*: 6, 251
*Invasion of the Saucermen*: 18
*Invisible Invaders*: 170
Irving Community Television Network (ICTN): 24, 100, 101
Irving, Texas: 94
Isfahan, Iran: 6
*It Came from Hunger*: 13, 14, 22
*It Conquered the World*: 19, 29, 38
*It's Alive*: 7, 11, 12, 22

jabootu.net: 61

Jamieson, Bruce: 25
Jamieson, Hugh: 109
Jamieson Film Company: 15, 25, 27, 109, 132, 140, 194
Jaws: 5, 32, 222
Jean de Florette: 103
Jefferson, Texas: 120, 121
Jenkins, Chris: 101
Jenkins, III, John H.: 160
Jenkins, Linda: 61
Jennings, Benton: 81
Jennings, Waylon: 17
Jennings, William Bryan: 86
Jennings III, William Bryan: 83
Jessup, Robert: 29
Jesus Christ: 23
Joe Bob Briggs: 101, 106, 107, 249
Johnson, Ben: 105
Johnson, Don: 44
Jones, Spike: 141, 143
Judge, Mike: 250
Juno: 233
Jurow, Martin: 119, 139
Justin, Louis: 198
JVC: 213

KABC-TV Channel 7: 220
Kael, Pauline: 9
Karloff, Boris: 43, 49, 220, 221
Katzman, Sam: 6, 24, 216
Kaufman, Lloyd: 235, 237, 244
KDAF Channel 33: 101
Keaton, Buster: 161
Keaton, Michael: 229
Keep My Grave Open: 7, 116, 119, 124-128, 132, 135
Keller, Billie: 163
Kelly, Jack: 19, 20
Kelly, Robert: 62
Kennamer, Gary: 67-71, 92
Kennamer, Hirom Monroe: 71
Kennamer, James: 68
Kenny, Tom: 229
KENS TV Channel 5: 58
Kentucky Fried Movie: 242
Kerouac, Jack: 10
Kier, Udo: 191
Killer Nerd movies: 244
Killer Shrews: 180, 251
Killers from Space: 170
Kinem, Dan: 196
King, Daniel: 206
King, Stephen: 250
Kings of the Bs: 6
Kinkade, Thomas: 100
Kip's Big Boy: 7, 8
Kirk, Tommy: 20, 26
KJH-TV: 220
Kjornes, Keith: 216
Klamath, Oregon: 51
Korg: 70,000 BC: 60
Krusz, Walter: 109, 110, 111, 112, 116, 133
Kubrick, Stanley: 36
KXAS Channel 5: 11, 219
Kushner/Locke: 156

Lake Dallas: 15, 16
Lake Tahoe: 23
Lang, Fritz: 49

Las Colinas, Texas: 7, 19, 175
Last Attraction, The: 222
Last House on the Left: 109, 111, 131
Last House on the Left: The Making of a Cult Classic: 119
Last Man on Earth: 1970
Last Picture Show, The: 124
Latham, Garl: 174
Laverne and Shirley: 137
Lean, David: 36, 37
Leave Me Alone: 62
Lee, Spike: 181
Legend of Boggy Creek, The: 28
Legend of 80-foot John, The: 154
Legend of the Hillbilly Butcher: 172, 173
Leggio, Jerry: 128
Lelouch, Claude: 102
Lennon, John: 94
Lenox, John Thomas: 137
Lentz, Jerry: 131
Leonard, Sean: 199
Leslie, Bill: 194
letterboxd.com: 115, 218
Letts, Billy: 176
Letts, Dennis: 164, 176
Letts, Tracy: 176
Lewis, Herschell Gordon: 115, 211
Lido Theater: 16
Lincoln, Abraham: 142
Linklater, Richard: 232
Lionsgate: 171
Little Shop of Horrors: 216
Lloyd, Christopher: 40
Loch Ness Horror, The: 23
Locke, Peter: 155, 156

Lofton, Terry: 183-195
Lorimar Home Video: 174
Los Angeles, California: 14, 161, 181, 220
Lost in Space: 204
Lost Prairie, Texas: 11
Lovecraft, H.P.: 249, 250
Lucas, George: 40, 102
Luckenbach, Texas: 17
Luckenbach Witch, The: 17, 140, 141, 142
Lugosi, Bela: 49, 220
Lugosi, Boris: 196
Lynch, David: 240

MacAdams, Annabelle: 112
MacAdams, Rhea: 112, 121
Macon County War: 130, 214
Mad Lab: 222
Magnificent Seven, The: 41
Magnum Entertainment: 190
Mahree, Diane: 86
Majorca, Spain: 36
Majors, Lee: 105, 217
Malloy, Catherine: 146
Malibu, California: 39
Man from Planet X, The: 50
Man Who Loved Inflatable Women, The: 153
Mandel, Ken: 218, 221, 226, 230
Manon of the Spring: 103
Manos Returns: 84
Manos: The Hands of Fate: 72-87
Manos: The Rise of Torgo: 84
Many Ghosts of Dr. Graves, The: 60
Marcum, Gary: 251
Marinaro, Ed: 217

*Mark of the Devil*: 109
*Mark of the Witch*: 95-107, 116
Marker, Russ: 61-71, 92, 93
Marquis de Sade: 16, 59
Marriott Corporation: 7
*Marrying Kind, The*: 15
*Mars Needs Women*: 7, 20, 21, 27, 179
Marvel Comics: 223
Maslansky, Paul: 251
*Massacre Video*: 198
Martin, Todd: 184
Matheson, Richard: 22, 170
*Mausoleum*: 154
Mayberry, William: 11
Max, Peter: 77
MBrown06: 199
McFarland and Company: 13, 14, 22
McCarthy, Joseph: 52
McCartney, Paul: 94
McCarty, John: 24, 215
McCormick, Brad: 211
McCormick, Bret: 196-217
McCormick, Jeremiah: 215
McCormick, Joseph: 215
McCormick, Joshua: 6, 215
McGahee, Geno: 219
McGhee, Bill: 112
McLain, Gary: 89
McLendon, Gordon: 180, 251
McLuhan, Marshall: 9
MCM Productions: 212
McNulty, William: 54
McVayne, Jane: 15
Meadowbrook Drive-In Theater: 108
Melies, Georges: 28

Mesquite, Texas: 70
Mesquite High School: 169
*Metropolis*: 49
Meyer, Michelle: 183
Meyer, Russ: 38, 71
Meyers, Thom: 162, 175, 176, 177, 179, 185
MGDSQUAN: 238, 245, 247
*Microwave Massacre, The*: 156, 158
Middleton, Greg: 229
Mikels, Ted V.: 24
Milan, Italy: 32
Milland, Ray: 176
Miller-Consolidated Pictures: 51
Millican, Joshua: 247
Milligan, Andy: 58, 140
millionmonkeytheater.com: 45, 61
Minasian, Steve: 109
Ministry: 109
Minton, Mike: 128, 166, 168, 218-232
Miramax: 181
*Mistress of the Apes*: 37
*Mole People, The*: 93
Molgaard, Matt: 108
mondo-digital.com: 95
*Mongrel*: 144-151, 154, 155, 160
Monopoly's Park Place: 223
Monroe, Marilyn: 10, 23
Monroy, Tania: 247
*Monster Bargains*: 220
*Monsters*: 219
Montalvan, Joaquin: 172
Monterrey, Mexico; 35
Montgomery Ward: 4, 49
Moore, Curtis: 211

*Moore, Rudy Ray*: 156
*Moore, Tom*: 24, 95-107, 116
*Moore, Tom T.*: 14, 174, 217
*Morgan, Lee*: 53
*moria.co.nz*: 62
*Morris, Chester*: 21
*Mortal Dilemma*: 232
*Motel Hell*: 244
*Movie Channel, The*: 101, 106
*Movie Macabre*: 220
*Mr. Dark*: 246
*MTV*: 139, 221
*Mudhoney*: 6
*Mulleur, Joyce*: 73
*Muppets, The*: 130
*Murray, Bill*: 9
*Murrow, Edward R.*: 25
*Museum of Horrors*: 219, 221
*My Dinner with Andre*: 210
*My Friends Need Killing*: 192
*Myers, T.J.*: 202
*Mystery Science Theater 3000*: 82, 83, 85

*Nail Gun Massacre*: 183-195
*Naked Witch, The*: 17, 18, 26, 29, 32, 58, 95, 131, 140, 141, 143
*NASA*: 52, 91
*National Enquirer*: 210
*Naughty Dallas*: 17
*Nazi(s)*: 9, 46, 52, 61, 64, 65, 66
*Neal, Tom*: 49
*Neiman Marcus*: 142
*Nervebreakers, The*: 242
*New Line Cinema*: 248
*New York, New York*: 14, 25, 231
*New Yorker*: 45
*Newsom, Ted*: 215
*Neyman Jones, Jackie*: 72, 81, 83-87
*Neyman, Tom*: 77, 79, 83, 84
*Nicholson, Jack*: 176
*Nicholson, Jim*: 26, 51, 110
*Nickelodeon Network*: 5
*Nicolau-Sharpley, Kris*: 163
*Night Chills*: 231
*Night Fright*: 62, 88-94
*Night Gallery*: 75
*Night of the Living Dead*: 162, 235
*NightCreeps*: 223, 224-226
*Nightmare on Elm Street*: 132, 184
*Nightmare Theater*: 219
*No Man's Land*: 59
*Norris, Chuck*: 202
*Norseman, The*: 103, 105
*Novak, Harry*: 16
*Nygard, Roger*: 229

*Oak Cliff, Texas*: 169
*Odem, Texas*: 247
*Odessa, Texas*: 175
*O'Dwyer, Larry*: 121
*oh-the-horror.com*: 109
*O'Hara, Quinn*: 21
*Oklahoma City, Oklahoma*: 7
*Old Style Beer*: 230
*Open Door Productions*: 214, 215
*O'Reilly, Cyril*: 217
*Out of Your Tree*: 153
*Outer Limits*: 4
*Ozone: Attack of the Redneck Mutants*: 6, 178, 197-201, 211-213

*Palace Theater*: 108
*Parsons, Zach*: 184
*Patterson, Rocky*: 185, 186
*Paulsen, Pat*: 174
*Peabody, Elizabeth*: 142
*Peacemaker, The*: 60
*Pearl, Daniel*: 248
*Peck, Bill*: 225, 226
*Pellegrino, Ann*: 62
*People Under the Stairs, The*: 132
*Perlman, Ron*: 216
*Perry Mason*: 4
*Peters, Bernadette*: 137
*Peters, Martha*: 96
*Petersen, Cassandra*: 220
*Petersen, Paul*: 21
*Phantom, The*: 60
*Philadelphia, Pennsylvania*: 161
*Phillips, Lou Diamond*: 176
*Pierce, Charles B.*: 28, 105
*Pierce, Jack*: 43
*Pierson, John*: 181
*Pileggi, Mitch*: 144, 153, 154
*Pistole, Roger*: 210
*Pitt, Ingrid*: 111
*Plan 9 from Outer Space*: 61, 80
*Planet of the Apes*: 42
*Plano, Texas*: 194
*Play Misty for Me*: 125
*Playboy Magazine*: 217
*playwithdeath.com*: 238
*Pocono Record*: 40
*Poe, Edgar Allan*: 58, 96, 109, 249, 250
*Polanski, Roman*: 16, 125
*Polaroid*: 8
*Poltergeist*: 232
*Poly Theater*: 4
*Polygrind Film Festival*: 173
*Poolville, Texas*: 211
*Poor White Trash*: 115
*Poor White Trash Part 2*: 7, 115-118, 132, 138
*Pope, Tim*: 109
*popmatters.com*: 233
*Porky's*: 217
*Pot Zombies*: 195, 233-244
*Pot Zombies 2*: 238-244
*Powell, Olga*: 65
*Power Rangers*: 205
*Powers, Justin*: 195, 233-244
*Price, Michael H.*: 153
*Producers Services Incorporated (PSI)*: 194, 195
*Productions West Communications*: 7, 67, 128, 129, 166, 222
*Protector, The*: 131, 217
*Project Paperclip*: 51
*Psycho*: 162
*Psychotronic Encyclopedia of Film*: 80
*Pulp Fiction*: 181

*Queen, Ron*: 185
*Quik-Print*: 218

*Raiders of the Lost Ark*: 222
*Rainone, Tom*: 157
*Ramming Speed*: 251
*Ramos, Octavio*: 125
*Ramsey, Jay*: 61

*Ray, Aldo*: 144, 160
*Ray, Fred Olen*: 130, 214
*RDM Productions*: 194
*Re-Animator*: 152, 153, 156, 161, 204, 215
*Rebel Without a Crew*: 250
*Redd, Bob*: 194, 195
*Redd, Daniel*: 141, 194
*Redmond, Mark "Boomer"*: 96
*Reed, Donna*: 21
*Reed, Lou*: 9
*Reeves, Steve*: 4
*Refugio, Texas*: 249
*Reis, George R.*: 96
*Ren and Stimpy*: 5
*Rennke, Dave*: 141, 195
*Repligator*: 172, 206-209, 216
*Replikator*: 216
*Repulsion*: 125
*Rescue Girls*: 180
*Return to Boggy Creek*: 106
*Revenge of the Creature*: 93
*Reynolds, Debbie*: 137
*Reynolds, John*: 85, 86
*RH Factor*: 157
*Riley, Joe*: 226
*Ripps, M.A.*: 115, 116
*Roarke, Adam*: 175, 176, 186
*Robert-A-Burns.com*: 153
*Robocop*: 249
*Rocking Reverend*: 244
*Rockwell, Norman*: 10
*Rodger, Kate*: 217
*Rodrigue, Eric*: 246
*Rodriguez, Robert*: 225, 232, 250

*Rogan, Seth*: 204, 206
*Roger Corman: Hollywood's Wild Angel*: 14
*Romero, George A.*: 218, 224
*Rosenblum, Bernie*: 73
*Ross, Gene*: 111, 116, 118, 119, 125, 137
*Roswell, New Mexico*: 203
*Rotten Riders*: 195
*Rowe, Kimberly*: 217
*Rumble in the Bronx*: 217
*Rumble in the Streets*: 217
*Rush, Richard*: 176

*Salisbury, James*: 229
*San Antonio, Texas*: 59
*Sandler, Adam*: 206
*Sands of Iwo Jima*: 93
*Santa Barbara, California*: 151, 218
*Santa Claus Conquers the Martians*: 80
*Santa Monica, California*: 30, 36, 213
*Santel, Marie*: 95, 96, 106
*Satan*: 29
*Sarasota Herald-Tribune*: 40
*Savage, Ann*: 49
*scaredstiffreviews.com*: 219
*Scheib, Richard*: 62
*Schneider, Dan*: 40
*Schooner Inn Donuts*: 220
*Scott, George C.*: 176
*Scott, Ridley*: 249
*Scream Test*: 153, 155
*Screamtime*: 219
*screenanarchy.com*: 72
*Scuderi, Phil*: 109
*Scum of the Earth*: 96, 115-118

*Seagoville, Texas*: 192
*Seale, Jr., Marcus Larry*: 11
*Seale, Maude Dove*: 11
*Serling, Rod*: 75
*Seventh Street Theater*: 108
*Shaffen, Matt*: 177, 210
*Shaye, Bob*: 248
*She Creature, The*: 21
*She's Gotta Have It*: 181
*Sherman, Jesse*: 67, 129, 166, 218-232
*Shimmer*: 35
*Shock Theater*: 169
*Shocker*: 154
*Sigel's*: 11
*Signs of Life*: 154
*silveremulsion.com*: 233
*Simon, King of the Witches*: 95
*Sitka, Emil*: 45
*Six Million Dollar Man*: 60
*Sixx, Kryten*: 163
*Slane, Rod*: 230
*slasherstudios.com*: 233
*slashingthrough.com*: 199
*Sleaze Merchants, The*: 24
*Smith Brothers Carpets*: 11
*Smith, Chad*; 175
*Smith, Dick*: 211
*Smith, Doug*: 124
*Smith, Will*: 170
*Smothers Brothers Comedy Hour*: 174
*Snatcher*: 229
*Sokolov, Vladimir*: 41
*something Weird Video*: 141
*Somethingawful.com*: 184
*Sons of Hercules*: 4

*Southeast Texas Filmmakers Hall of Fame*: 159
*Southern Methodist University*: 142
*Southside Twin Drive-In Theater*: 108
*Speer, Connie*: 186, 187
*Spider-Man*: 223
*Spielberg, Steven*: 102, 222, 249
*Spindletop Productions*: 105
*Splot*: 5
*Sponge Bob Squarepants*: 229
*Spurling, Ben*: 197
*Stafford, Ann*: 117
*Stang, Reverend Ivan*: 124
*Star Trek*: 213
*Star Wars*: 40, 107
*Stars and Stripes*: 5
*Staten Island, New York*: 58
*Stealth Hunters*: 215, 251
*Steckler, Ray Dennis*: 9
*Steele, Barbara*: 111
*Steinfeld, Adam*: 128
*Steve Allen Show*: 142
*Stevens, Brinke*: 206, 216
*Stouffer, Larry*: 7, 124, 127, 128, 251
*Streets*: 217
*Striking Point*: 214
*Strongsville, Ohio*: 192
*STX Media*: 248
*Sucker*: 230
*Sugar Hill*: 251
*Sullivan, Jim*: 68, 88-94
*Sumner, Jane*: 216
*Super 8*: 13, 71, 199, 212
*Superman Lives*: 223
*Support Your Local Monsters*: 219, 220,

222
*Swamp Rose*: 17
*swampflix.com*: 96
*Synapse*: 195
Synodis, Greg: 14
*System of Dr. Tarr and Professor Fether, The*: 109
Szulkin, David: 118, 119

*Tabloid!*: 8, 14, 168, 175, 177, 210, 211, 213, 221, 245
*Tahiti's*: 14
*Takedown*: 216
*Tales from the Crypt*: 221, 245
*Tales from the Darkside*: 224
*Tarantula*: 19, 32, 93
*Tarzan*: 4
*Teacher, The*: 188
Telly Awards: 35
Temple, Shirley: 20
*Ten Commandments, The*: 224
*Terminator, The*: 222
Texarkana: 101, 244
Texas A&M Commerce: 175
*Texas Chain Saw Massacre*: 28, 71, 147, 152-158, 161, 179, 184, 224, 244, 247, 251
Texas Christian University: 96
Texas Frightmare Weekend: 189, 191, 244
Texas Ranger: 161
Texas State Fair: 51
*Theater of Blood*: 170
*theaterofguts.com*: 145
*thebloodsuckinggeek.wordpress.com*:

162
*thebloodypitofhorror.blogspot.com*: 218
*thespinningimage.co.uk*: 40
*thirdeyecinema.wordpress.com*:
*Thirteen Clocks*: 158
Thompson, Blue: 6, 198, 199
Thompson, Carolyn: 6
Thornton Model Agency: 14
Three Stooges: 4, 45, 78
*Through the Fire*: 251
Thrower, Stephen: 120, 125
Thurber, James: 158
Thurman, Bill: 11, 28, 63, 64, 68, 70, 89, 93, 124
Tiennan, Andy: 144
*Time Tracers*: 204-206, 215, 216
*Time Trap*: 182, 204-206, 215
*Tim's Horror Tweet*: 233
*Title Rune, The*: 96
TNT Monster Vision: 249
Tompkins, Darlene: 41
*Topper*: 48
*Topsy Dingo Wild Dog*: 137
*Torture Dungeon*: 58
*Total Recall*: 28
Touchstone: 181
*Tourist Trap*: 153, 156
*Town that Dreaded Sundown, The*: 101, 105, 244
*Toxic Avenger*: 242
Tracey Locke: 194
*trashfilmguru.wordpress.com*: 115
*Trekkies*: 229
*Trekkies 2*: 229
Tremayne, Les: 21

*Treasure of the Sierra Madre*: 69
*Trial of Lee Harvey Oswald, The*: 17
*Triesault, Ivan*: 45
*Trip with the Teacher*: 188
*Troll 2*: 162
*Troma Entertainment*: 235
*Trotter, Matt*: 215, 251
*Tucson, Arizona*: 39
*Tulsa, Oklahoma*: 7, 224
*Turner, Ted*: 106
*Twilight Zone*: 4, 40, 176
*Tyfus, Kries*: 199

*UFO(s)*: 18
*U-Haul*: 7
*Ulmer, Arianne*: 43
*Ulmer, Edgar G.*: 40-52, 209
*Ulmer, Shirley*: 51
*Ultra Violent Magazine*: 174, 191
*Under Age*: 17
*United Artists*: 15
*Universal Cine Photo*; 195
*Universal Studios*: 19, 49, 168, 169, 176, 220, 249, 250
*University of Texas*: 158, 161
*University of Texas at Arlington*: 5, 6
*USA Film Festival*: 232

*Vampira*: 220
*Vanilla Ice*: 14
*Variety Club*: 25
*Venkman, Peter*: 9
*Venus in Furs*: 15, 16
*Vestron*: 6
*Vhscollector.com*: 28, 37

*vhshitfest.tumblr.com*: 196
*Victorville, California*: 156
*Video Post and Transfer*: 129, 230
*Vimeo*: 182
*Virus*: 223

*Waco, Texas*: 14, 25
*Walker, Samantha*: 166
*Wallace, Dee*: 156
*Walpurgis night*: 95
*Walsh, Anitra*: 96
*Ward, Burt*: 20
*Warhol, Andy*: 10
*Warner Brothers*: 23, 192
*Warner Home Video*: 174, 194
*Warped*: 229
*Warren, Hal P.*: 72-87
*Warren Publishing*: 60
*Watts Riots*: 199
*Wayne, John*: 52, 107, 224
*Wayne, Patrick*: 107, 224
*WBS*: 195
*Webb, John*: 163
*Weekly World News*, 210
*Weems, T.G.*: 216
*Weenick, Annabelle*: 11, 112, 119, 127, 137
*Weird Ones, The*: 59
*Weldon, Michael*: 80
*Wells, Darryl*: 96
*Wells, Dawn*: 105
*West, Adam*: 20
*Wetback, The*: 25
*Whacked! Skewed Views of Horror Movies that Simply Refuse to Die*: 196

Whacked Movies: 172, 173, 182
Where the Heart Is: 176
White Noise: 229
White Noise 2: 229
White Rock Lake: 27
Wichita, Kansas: 7
Wild Eye Releasing: 173, 244
Wild Turkey: 130
Wilde, Cornel: 105
Williams, Tennessee: 119
Wilson, Luke: 206
Wilson, Owen: 206
Winberg, Ted: 216
Winberg, Wynn: 216
Winfree, Rachel: 145
Wizard of Oz: 5
Wolfman: 249
Wood, Ed: 9, 206, 208, 209
Woodland Hills, California: 52
Woodstock: 107
World War II: 41
Worth Theater: 108

X-Files, The: 153, 154

Yesterday Machine, The: 61-71, 93
Young Producers: 231
Youngstein, Max: 15
You're a Good Man, Charlie Brown: 222

Zanuck, Darryl: 25
Zappa, Frank: 85
Zavala, Sebastian: 72
Ziemba, Joseph: 217
Zontar, the Magazine: 22
Zontar, the Thing from Venus: 7, 15, 19, 20, 22, 28, 29, 38, 194

# Buy these TEXAS SCHLOCK classics now!

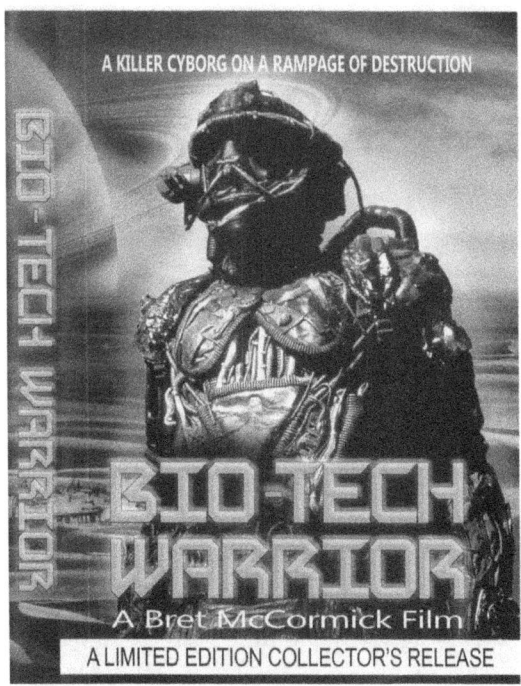

A top secret government experiment is unleashed on the world! This extra-terrestrial cyborg leaves a trail of death and devastation in **BIO-TECH WARRIOR!**

A team of daring explorers are hurled into a terrifying time-space paradox in **TIME TRAP!** Featuring Jeffrey Combs of *Re-Animator!*

Only 1,000 DVDs of each title will EVER be released! All are hand-numbered and autographed by the director. Order yours today at **collectorsreleases.com**

www.ingramcontent.com/pod-product-compliance
Lightning Source LLC
Chambersburg PA
CBHW081211230426
43666CB00015B/2716